TOLKIEN AMONG THE MODERNS

TOLKIEN
AMONG THE
MODERNS

Edited by
RALPH C. WOOD

University of Notre Dame Press
Notre Dame, Indiana

University of Notre Dame Press
Notre Dame, Indiana 46556
undpress.nd.edu
All Rights Reserved

Copyright © 2015 by University of Notre Dame
Published in the United States of America

The publisher gratefully acknowledges the generous support
of the Lilly Fellows Program in Humanities and the Arts
toward the publication of this volume.

Library of Congress Cataloging-in-Publication Data

Tolkien among the moderns / edited by Ralph C. Wood.
     pages   cm
Includes bibliographical references and index.
ISBN 978-0-268-01973-0 (paperback) —
ISBN 0-268-01973-8 (paper)
1. Tolkien, J. R. R. (John Ronald Reuel), 1892–1973—Philosophy.
2. Tolkien, J. R. R. (John Ronald Reuel), 1892–1973—Knowledge—Literature.
3. Philosophy in literature.   4. Postmodernism in literature.
I. Wood, Ralph C., editor.
PR6039.O32Z8383   2015
823'.912—dc23

2015023726

∞ *The paper in this book meets the guidelines for permanence and
durability of the Committee on Production Guidelines for
Book Longevity of the Council on Library Resources.*

CONTENTS

INTRODUCTION

Tolkien among the Moderns

Ralph C. Wood

J. R. R. Tolkien is neither an escapist nor an antiquarian writer. On the contrary, his work addresses the most clamant questions of our age. This collection of essays is devoted to the proposition that Tolkien's work is animated and undergirded by a profound moral and religious vision. It has been made evident not only by its many formal interpreters but also by the millions of readers who have been braced by it. *The Lord of the Rings*—like all of Tolkien's other major texts: "The Monsters and the Critics," "On Fairy-Stories," *The Hobbit*, and, chiefly, *The Silmarillion*—is imbued with profound ethical and theological concerns. What has gone largely unnoticed, however, is that Tolkien's work also engages with major literary figures and philosophical movements of our time. Tom Shippey, in *J. R. R. Tolkien: Author of the Century*, has given glancing notice to Tolkien's kinship with such apocalyptic writers as George Orwell and William Golding, Kurt Vonnegut, Ursula Le Guin, and Thomas Pynchon.

Yet Shippey does not explain how Tolkien's moral vision engages the specific concerns that animate the work of such major modern writers. This book seeks to fill this considerable gap. It does so, not by claiming any literary or historical influences on Tolkien, nor does it take a "view from nowhere," as if his work could be read while hovering in the ether. Instead, it offers a quite particular "listening from somewhere." This is to say that we place modern writers and modern quandaries in lively engagement with the textual particularities of Tolkien's masterpiece, in the conviction that we can thus illumine *Lord of the Rings* in provocative and constructive ways.

We begin with Germaine Walsh's contention that Tolkien is strangely modern in his very recourse to things ancient. For in taking up the celebrated quarrel between poetry and philosophy, Walsh maintains that Tolkien answers both of Plato's objections to creative art: not only the conviction that poetry offers beautiful lies masquerading as truth, but also that poetry undermines morality by depicting both gods and heroes as overcome by passion and thus as living subrational lives. On the contrary, argues Walsh, Tolkien gives us no mere "likeness" of the world but rather a profound experience of its inherent wonder. Even more importantly, Walsh shows that Tolkien depicts the subtleties of moral virtue and its proper development—especially in engaging with the huge and vexed question of the role of women. In a surprising defense of *Lord of the Ring*'s primary female character, Éowyn, Walsh demonstrates that Tolkien is indeed a writer for our time.

Bringing us further toward our own era, Helen Lasseter Freeh (in chapter 2) traces Tolkien's abiding concern with fate and thus with the seeming helplessness of human beings in the face of circumstances that repeatedly overwhelm them. Under the hegemony of modern science, most of us moderns have come to regard ourselves as creatures whose destiny is largely determined by our social and bodily conditions. From a Newtonian kind of determinism, we have adopted another kind of impotence—the kind born of the conviction that the universe is both unsponsored and undirected. On the contrary, Freeh's analysis of Tolkien's *Silmarillion* reveals that all people remain free, not to determine their own destiny in autonomous ways but rather to shape their lives in accord with the deep providential intentions that order the universe.

Approaching our late age still further, Michael Thomas (in chapter 3) links Tolkien to Cervantes in unanticipated ways, showing that—as knights accompanied by comic companions, as heroes doing battle with evils both real and imagined—Don Quixote and Sancho Panza have odd resemblances to Frodo Baggins and Samwise Gamgee. Their improbable comic heroism, Thomas argues, is of their very essence. Yet theirs is not a valor and intrepidity of the antiheroic kind that pervades much of modern literature. Cervantes's and Tolkien's heroes serve, albeit often inadvertently, to shore up our confidence that the human quest is indeed a road worth traveling.

In chapter 4, Peter Candler demonstrates that Tolkien answered Friedrich Nietzsche's critique of Christianity as unconsciously nihilistic because it was necessarily linguistic. Nietzsche believed that once the language of Christians had been thoroughly deconstructed their faith would collapse. Turning the tables on Nietzsche, Candler argues that Tolkien is not at all troubled by the linguistic character of both divine revelation and human truth. Rather than leading to nihilism, our irreducible linguisticality proves, in Tolkien's work, to be our abiding hope, since human beings are sacramentally created to participate in the life of the triune God, who creatively speaks all things into being.

Phillip Donnelly argues in chapter 5 that Tolkien's inset verse narratives in *Lord of the Rings* embody an alternative to some of the aesthetic and ontological assumptions typical of literary modernism. Three inset narratives in *The Fellowship of the Ring*, when taken together, imply the artistic development of Bilbo Baggins, from a composer of traveling lyrics and bathing songs to a composer of heroic court poetry on the myth of Eärendil. This alternative story of development in poetic skill ultimately reveals a deeper contrast between Tolkien's ontology and the vision of reality most commonly assumed by modern authors, including James Joyce.

Dominic Manganiello returns to Joyce again in chapter 6. He argues that Tolkien shared with Joyce the fundamental premise that the great book can serve as an image of the cosmos itself. But whereas Joyce's *Ulysses* turns the artist into a countercreator and thus an epic maker of a world without God, Tolkien's *Lord of the Rings* revives the ancient trope of the world as a book written by human scribes or "subcreators" and thus as glossed by the hand of providence. Tolkien's paradigm of collaborative authorship, when set alongside Joyce's antitheological bias, also issues in radically opposed notions of heroism.

In chapter 7, Scott Moore explores still further startling evidence of Tolkien's link to non-Christian figures—namely, to the novelist and philosopher Iris Murdoch. She was fascinated with Tolkien's work, Moore reveals, for very good reason. They were both interested in the remarkable kinds of moral and spiritual consolation that are to be found in fantasy, but they construed the term in almost diametrically opposed ways. Murdoch believed that Tolkien's work belonged among those few compelling works of art that not only legitimately console their readers but also embody the moral vision that Murdoch thought was indicative of authentic virtue and that she sought to show in her own fiction.

Joseph Tadie in chapter 8 brings us into the contemporary arena of ideas by showing the link between the philosophical work of Emmanuel Levinas and the fantasy fiction of Tolkien—especially, though perhaps also surprisingly, *The Hobbit*. From Levinas, Tadie has learned how dreadfully difficult it is to attend to the other without reducing them to our own comfortable categories. This conundrum is made acute when dealing with those who are deemed weak and dependent, since we are likely to treat them as creatures in need of our help. Tadie demonstrates, exactly to the contrary, that Tolkien joins Levinas in regarding the allegedly strong and wise as those needing to be transformed by the lowly and the broken. In their very powerlessness, they help prevent the mighty from "usurping the world," a fine phrase from Pascal that Tadie explicates in the texts of both Levinas and Tolkien.

My own essay, chapter 9, seeks to establish Tolkien's surprising relevance to the vexed question of postmodernity—how he shares many of its questions while embracing almost none of its solutions. There I attempt to show that Tolkien does not begin, in standard Enlightenment fashion, with abstract universal principles that he then seeks to instantiate in his fiction, but that he always proceeds from the particular and the historical and the linguistic, locating his deepest beliefs in the habits and practices of specific communities, especially the hobbit world of the Shire.

These nine essays were born of a seminar sponsored by the Lilly Fellows Program in Humanities and the Arts held at Baylor University. For four weeks, a group of scholars from a variety of U.S. colleges and universities—and also from a variety of disciplines: English, philosophy, political science, Spanish, theology—met daily to discuss the various ways in which the work of J. R. R. Tolkien impinges on the modern world. Our seminar was entitled "Reading Tolkien and Living the Virtues," for we sought to discern how Tolkien's work offers a fresh imaginative vision of the moral and religious life as it might yet be lived in the early twenty-first century. Yet our conversations soon revealed that Tolkien's *legendarium*—the huge mythological and linguistic world that he spent his entire adult life creating—has resonances that extend well beyond the seven classical virtues, though never excluding them. We discovered, in short, that Tolkien's work trenches unexpectedly on our various disciplines and that it participates in a conversation that is altogether as much modern as it is classical. This volume is the result of our firm conviction that Tolkien has a permanent dwelling place "among the moderns."

CHAPTER 1

PHILOSOPHIC POET

J. R. R. Tolkien's Modern Response to an Ancient Quarrel

Germaine Paulo Walsh

Perhaps more deeply than any other twentieth-century author, J. R. R. Tolkien reflects on the problematic question of human creativity, of man as maker. Tolkien maintains that the calamitous events of the twentieth century, events he witnessed firsthand, were due, at least in part, to a fundamental misunderstanding of human creativity. In accepting the notion that human beings are makers but not that they are made, that human beings are creative but not that they are created, modernity places man in the position of God, an arrogation that is both futile and self-destructive. What is needed, Tolkien suggests, is a reintroduction to an older view of human creativity, one recognizing both the dignity and the limits of man's capacity as maker. Considered in this light, one may understand Tolkien's work as being an attempt to reacquaint the modern mind with that complex human capacity referred to by the ancient Greeks as *poiesis*.[1]

The creativity theme underlies the whole of Tolkien's *legendarium*, the vast collection of writings conveying the history of the mythical elves, recounting their origin, deeds, and final passage from Middle-earth. The primary focus of the saga is on one particular elvish clan, the Noldor, who are distinguished from the other clans by virtue of their extraordinary creative ability, their "maker's power" (*S*, 68).[2] In telling the history of the Noldor, Tolkien explores the

7

sense in which the possession of this power is a gift, albeit a perilous one. As the Noldor develop their creative capacity in many and various ways, they forget that, although they are responsible for the use to which they put this ability, they are not responsible for the fact that they possess it in the first place. They forget that the source of their extraordinary power in making is not themselves but their creator, Eru, called Ilúvatar, who has gifted them, above all others of their kind, with a share in his own creative power; and so they become increasingly proud of their accomplishments in making "many new things fair and wonderful" (*S*, 63). Failing to recognize the inexorable contingency of their creative ability, the Noldor fail to recognize its limits, and they suffer for it.

In his essay "On Fairy-Stories," Tolkien argues that, properly understood, all art, all *poiesis*, is "sub-creation." In defending the often derided form of literature known as fairy story, from which the genre of fantasy emerged, Tolkien argues that the poetic art, like all human making, is not purely and simply "creative." Given that human beings cannot bring forth something from nothing, the ability to "create" is, strictly speaking, limited to God. Yet within the limits and possibilities of the world established by God, human beings are capable of re-forming and reordering the objects of the world, and in this more limited way, share in the divine creativity. Tolkien's deep reflection on the biblical teaching that human beings are made in the image and likeness of God underlies his own mythopoetic vision. For Tolkien, the human likeness to God is expressed most fully in the capacity for creativity. Furthermore, it is in light of this teaching, Tolkien maintains, that the underlying order of the world—which so often appears, paradoxically, as disorder—is most fully and comprehensively disclosed. As Tolkien writes in his poem "Mythopoeia":

Although now long estranged,
Man is not wholly lost nor wholly changed.
Dis-graced he may be, yet is not dethroned,
and keeps the rags of lordship once he owned. . . .
. . . though we dared to build
gods and their houses out of dark and light,

and sow the seeds of dragons—'twas our right
(used or misused). That right has not decayed.
We make still by the law in which we're made.[3]

Tolkien's account of subcreation, as with many aspects of his
work, entails a reconsideration of modern conceptions and presuppositions in light of the older, deeper tradition of Western thought.
In arguing that the artist is a maker, not a creator, Tolkien tacitly rejects one aspect of the modern view. Similarly, he stands in accord
with ancient thought in viewing the poet as the quintessential
maker,[4] even as he also holds that the activity of the poet involves
not just making[5] but discovering. That is, Tolkien maintains that poetry entails the making of stories, but the stories disclose the poet's
vision, the poet's discovery, as it were, of an intelligible order—despite the appearance of disorder—that underlies the world. In order
to arrive at an understanding of this intelligible order, the poet must
confront several central concerns of both philosophy and theology.

I shall explore Tolkien's *legendarium*—the huge mythological
system that he created over more than fifty years of labor, and that is
found in *The Silmarillion* and in the twelve volumes of *The History of
Middle-earth*, along with *The Lord of the Rings* and *The Hobbit*—in
light of what is commonly regarded as the most famous philosophical
analysis of poetic art, Plato's critique of poetry in the *Republic*, which
culminates in his discussion of the "ancient quarrel between poetry
and philosophy." I shall proceed by providing a brief discussion of
each charge that Plato raises against poetry, followed in turn by
some reflections on how Tolkien's *legendarium* may be regarded as
offering a response, as it were, to each charge.

Approaching Tolkien through the lens of Plato's two-pronged
critique of poetry, I shall argue, leads to some previously overlooked
insights into the philosophic character of Tolkien's work. In particular, this approach may enable us to acknowledge and more fully
grasp Tolkien's comprehensive vision of the whole, a poetic achievement intended both to rekindle the experience of wonder and to defend its enduring value. Furthermore, this approach may lead us to
more fully appreciate Tolkien's deft and complex depiction of moral

virtue and its development. In following this approach, we will eventually be drawn to the character of Éowyn of Rohan, and thereby, perhaps most surprisingly, to consider the aspects of Tolkien's work that deal most directly with the claims of modern feminism.

PLATO'S CHARGE THAT POETRY OFFERS "LIES" MASQUERADING AS TRUTH

In book 10 of the *Republic*, Socrates states that there is an "ancient quarrel between philosophy and poetry" (607b).[6] It proves to be a long-standing quarrel, predating Socrates and his contemporaries. Plato suggests, by having Socrates report several seemingly well-known statements made by poets against philosophers, but none by philosophers against poets, that the poets have been the more contentious parties to the quarrel.[7] Subjecting the poetic art to philosophical questioning, and arguing presumably on behalf of philosophy, Socrates raises two distinct but related charges against poetry. The first charge is that by producing images of things rather than providing direct access to the things themselves poetry offers lies masquerading as truth. This charge, which centers on the role of imitation (*mimesis*)[8] in poetry, is connected to what is generally known as the Platonic theory of forms, or ideas, the most explicit discussion of which occurs in the *Republic*. The second charge is that poetry undermines morality, and thus the good of the political community, by supporting the rule of desire rather than the rule of reason. Poetry on its surface seems to exalt models of heroic virtue, but Plato holds that a deeper examination of poetry reveals that it does not ultimately support virtue.

In considering these charges, there are several matters of which one should be mindful. First, in speaking of poetry, Socrates refers to the whole tradition of ancient Greek poetry, including epics, tragedies, and comedies. However, given the preeminent place held by the Homeric epics, Socrates' comments about poetry are often aimed directly at Homer. Furthermore, Plato conveys his critique of poetry in a text that is itself a work of poetry. Although Plato offers, through Socrates, a sharp criticism of the role of imitation in poetry, he himself engages in imitation. In reading the *Republic*, as in reading all of the Platonic dialogues, one encounters an author who excels at the poetic art, revealing himself to be a master at imitating a variety of characters, from Socrates to Thrasymachus, and at employing an array of images and myths, from the Allegory of the Cave to the Myth of Er. With this in mind, it may not be surprising to find that, the more deeply one examines the charges made against poetry, the more ambiguous and insufficient these charges seem. Hence one must consider not only the arguments themselves but also Plato's intent in raising them.

In discussing the first charge against poetry, Plato explores the question of whether poetry is, given its very nature, necessarily detrimental to human life. Book 10 opens with Socrates expressing approval of the interlocutors' earlier decision to ban all imitative poetry from the city-in-speech, since such works "maim the thoughts (*dianoia*) of those who hear them and do not have knowledge of how they really are as a remedy (*pharmakon*)" (595b).[9] As Socrates proceeds to explain why this is the case, he alludes to his earlier discussion of the "forms" or "ideas," according to which all sensible objects are understood as being images or representations of real things. Each particular thing we see in the world is in fact an image, participating in some way in the unseen original, which is the form or idea of the thing. For example, in regarding a flower as beautiful, what we see with our eyes is an image that participates in the form or idea of Beauty. With this theory in the background, Socrates alleges that the poetic imitation of being, by its very nature, is a form of deception. Poets, by producing false images, intentionally deceive people about reality.

Likening poets to painters, Socrates uses the rather curious example of a painting of a bed. Such a painting would be an image of a particular bed, which is itself an image of the "idea" of bed.[10] Thus the poet, like the painter, is "at the third generation from nature" (597e), a maker of a "phantom" (601b). Though Allan Bloom concedes that there is "a kind of surface plausibility" to this argument, he maintains that one nevertheless gets the sense that it is "somehow very wrong."[11] What, precisely, is wrong with this argument begins to come into focus in considering the next step in Socrates' argument. He acknowledges that Homeric poetry refers to many subjects— such as military strategy, legislation, and education (599c–d)—but Socrates faults Homer for failing to offer any specific, practical knowledge of such subjects that could be passed on for the good of society. However, as discussed earlier in the dialogue, practical use-lessness is one of the two most common accusations made against philosophy (487c3), and so the objection applies to Socrates as well as it does to Homer. In showing that from the point of view of prac-tical knowledge or skill neither poetry nor philosophy seems to con-tribute anything essential, Plato may intend to point out the simi-larity, rather than the differences, between poetry and philosophy, and thereby to reveal the flaw in Socrates' initial argument about po-etry's deceptiveness. When one begins to reflect on Socrates' argu-ment, one realizes that it is patently false to claim that poets provide images that are mere copies of objects within the sensible world. On the contrary, with respect to the most interesting and significant images that poets provide, such as those of the gods and the after-life, there are no corresponding objects within the sensible world. Furthermore, the poet does not simply present copies of objects within the sensible word but rather provides a vision of the world that accounts for the *interrelatedness* of the objects within it. Because a poem manifests the poet's comprehensive vision, the activity of the poet cannot be wholly different from the activity of the philosopher, who, by definition, seeks comprehensive wisdom.[12] If there is a dif-ference between them, Plato suggests, it is that the poet, in contrast to the philosopher, cannot provide a defense of his own activity. Hence the real criticism Plato offers here may be that the philosopher can provide a better defense of poetry than the poet himself can.[13]

With respect to the heart of the first charge against poetry, the al-legation that poets produce false images, Plato would need to show that there is a difference between false and true images, and that there is someone who has knowledge of this difference. Such knowledge could be reached only by one with direct access to the originals, that is, the forms or ideas. Yet, as Plato indicates in the *Republic* and elsewhere, direct apprehension of the forms is not possible for human beings.[14] Human access to the ultimate ground of being is limited, in Stanley Rosen's words, to "hypotheses . . . which are based on the use of perceptible things as images of presumed originals."[15] Given that such "hypotheses" can be described only through figurative language, it follows that human wisdom, or human reflection on the highest things, must take poetic form. As Joseph Pieper argues, Plato's own dialogues attest to this fact:

> [Plato's] figurativeness does not spring from a poetic "carelessness" toward exact rendition of reality, or from the reckless play of the creative imagination. Rather, Plato himself expressly terms it a kind of acquiescence in inadequacy, an expedient, a confession of failure. We are not able to speak of matters such as soul, spirit, deity, with any claim to direct description. This is Plato's excuse for attempting to explain the same thing by *several* analogies, as he is wont to do. The implication is that a matter is difficult or impossible to grasp by direct, non-metaphorical statement, and that no single metaphor is in itself completely adequate, none fully accurate.[16]

Although Plato defines the task of philosophy as the study of the whole, of the intelligible order standing behind or underlying the world, he insists that, given the limits of the human mind, the precise nature of this order can never be fully grasped. This means that any particular claim about the nature of the whole would be, in a sense, a "lie." However, such a "lie" would be detrimental only to someone who does not recognize that it is, in fact, a "lie." Plato indicates it is precisely the knowledge of this fact—of the inability of any particular image of the whole to accurately depict the whole—that is the "remedy" against poetry's potential to "maim thoughts" (595b).[17] Yet how does one acquire this knowledge? Can it be gained only through philosophy, or can poetry somehow provide it? Does philosophy alone serve to inoculate individuals against the "lies" of poetry, as it were, or can poetry itself provide such inoculation? In other words, is it possible for poetry to present a vision of the whole that somehow communicates the limitations of that vision? At the very heart of his argument in book 10, Plato suggests that this might be the case. Immediately before stating that there is an "ancient quarrel between poetry and philosophy," Socrates remarks that he and his interlocutors have provided an apology to the poets that justifies their being banished from the city (607b). Immediately thereafter, he invites the poets—or, if not the poets themselves, then perhaps the "lovers of poetry," who can speak on its behalf—to provide an apology that would persuade him to "receive them back from exile" (607c–d). Hence Plato suggests that there are grounds for such an apology and consequent return from banishment, but he does not himself provide one. Yet in the spirit suggested by Plato, Aristotle later takes up this invitation, as it were, arguing that because philosophy begins in wonder, and wonder is sparked by poetry, the "lover of myth or story (*philomuthoi*) . . . is in a sense a philosopher" (*Metaphysics* 982b12–19).[18]

TOLKIEN'S "RESPONSE" TO PLATO'S FIRST CHARGE

To understand Tolkien's poetic art, one must have some grasp of the vast compilation of texts he referred to as the *legendarium*. Over the course of virtually his entire adult life, Tolkien composed an immense number of complex texts, employing a variety of literary genres, in order to chronicle the history of the mythical elves, focusing primarily on the Noldor, the most gifted and most long-suffering elvish clan. He came to refer to these texts, taken together, as the *legendarium*, and he described this compilation as "a body of more or less connected legend, ranging from the large and cosmogonic, to the level of romantic fairy-story."[19] The history chronicled in the *legendarium* involves four distinct eras: (1) the prehistorical period, which tells of certain events, including the creation of the world, that occur before the elves come into being, which they learn about from the Valar; (2) the First Age, during which the elves dwell with the Valar in Aman, the Blessed Realm, but eventually return to Middle-earth in pursuit of the silmarils, the precious gems stolen by the rebel vala, Morgoth; (3) the Second Age, during which the civilization of Númenor is established by those men who have aided the elves in the long battle against Morgoth, as the elves of Middle-earth fashion the Rings of Power and as Sauron fashions the One Ring; and (4) the Third Age, during which the final conflict pits the elves and their allies among the other Free Peoples against Sauron. *The Hobbit* and *Lord of the Rings* recount the events that occur at the end of the Third Age.

Understanding the composition of the *legendarium* is no simple task, given both the tremendous scope of the texts and their fragmentary condition at the time of Tolkien's death in 1973. With the exceptions of *The Hobbit* and *Lord of the Rings*, most of the texts constituting the *legendarium* were, when Tolkien died, left both unfinished and unorganized. To further complicate matters, Tolkien repeatedly left several versions of the same text, often with alterations penciled over existing manuscripts. After Tolkien's death, his son and literary executor, Christopher, devoted more than twenty years to preparing these texts for publication. This massive effort required painstaking organization and editing and, in most cases, Christopher's extensive explanatory notes. Christopher published the first of his father's posthumously published works in 1977 with *Silmarillion*, followed in 1980 by *Unfinished Tales*. From 1984 to 1996, Christopher brought forward, one by one, what would in the end become the twelve-volume *History of Middle-earth*. Following Christopher Tolkien's practice,[20] I shall refer to the vast compendium of texts telling of the earlier part of the history of the elves (dealing primarily with the events of the prehistorical period and the First Age) as the "Silmarillion," to be distinguished from *Silmarillion*, the selections from this vast compendium that Christopher Tolkien put into print in 1977.

Tolkien's poetic vision of the whole is communicated throughout his *legendarium*, but he presents his most succinct and straightforward account of the nature of the whole in the *Ainulindalë*, which tells of the creation of the universe by the one god, Eru, called Ilúvatar, together with the cooperation of the Ainur, a race of demiurgic, spiritual beings previously created by Eru. According to the *Ainulindalë*, Ilúvatar bids the Ainur to join with him in the world's creation, and, once this process is set in motion, he invites those Ainur who so desire to enter directly into the newly created world and to take up the twin tasks of completing the formation of the world and governing it in accord with his will. The greatest among these divine beings become known as the Valar, the powers of the world, and the others among them who are like the Valar, but of lesser degree, are called the Maiar. The Valar and Maiar participate in all aspects of the world's creation, with one exception: Eru alone creates the two races of incarnate rational beings known as the "Children of Ilúvatar," namely, elves and men. In completing the formation of the world, the Valar are in fact preparing all things for the eventual coming of these two "Children."

According to Tolkien's poetic vision, there is hierarchy and distinction between the members of these different races, but all are alike in dignity because all have been given a share in the divine creativity. That is, despite the differences between them, the Valar, elves, and men are alike in that all have, to some degree, the capacity to make or "sub-create." Tolkien indicates that one's character—vala, elf, or man—is determined by one's exercise of this capacity. That is, the most important and difficult task each individual faces is to properly understand and use his or her maker's power, since the act of making entails a recognition of the limits of one's powers, something that is not, Tolkien indicates, simply or obviously evident. As we see in the tales that unfold in the "Silmarillion," all of the rational beings created by Eru are at first uncertain of their abilities, and so must test them in order to know them, that is, in order to acquire self-knowledge. However, these rational creatures are prone to mistake their creaturely power to make or to sub-create for the divine power actually to create. Although Tolkien attributes this mistake to a number of different causes, such as ignorance, impatience, possessiveness, and envy, he maintains that, at its root, this failure results from the desire for self-aggrandizement. Tolkien makes this clear in describing the archetypical fall—the fall of the greatest vala, Melkor, later known as Morgoth. Tolkien mentions a number of reasons for Morgoth's fall, but the central reason is Morgoth's desire "to increase the power and glory of the part assigned to himself" (*S*, 16).

Plato claims that all poetry offers a particular vision of the whole, and Tolkien offers such a vision in the "Silmarillion." Yet within the "Silmarillion" itself, Tolkien indicates that the vision it presents is imperfect. By doing so, Tolkien responds, as it were, to the Platonic warning about the power of poetic imagery to tell "lies," and thus to dampen, rather than spark, wonder. The continuing popularity of Tolkien's work attests to its power to charm, but Tolkien seeks to move his readers away from complacency by communicating, in several ways, the limitations of his poetic vision of the whole.

First, he presents the early history of the elves primarily in the form of legends or tales, all of which are to be understood as having been handed down by human beings, over the course of many generations. Tolkien thereby moves his readers to ponder how, over time, the tales may have been subject to alteration and corruption, even to becoming "blended and confused" with "Mannish myths and cosmic ideas" (*MR*, 370).[21] Furthermore, the very structure of the "Silmarillion" reflects Tolkien's acknowledgment of the limitations of its vision. With respect to almost all of the major legends told in the "Silmarillion," Tolkien crafted several different versions of the same tale. In so doing, Tolkien suggests that the same events may be viewed in different ways by different peoples in different times, and thus that no one version of a legend can ever provide a comprehensive account of the events it relates.[22]

Second, though it is true that Tolkien provides, in many respects, a defense of the dignity of the human capacity for language,[23] he also points out the limitations of this capacity. Like Plato, Tolkien associates the limited character of all human speech with the limitations of the human mind. This point comes across forcefully in his fascinating essay "Quendi and Eldar," which is presented as a learned commentary on the origin and early development of the elvish languages, written sometime during the Third Age (i.e., near the end of the time in which the elves dwelt in Middle-earth) and based largely on the lore of an elvish scholar named Pengolodh (*War of the Jewels*, 396–97).[24] At one point, the essay addresses the difficult matter of rightly interpreting the *Ainulindalë*, the text that tells of the creation of the universe. Reflecting on the tradition that the *Ainulindalë* was composed, in its earliest form, by Manwë, lord of the Valar, the learned Pengolodh offers judgments that are reminiscent of Plato's point that the highest expression of human wisdom must take poetic form, the form of a "lie." Pengolodh reports that, in composing this story, Manwë did not simply tell the elves exactly what happened, for that, Pengolodh maintains, would have been both impossible to put into the language of the elves, and incomprehensible to the more limited elvish minds. Hence, Pengolodh concludes, Manwë must have presented the *Ainulindalë* "to us not only in the words of Quenya [the original elvish language], but also according to our modes of thought and our imagination of the visible world, in symbols that were intelligible to us" (*Jewels*, 407).

Third, throughout the *legendarium*, Tolkien refers repeatedly to the experience of "wonder," and he treats it in a way that is quite similar to Plato's treatment of it. The experience of wonder brings on a kind of surprise, even astonishment, upon realizing that one stands in the presence of something previously unknown or unrecognized. In most cases, the experience of wonder sparks the desire to know or understand. Within the *legendarium*, the experience of wonder is attributed to beings of all kinds, including the Valar, elves, men, dwarves, and hobbits. Let us consider a few examples. The Valar experience awe when Ilúvatar grants them a vision of the unfolding world (*S*, 17). Even though they have foreknowledge of the elves, they are "filled with wonder" when they actually see the elves for the first time (*S*, 49). Similarly, when the elves first come into being, they walk the earth "in wonder" (*S*, 49), and during their long march across Middle-earth to reach Aman, they are "filled with wonder" at all they see (*S*, 53). Upon seeing the silmarils for the first time, all who dwell in Aman are "filled with wonder and delight" (*S*, 67). When Beren calls out to the fair elf-maid Lúthien for the first time, she halts "in wonder" (*S*, 165), and when, at the end of their quest, Lúthien brings Beren before Thingol's throne, Thingol looks "in wonder upon Beren, whom he had thought dead" (*S*, 184). When Finrod Felagund encounters the first men who have entered into Beleriand, he sings to them, and they are utterly enchanted by "the beauty of the music and the wonder of the song" (*S*, 140). When the dwarf Gimli realizes that, unlike all of the other elves he has encountered, Galadriel holds no resentment against the dwarves, and in fact offers him her understanding and friendship, he is filled with "wonder" (*LOTR*, 356).[25] The hobbit Frodo, as he gazes for the first time upon the land of Lothlórien, is "lost in wonder" (*LOTR*, 350). For Tolkien, as for Plato, the experience of wonder is a necessary step in the direction of wisdom, and thus, for the most part, Tolkien portrays the experience of wonder as indicating a character's potential for wisdom.

Tolkien provides very few instances in which wicked characters experience wonder, but what he conveys, in these rare cases, is quite instructive. In explaining how Gollum came to reside in the caves at the base of the Misty Mountains, Gandalf provides what might be deemed as a kind of reverse account of the Allegory of the Cave in Plato's *Republic*. After being exiled from his community, Gandalf explains that Gollum had wandered for a long time alone, preferring the dark. One day, while "bending over a pool," he felt "a burning on the back of his head," and when he looked upon the "dazzling light" reflected in the water, his eyes were pained (*LOTR*, 54). He "wondered at it, for he had almost forgotten about the Sun" (*LOTR*, 54). But significantly, rather than moving him to reflect on the existence of the sun, and thus in its splendid light to reflect on the truth of his situation, Gollum's experience of wonder renders him angry and resentful. "For the last time," Gandalf declares, he looked at the sun and "shook his fist at her" (*LOTR*, 54).

Similarly, Tolkien writes of one occasion on which the treacherous wizard Saruman also experiences wonder. Even after he has tried to kill Frodo, Frodo refuses to allow Sam, or any of the other hobbits, to harm Saruman. Saruman, Frodo explains, "was great once, of a noble kind that we should not dare to raise our hands against" (*LOTR*, 1019), and though he "is fallen, and his cure is beyond us," he should still be spared, "in the hope that he may find it" (*LOTR*, 1019). Perhaps recognizing that Frodo's reasoning is based not on weak sentimentality or hobbit naiveté, Saruman experiences "wonder" at Frodo's words. Yet Saruman's wonder is "mingled" with both "respect and hatred" (*LOTR*, 1019). As with Gollum, Saruman responds to the experience of wonder not by pondering how it is that Frodo has come to be so wise, or by considering the truth of Frodo's words about Saruman and his need for a "cure," but rather with anger and resentment. Figuratively, if not literally, Saruman, like Gollum, raises his fist in defiance against the agent that has brought on the experience of wonder, telling Frodo, in the form of something like a curse, that he will face terrible suffering, despite his seeming victory.

PLATO'S CHARGE THAT POETRY
UNDERMINES MORALITY

The charge that poetry undermines morality is introduced in Socrates' discussion of the poets' portrayal of "what the gods and heroes are like" (*Rep.* 377e–378a), those who serve as models in the moral education of the city's rulers. Arguing that the poetic depictions of the gods and heroes do not provide consistently good models for the education of the city's rulers, Socrates condemns much of what the poets offer. By depicting the gods as being in conflict with each other, sometimes punishing good men and rewarding bad ones, the poets undermine the practice of virtue. Similarly, in depicting heroes such as Achilles, Agamemnon, and Odysseus, the poets portray them as at times being overcome by passion and engaging in shameful acts, thus living their lives not according to reason, at least not consistently, but according to passion.

Socrates attributes the poets' depiction of character to a combination of ignorance and desire for good repute. This leads them to engage in what is, essentially, a kind of pandering. Rather than providing models who exemplify wise judgment, poetic imitation "keeps company with the part of us that is far from wise judgment or prudence (*phronesis*)" (603a–b). Taking as his standard "whatever looks to be beautiful or noble (*kalos*) to the many—those who do not know anything" (602b), the poet "awakens" and "nourishes" the passionate part of the soul while destroying the reasoning part (605b). Socrates indicates the potential danger of poetry's charm when, explicitly including even himself, he states that "we enjoy" observing the characters who appear in poetry, the suffering characters in the tragedies or the ridiculous characters in the comedies, and we praise "as a good poet the man who most puts us in this state" (605d). Hence Plato indicates that the heart of the moral threat posed by poetry lies in its encouragement—both subtle and charming—of unrestrained desire. This explains, as Rosen argues, Plato's association of poetry with tyranny throughout the dialogue:

> In the extreme case, man desires to become, not merely the master and possessor of nature, but the producer of nature. He wishes to transform nature into an artifact or poem . . . In order to satisfy his desires completely, man must recreate the world in his own image.[26]

Although he acknowledges that he has long felt "a certain friendship for Homer, and shame before him" (595b) that made him unwilling to criticize, Socrates nevertheless subjects Homer, the "teacher and leader of all these fine tragic things" (595c), to philosophic questioning. In doing so, Plato shows that there are two levels to Homer's poetic teaching. On its surface, Homer's poetry provides support for the moral virtues. However, upon more careful examination, one sees that Homer's poetry does not provide any ultimate support for the practice of virtue.[27]

Presenting his own poetic account of death, the Myth of Er, as an alternative to the account of death Homer presents in the *Odyssey*, Plato invites his readers to compare the two. Central to Homer's account, Plato indicates, is Odysseus's encounter, in his journey to the underworld, with Achilles, the greatest of all the Greek heroes. Achilles communicates nothing but despair over death, saying that he would rather be "a slave to another . . . than rule over all the dead who have perished."[28] Homer is tragedy's "leader" (598d), Plato suggests, not only because he serves as the source and inspiration for the whole tradition of Greek tragedy, but also, and more importantly, because his work supports the notion that human life is inherently and unalterably tragic. Human beings long for justice, but the cosmos is wholly indifferent to this longing. Hence human belief in ultimate justice is groundless. Everyone suffers, some greatly. Suffering can be faced with nobility, but it has no ultimate meaning, no greater purpose. The fate of all, regardless of how they bear the sufferings of life, is essentially the same, to be thrust into the great void of death.

Plato, like the poets he criticizes, recognizes the ineradicable nature of suffering in human life, but he proposes a response unlike that of the tragedians. Referring to the suffering of a man who experiences the death of a beloved child (603e), Socrates alludes to our inability to judge whether any particular event or deed is truly good or bad without placing that event within the context of the greater whole. That is, our ability to properly judge events is dependent on having knowledge of the whole. Although he acknowledges that it is impossible for a human being to ever achieve knowledge of the whole, Plato nevertheless suggests that, with the passage of time, one may grow in understanding. For Plato—and, as we shall see, for Tolkien—it is in looking back, in gazing retrospectively, that human wisdom reaches its highest potential. For this reason Socrates advocates "quiet" (604b) and "deliberation" (604c) in response to suffering, even the terrible suffering that comes with the loss of a beloved child. Such a response indicates recognition that the meaning of the event, however painful, cannot be known, at least not yet. What Socrates seems most concerned about is the tendency, encouraged by poetry, to become emotionally and unreflectively fixated on the sufferings and injustices of life, "like children who have stumbled and who hold on to the hurt place and spend their time in crying out" (604c). By encouraging this unmediated response to suffering, poetry prevents us from having the patience necessary for growth in understanding. Poetry discourages us from developing the kind of disposition that would enable us to respond to suffering in a reasonable way. Yet in pointing out how poetry discourages a philosophic approach to life, Socrates hints that such discouragement might not be a necessary characteristic of poetry per se. That is, some other kind of poetry may be possible, a kind of poetry that, in providing models of genuine human goodness and wise judgment, is beneficial rather than detrimental to human life. Socrates indicates that this would be an immensely difficult endeavor, given that, unlike the "irritable" character, the prudent character "is neither easily imitated nor, when imitated, easily understood" (604e).

TOLKIEN'S "RESPONSE" TO PLATO'S SECOND CHARGE

Tolkien answers, in two distinct ways, Plato's charge that poetry undermines morality by revealing that the cosmos provides no ultimate support for virtue: Tolkien offers a vivid and unequivocal condemnation of the practice of vice and presents a clear though subtle defense of the practice of virtue.

Tolkien's Depiction of Vice

Tolkien's depiction of wicked character responds, as it were, to Plato's claim that, through its power to charm, poetry tends to make wickedness appear sympathetic, even alluring. In agreement with Plato, Tolkien regards poetry as being very susceptible to making wickedness appear attractive. Acutely aware of this difficulty, Tolkien takes great care in his depiction of bad characters, so that they do not attract but repel.[29] Although Tolkien clearly is not the first writer who seeks to avoid portraying evil as attractive, he is arguably one of the most successful, given that he so convincingly associates evil with misery. That is, the characters in the *legendarium* powerfully exemplify the Augustinian principle—rooted in Platonic philosophy transformed by Christian theology—that evil is essentially a privation of being, an absence of good, and thus that those who pursue evil ultimately end up in a condition of abject misery.

The power of Tolkien's depiction of vice-ridden characters as miserable—and, indeed, the strength of his depiction of character in general—stems, at least in part, from the fact that many of the characters within the *legendarium* are either immortal, as in the case of the Valar and the elves,[30] or, in certain circumstances, have an extraordinarily long life, as in the case of the Númenóreans and those mortals who come into possession of a Ring of Power. By depicting characters who have extraordinarily long lives, Tolkien is able to vividly and meticulously convey something that is generally hidden from view, and thus extremely difficult to convey—the transformation of soul that occurs in the doing of evil. Tolkien communicates this inner transformation largely through his depiction of the outer transformation of evil characters. By means of showing how one's outer condition is altered, Tolkien conveys how, in choosing evil, one's inner condition is also altered. The outer transformation is thus a dramatic representation of the inner change. All of the evil characters in the *legendarium* undergo a process of physical alteration, losing their original beauty and wholesomeness, and this loss is a sign of more fundamental loss of the capacity for wisdom and sympathetic understanding, for creativity, for love and friendship.

In the case of Morgoth, the prototype and greatest of all wicked characters within the *legendarium*, Tolkien shows how, in rejecting the fundamental order established by Ilúvatar, Morgoth's physical and psychological characteristics are gradually diminished. Over the course of the vast ages in which he strives for domination of the world, Morgoth is transformed from the most magnificent, skillful, and noble of beings into the most repulsive, foolish, and ignoble. Tolkien conveys this point most forcefully in his description of Morgoth, beginning with his original theft of the silmarils from the elves and ending thousands of years later with his defeat by the army led by the Valar. What does Morgoth do throughout all these years, years in which he believes himself to be "free," referring to himself as "King of the World" (*S*, 81)? Tolkien's imagery is striking: Morgoth sits on a throne in a room at the bottom of a deep dungeon, wearing a crown in which he has set the stolen silmarils. His hands, having been burned by the silmarils, are blackened, causing him constant pain. Though he suffers great weariness from the weight of the crown on his head, he never removes it. The great majesty of his person has been transformed, such that the sight of his face inspires nothing but sheer terror (*S*, 81–82). When the Valar finally make war upon Morgoth, he remains hidden in the depths of his dungeon. Once they finally reach him, he reveals how small-minded and wretched he has become, cowering before them and begging for clemency (*S*, 252).

One sees a similar approach in Tolkien's depiction of the character Gollum from *Lord of the Rings*. Gollum's possession of the One Ring greatly extends the length of his life, but in adding immense quantity to his years the Ring provides no increased quality. On the contrary, it makes Gollum utterly wretched. As in the case of Morgoth, the long transformation of Gollum's outer condition—whereby his original hobbit appearance is almost entirely altered for the worse—provides Tolkien's readers with a glimpse into Gollum's inner condition, his soul. Terribly pale and gaunt, no longer walking upright on two legs but rather moving about in a crouched position, using his hands and his feet, Gollum's original hobbit shape has become virtually unrecognizable. Having been denied light for so many years, his eyes have become sharp-sighted, gleaming in the dark like a cat's. He continually sniffs the ground, like a dog, frequently making hissing sounds and eating only raw meat and fish.

Gandalf, in the course of his quest to determine whether the ring in Bilbo's possession is in fact the One Ruling Ring, learns that the creature now known as Gollum is a hobbit, originally named Sméagol. He is from the clan of hobbits known within the Shire as the Stoors, who, long before settling in the Shire had lived along the banks of the river Anduin.[31] The transformation from Sméagol to Gollum began, Gandalf learns, with Sméagol's decision to commit the most horrific and antisocial of crimes in order to gain possession of the Ring for himself: Sméagol murdered Déagol, his companion and likely his close relative, who had found the Ring while fishing. Once he gains possession of the Ring, Sméagol uses the invisibility conveyed by the Ring for "crooked and malicious" purposes (*LOTR*, 53), thereby coming to be shunned, and eventually exiled, by the members of his clan. Yet though cut off from hobbit companionship, he is unable to overcome his need for it. In the period just before his exile, he had begun to mutter to himself and make gurgling sounds in his throat, a habit that led his relatives to begin referring to him as "Gollum." He continues his muttering during the long years of his isolation, at first calling the Ring "my Precious" but eventually identifying with it so closely that he also refers to himself as "my Precious." That is, he becomes so deluded as to think of himself no longer as an individual, as "I," but rather as a duo, as "we." In moments of relative lucidity, he is aware of the misery of his condition. He refers to the supposed "we" as "lonely" and "wretched" (*LOTR*, 614–15), and he responds to Frodo's use of his real name, Sméagol, by remarking that this person "went away long ago" and is now "lost" (*LOTR*, 616). Through this depiction of the perversion of Gollum's natural sociality, Tolkien illustrates the Augustinian argument that evil can express itself only as a distortion of the good.[32]

Like Plato, Tolkien associates the desire for tyranny, for "[mastery] over other wills" (*S*, 18) with a failure to appreciate one's limits. Though Tolkien is critical of such failure, he nevertheless conveys a sympathetic understanding of it. That is, without in any way indicting the creator, Ilúvatar, Tolkien shows that, in giving his creatures a share in the divine creativity, the creator has endowed them with a dangerous gift, one that even the best-intentioned among them are likely at times to misuse. Nevertheless, Tolkien emphasizes that the way to respond to this gift is to use it as well as one can, and, when one fails to use it properly, to admit failure, ask for pardon, and learn from the experience. Tolkien conveys this point, for example, in the story of the vala Aulë's making of the dwarves. Desirous of having pupils to teach, and impatient while awaiting the arrival of the Children of Ilúvatar, Aulë attempts to bring to life a race of beings modeled after the Children. But because he does not possess a full understanding of the Children whom Ilúvatar will create, Aulë originates a lesser creature known as the dwarves. Ilúvatar is greatly displeased with Aulë's act, yet, in light of Aulë's motives, his admission of wrongdoing, and his willingness to give up the dwarves, Ilúvatar not only forgives Aulë but grants the dwarves what Aulë sought but could not provide for them: independent life and a place within the world (*S*, 43–44). The differences between the dwarves and the elves are a source of constant tension, and sometimes outright conflict, between the two races. Nevertheless, the culture developed by the dwarves is admirable in many respects, as the dwarves' skills in metallurgy and mining provide great benefits both to themselves and to those with whom they interact, such as the elves of Nargothrond during the First Age and the elves of Eregion during the Second Age.

Those who continuously misuse their divinely given creativity, Tolkien maintains, are in danger of destroying it.[33] In "Notes on Motives in the *Silmarillion*," Tolkien remarks that Morgoth's lying, even and especially to himself, eventually leads him to lose his capacity for "rational thought" (*MR*, 395) and to become subject to "nihilistic madness" (*MR*, 396). Enraged over the fact that much in the world "was not from his own mind and was interwoven with the work and thoughts of others" (*MR*, 396), Morgoth gradually reaches the point of madness, seeking to annihilate all things, to "destroy their being" (*MR*, 395). Yet even if Morgoth had succeeded in wreaking the havoc he wished, bringing about the "destruction and reduction [of the world] to *nil*" (*MR*, 397), he still "would have been defeated," Tolkien writes, "because [the world] would still have 'existed' independent of his own mind, a world in potential" (*MR*, 396).

The condition of Denethor, the Steward of Gondor, comes, in some respects, to resemble Morgoth's "nihilistic madness." Rejecting Gandalf's attempts to persuade him that his judgment, being rooted in "pride and despair" (*LOTR*, 853), is severely impaired, Denethor declares that, if he can no longer have things as he wishes, "as they were in all the days of my life," then he will have *"naught"* (*LOTR*, 854). As with Morgoth, in choosing "naught" Denethor rejects life and creativity in favor of death and destruction. Believing that there is no hope for his family or his kingdom, he defiantly rejects them both, attempting to kill himself and his only remaining son, abandoning his duties while the city is under attack.

Saruman also moves in the direction of "nihilistic madness." Once his hopes of ruling Middle-earth have been defeated, he is consumed by malice and a desire for revenge against those he believes responsible. After meeting the hobbits as they journey back to the Shire, he decides to enter the Shire himself, not out of a desire to rule or subdue it, as had been his previous intent, but only out of malice, to harm its inhabitants as much as he can. Although he does not, like Denethor, die by his own hand, his actions nevertheless bring about his death, at the hand of his lone remaining companion, Gríma Wormtongue. In death, the true wretchedness of Saruman's condition is revealed. In one of the most remarkable passages in the whole of the *legendarium*, Saruman's soul is portrayed as being momentarily visible, appearing as "a grey mist . . . rising slowly to a great height like smoke from a fire" (*LOTR*, 1020). After wavering for a moment as it gazes toward the West, Saruman's soul bends away and dissolves "into *nothing*" (*LOTR*, 1020; emphasis added). The condition of his maddened soul corresponds to the hideous transformation of his body. As Frodo gazes upon it, "long years of death" are "suddenly revealed in it," his "shriveled face" becoming "rags of skin upon a hideous skull" (*LOTR*, 1020).

Tolkien's Depiction of Virtue

As with his evil characters, so too with his virtuous ones, Tolkien depicts their outer, bodily transformation in a way that helps to dramatize their inner, spiritual transformation. The choice of evil leads to physical alteration in the direction of ugliness and revulsion, but the choice of good leads in the direction of beauty and splendor. Nevertheless, Tolkien does not provide a precise parallel between the two, for he does not portray even his most virtuous characters as being wholly and permanently transformed, as is the case with the most wicked. That is, whereas Tolkien suggests that the physical alteration of wicked characters is both clearly visible and permanent, he is more tentative in his depiction of the physical alteration of virtuous characters. The virtuous do, at times, exhibit extraordinary beauty or splendor, but only intermittently. In the case of a character such as Gandalf, this seems to be intentional, so as purposefully to conceal the wizard's extraordinary qualities. For example, after returning from his battle with the Balrog, Gandalf is portrayed as having been physically transformed, such that he appears to shine "as if with some light kindled within . . . holding a power beyond the strength of kings" (*LOTR*, 501). His physical transformation is meant to reveal his greatness of soul, indicating his fitness to lead the Free Peoples against Sauron. Having been "sent back," he tells his friends—by whom, he does not say—in order to complete his "task" (*LOTR*, 502), he has been granted what, in a letter, Tolkien refers to as "an enhancement" of "wisdom and power" (*Letters*, 202) that he reveals only at certain key moments. In response to Gimli's surprise at seeing him clothed no longer in grey but in the former guise of Saruman, "all in white," Gandalf states, "Indeed I *am* Saruman, one might almost say, Saruman as he should have been" (*LOTR*, 495). Yet despite this permanent enhancement of his powers, Gandalf continues to reveal his true nature only as needed, for example, when he rides forth to aid Faramir, "*shining, unveiled* once more, a light starting from his upraised hand" (*LOTR*, 820; emphasis added).

In other cases, however, Tolkien depicts the virtuous as exhibiting—again intermittently, and only temporarily—certain extraordinary physical characteristics. In such cases, Tolkien indicates not so much the precise nature of their soul at present but rather the end toward which they are headed if they persevere in virtue. For example, at numerous points Frodo manifests physical characteristics that are meant to reveal the condition of soul he may eventually achieve, so long as he continues along the path meant for him. As he recovers from his injuries in Rivendell, for instance, Gandalf perceives the effect of the Ring on him, discerning "a hint . . . of transparency about him" (*LOTR*, 223). This effect may bode ill for Frodo, insofar it reveals his potential to be defeated by evil and thus permanently to "fade," but it also points toward his potential to become a transparent embodiment of virtue, if he remains faithful to his quest. Gandalf ruminates that, in the end, Frodo will not "fade" but rather "become like a glass filled with a clear light" (*LOTR*, 223). Like Gandalf, Sam also notices "a light" that seems "to be shining faintly within" Frodo as he recovers in Rivendell from the ringwraith's attack (*LOTR*, 652). In the course of their journey to Mordor, Sam perceives an increase of this "light" within Frodo, a sign of Frodo's growth in virtue even as he struggles against the terrible power of the Ring. While in Ithilien, as Sam watches Frodo sleeping, Sam perceives that "the light" shining within Frodo is "even clearer and stronger than it had been in the house of Elrond" (*LOTR*, 652).

Given the differences between his depictions of wickedness and goodness, Tolkien suggests that, within this mortal life, the achievement of wholesale wickedness is possible, but the achievement of wholesale goodness is not. Those who choose evil may eventually become fixed in their character, wholly bound by the evil choices they have made, whereas those who choose goodness, however virtuous they become, are never wholly free of the potential for evil. However paradoxical it may seem, it is the wisest and most virtuous who are most aware of their own potential to succumb to evil, and thus most vigilant against it.

Plato claims that, in addition to making wickedness seem attractive, the poets are unable to portray genuine goodness or virtue. The root of this failure, Plato indicates, is in their inability to provide any models of "prudential wisdom" or "wise judgment" (*phronesis*), the intellectual virtue that provides proper guidance to human action. The poets' failure to depict characters who exhibit prudential wisdom may be the result of the fact that, as Plato repeatedly points out in his dialogues, this virtue is very difficult both to define and to exercise. There are general principles providing human beings with guidance for action, but these principles are not rules—they cannot simply be used to determine what particular action to take or to avoid. Deciding how to act rightly requires consideration of the entire context in which one acts, and, in some cases, the best choice may be in tension with what is generally true. As Socrates famously argues in book 1 of the *Republic*, although it is generally true that a man should "give back what he takes," it is nevertheless the case that a man should not return a weapon to its owner if the owner is in a fit of madness (331c).

Despite Plato's assertion that poetry is unable to adequately depict the virtue of prudential wisdom, Tolkien provides a rich and compelling account of this virtue. He achieves this in two distinct though related ways. First, Tolkien illustrates the *process* of prudential judgment. He depicts a number of scenes in which certain honorable, well-intentioned characters—who seek to be virtuous even if they have not yet acquired the virtue of prudential wisdom in the complete sense—must make difficult choices in times of crisis. By depicting the struggles in judgment undergone by characters such as Éomer, Marshall of Rohan, and Beregond, tower guard of Gondor, Tolkien demonstrates how wise judgment requires a careful manner of reasoning that takes into account both general principles and particular circumstances. Second, Tolkien explicates the fundamental *character* of prudential wisdom. He exposes what prudential wisdom is, and what it is not; what resembles it, in certain key respects, yet falls short of it. Tolkien achieves this by providing an in-depth portrayal of characters, some of whom exhibit prudential wisdom in the complete sense, such as Gandalf and Aragorn; some exhibit cunning, a vice that resembles prudence, such as Saruman and Denethor; and some exhibit a mode of judgment that is not vicious as such but that falls short of prudential wisdom out of zeal for honor, such as Éowyn and Éomer.

The Process of Prudential Reasoning

In the first place, to illustrate the process of prudential reasoning, Tolkien provides a number of cases in which certain characters must consider whether the best course of action requires the violation of a law or custom that, in itself and on the whole, is just and reasonable. Haldir, the elf who guards the borders of Lórien, decides to allow the members of the Company of the Ring to enter into Lórien, even though such entry violates the law prohibiting admittance to uninvited strangers (*LOTR*, 343–47). Upon meeting Aragorn, Legolas, and Gimli wandering the lands of Rohan in pursuit of their kidnapped friends, Merry and Pippin, Éomer decides to allow them to continue their pursuit, even to actively aid them, even though such aid violates the law prohibiting strangers from roaming freely without the leave of the king (*LOTR*, 438). Háma, King Théoden's door warden, allows Gandalf to bring his staff into the king's presence, despite the custom whereby weapons must be left behind (*LOTR*, 511). After meeting Frodo and Sam in Ithilien, Faramir allows them to continue their quest, despite the law commanding that all who wander through Ithilien without the Lord of Gondor's permission be slain (*LOTR*, 665–68). Upon learning from Pippin that Denethor intends to kill himself along with his injured son, Faramir, Beregond violates the law prohibiting any member of the tower guards from leaving his post without the permission of the steward in order to try to save Faramir (*LOTR*, 827). In all of these cases, Tolkien illustrates the process whereby various well-intentioned characters struggle to weigh and sort out various arguments with respect to some particular action, in order to arrive at the best judgment.

THE DISTINCTION BETWEEN WISDOM AND CLEVERNESS

In the second place, Tolkien enables his readers to discern the differences—sometimes glaring, sometimes subtler—between those who are wise and those who are not. Tolkien depicts key differences between characters such as Gandalf and Aragorn, who exhibit prudential judgment in the complete sense, and characters such as Saruman and Denethor, who exhibit not the virtue of prudence but rather the vice most closely resembling it, "cunning" or "cleverness."[34] Tolkien maintains, in accord with Platonic teaching, that prudential judgment entails the ability to recognize and attain those ends that are in accord with what is truly good, and to do so using only good or proper means. Hence those with prudential wisdom remain steadfast with respect to their highest goals or purposes, and to the means they are willing to use in pursuit of such ends. The clever or cunning, by contrast, pursue wicked ends and are willing to use wicked means to achieve them. Tolkien contrasts prudence and cunning through his depiction of the confrontation between Gandalf and Saruman at Isengard. Saruman seeks to persuade Gandalf that they should join together in forming an alliance with Sauron, arguing that doing so would entail a change only of means, not ends. Though they would "[deplore] maybe the evils done along the way," Saruman states, they would still pursue their long-held "high and ultimate purpose: Knowledge, Rule, Order" (*LOTR*, 259). Gandalf, however, recognizes that Saruman's proposal entails a fundamental alteration of both means and ends. Gandalf sees that Saruman "has left the path of wisdom" (*LOTR*, 259), his highest purpose now being to gain possession of the Ring for himself and thereby to achieve absolute mastery over Middle-earth.

Tolkien indicates that the wise judgment exhibited by characters such as Gandalf and Aragorn is due largely to the steadfast effort and patience they exhibit in learning as much as possible about the world and the course of history. It is striking to consider, for example, that Gandalf devotes roughly seventeen years to investigating whether the ring Bilbo found is indeed the One Ring. This is not to imply, however, that prudential judgment always necessitates a lengthy assessment of a situation in order to reach a conclusion. On the contrary, especially in the face of unforeseen circumstances, those with prudential wisdom will respond quickly or even immediately. Aragorn, for example, displays this kind of judgment in his decision to peer into the Stone of Orthanc (the *palantír* that had been used by Saruman). He properly judges that, in the present circumstances, he should hazard the risk and use the Stone in order to focus Sauron's attention on him rather than on Frodo. Gimli, upon learning what Aragorn has done, reproves him, reminding him that "even Gandalf feared that encounter" (*LOTR*, 780). Yet although Aragorn would be the first to admit Gandalf's overall superiority in prudential wisdom, he nevertheless judges that he, not Gandalf, is "the lawful master of the stone," having "both the right and the strength to use it" (*LOTR*, 780). Gandalf, correctly guessing what Aragorn has done, confirms the wisdom of his decision, praising him for being "bold, determined, able to take his own counsel and dare great risks at need" (*LOTR*, 815). Prudential judgment, as we see in this example, requires that one have a proper understanding of one's true capacities and thus of one's limits. Without falling prey to arrogance, Aragorn properly judges that he will be able to look into the Stone without falling under the mastery of Sauron. In other circumstances, however, we see prudential judgment exercised not in the acceptance of risk but in the refusal to take a risk, however great the need of the moment may be. For example, each of the characters to whom Frodo offers the Ring—Gandalf (*LOTR*, 61), Aragorn (*LOTR*, 247), and Galadriel (*LOTR*, 365)—display wise judgment in refusing to take it, recognizing that, however intelligent and well-intentioned, their taking of the Ring would lead not to their mastery of it but rather its eventual mastery of them.

THE DISTINCTION BETWEEN WISDOM AND HONOR: THE CASE OF ÉOWYN

In addition to contrasting prudential wisdom and cunning, Tolkien explores the subtler differences between prudential wisdom and another mode of judgment that, without being vicious, still falls short of prudential wisdom. In the characters of Éowyn and Éomer, we encounter a particular mode of judgment exercised by individuals who, though gifted with respect to intelligence and nobility, have not as yet developed prudential wisdom in the complete sense. Their capacity to judge is hampered, Tolkien indicates, by their tendency to regard honor—specifically, the honor won through courage in battle—as the greatest good. This desire for valor in warfare is, Tolkien emphasizes, one of the most distinctive traits of the people of Rohan, a desire that both Éowyn and Éomer seem to cultivate, at least initially, without question. Tolkien maintains that there is much that is praiseworthy about the Rohirrim, but at the same time he subtly indicates their characteristic deficiencies. In his portrayal of Éowyn, he provides his most pointed ruminations about the strengths and weaknesses of the Rohirrim, focusing primarily on their understanding of honor.

To understand what is problematic about the Rohirrim, it may be helpful to consider Aristotle's commentary on honor, which he discusses in the context of examining the meaning of happiness, or the good life. Noting that the "cultivated and active" identify the good with honor (*NE*, 1095b22–23),[35] Aristotle remarks that they are mistaken in their thinking, since honor "depends on those who bestow it rather than the one who receives it," whereas goodness must be something that "belongs to the one who possesses it and cannot be taken away from him easily" (*NE*, 1095b25–28). Those who identify honor with goodness are mistaken, Aristotle goes on to argue, but they are not wholly wrong. In pursuing honor, they are in fact seeking something else, such as assurance of their own goodness or virtue. This explains, Aristotle states, why they seek to be honored by the wise or prudent (*ton phronimon*), those who are truly capable of judging their goodness (*NE*, 1095b28–29). Offering both praise and subtle correction, Aristotle concludes that the end sought by the "cultivated and active" is indeed virtue rather than honor. Through his depiction of the Rohirrim in general, and of Éowyn in particular, Tolkien offers a similar combination of praise and correction. Éowyn becomes capable of developing prudential wisdom, Tolkien shows, only insofar as she comes to recognize her deficiencies of judgment, recognizing that these deficiencies stem largely from her identification of goodness with honor rather than with virtue as such.

Éowyn's mode of judgment is similar to Éomer's, yet her circumstances are quite different from his, a difference that helps to explain her seemingly more serious mistakes in judgment. Tolkien depicts instances in which both Éomer and Éowyn manifest deficient judgment,[36] but there are no instances in which Éomer's judgment results in his taking, or commanding others to take, a morally objectionable action. In one particular action, however, Éowyn seems guilty of grave moral failure—her decision to abandon her position of stewardship in the king's stead in order to accompany Théoden into battle in Gondor. Tolkien clearly indicates the moral deficiency that underlies this decision, and he provides a sympathetic explanation that serves as a correction not only for Éowyn but also for Éomer, and for the Rohirrim in general, given that Éowyn's decision relates directly to her misunderstanding of honor.

To understand Éowyn's character, Tolkien suggests, we must take into account her circumstances. Her parents died when she and her brother, Éomer, were both children,[37] at which time Théoden, their uncle, "took [them] into his house, calling them son and daughter" (*LOTR*, 1070). From this point on, Éowyn is without the companionship of any female family member, since all the others within the household are male: Théoden, his only child, Théodred,[38] and Éomer. One wonders whether this lack of feminine guidance contributes to Éowyn's difficulties in understanding her proper role in life. It is also clear that Théoden dearly loves both the niece and nephew he has adopted, but he tends to take Éowyn for granted, to overlook her, and Éomer tends to do likewise. This fact is made plain in the remarkable scene in which Théoden, immediately after recovering from Saruman's spell, decides that he will accompany his men into battle. Determining that he should appoint someone to govern in his absence the people left behind, he asks his men to identify someone worthy of trust. Háma responds that the people trust in "the House of Eorl" (those of the line descended from Eorl, the first king of Rohan), to which Théoden replies, "Éomer I cannot spare, nor would he stay . . . and *he is the last of that House*" (*LOTR*, 523; emphasis added). One can only wonder what goes through Éowyn's mind—given that she is also of the House of Eorl—upon hearing Théoden speak these words. Correcting Théoden, Háma states that Éomer is not the last of the line. There is also his sister, Éowyn, who is "fearless and high-hearted" and loved by all (*LOTR*, 523). Théoden, recognizing the truth of Háma's words, immediately appoints Éowyn to rule in his stead. Yet this does not erase the fact that he failed to consider her earlier, even after Háma's initial suggestion, nor the fact that Éomer also overlooked her; it is Háma, after all, not Éomer, who reminds Théoden that Éowyn is also of the House of Eorl. Hence, even though Théoden and Éomer clearly love and esteem Éowyn, they also tend to overlook her, to take her for granted. Their reasons for doing so, Tolkien indicates, stem from their own deficiencies in judgment, and these contribute directly to Éowyn's deficiencies.

Éowyn's mode of judgment is revealed most vividly in her encounter with Aragorn, just before he sets out for the Paths of the Dead. In making her points, Éowyn frequently refers to the value of winning "renown" or "honour." She compliments Aragorn in what, for her, is the highest possible manner, referring to him as a man of "renown and prowess" (*LOTR*, 783). It is significant to note that here as elsewhere she places "renown," or receiving honor from others, before "prowess," or the actual skill or excellence one displays. In the course of their conversation, we see that they speak to each other on two levels. On one level, they speak directly, arguing about what course of action, what "path," each of them should take. On another level, they communicate indirectly, as Éowyn seeks to convey her love for him, and her hope that he returns it, and Aragorn seeks to convey that his heart is already given to another. Let us focus, for the moment, only on their arguments about their respective courses of action.

Upon learning what Aragorn intends to do, Éowyn first seeks to dissuade him, telling him that to seek the Paths of the Dead entails a mad desire to "seek death" (*LOTR*, 783). However, once it becomes clear to her that he will not change his mind, she asks him to let her accompany him, a request that he refuses. In explaining why she wishes to accompany him, she says that she is "weary of skulking in the hills," of performing what, to her way of thinking, is the relatively unimportant task of "mind[ing] the house" while the warriors "win renown" (*LOTR*, 784). In refusing her request, Aragorn makes two main points. First, he reminds her that she has been appointed to rule in Théoden's place, and, second, he tries to persuade her that the fulfillment of this "duty" is not, as she seems to think, something relatively unimportant. Speaking to her in a way that reveals a sympathetic understanding of her mode of judgment, along with a gentle correction of it, he tells her that, if honor is what she seeks, she will not gain it by abandoning her position of rule in order to accompany him. Even more importantly, he tries to persuade her not only to do what is right for its own sake, rather than for the sake of gaining honor, but also to recognize that her understanding of virtue, of what is truly worthy of honor, is much too narrow. If the armies of Rohan and Gondor are defeated, he tells her, she, along with the other survivors, may have to perform acts of "valour without renown." In a crucial corollary, Aragorn adds that such "deeds will not be less valiant because they are unpraised" (*LOTR*, 784). Not understanding Aragorn's true character—namely, that he himself has willingly performed countless acts of "valour without renown"—Éowyn is not persuaded. Rather, she assumes that Aragorn does not really believe what he says, speaking this way only because she is a woman, and thus incapable of performing any genuinely "valiant" actions. Hence she responds by asserting that, though a woman, she has a royal lineage and possesses the qualities most highly regarded within her culture: "I am of the House of Eorl and not a serving-woman. I can ride and wield blade, and I do not fear either pain or death" (*LOTR*, 784). Her point is that she could do more good by using her skills in the war against Mordor and not "wasting" them—as, she is keenly aware, both Théoden and Éomer refused to do—by remaining behind with those unable to make war. Recognizing, it would seem, that there is nothing further he can say to persuade her, Aragorn responds not by continuing to argue with her but by asking whether there is anything that she does fear. She answers, in complete accord with the line of reasoning she has employed thus far, that she fears only a "cage," having "to stay behind bars, until . . . all chance of doing great deeds is gone beyond recall or desire" (*LOTR*, 784).

Once Aragorn departs, Éowyn despairs, convinced that, with his decision to take the Paths of the Dead, all hope of victory over the forces of Mordor is now lost. In her mind, it is now a certainty that Théoden, along with Éomer and all those she loves, will die on the field of battle in Gondor, after which loss the victorious army of Mordor will invade Rohan and slaughter or enslave all those who remain. Convinced of the inevitability of these events, and with her pride stung by Aragorn's refusal to return her love, she decides that it would be better to die in battle at Théoden's side than to remain and await an inglorious death. Thus she disguises herself as a man, "Dernhelm," and secretly accompanies Théoden into battle.[39] When Théoden is killed by the chief ringwraith, Éowyn alone withstands the terror of the ringwraith in order to defend the fallen king. Amazingly, she kills the ringwraith's flying steed, and, with the assistance of Merry, the ringwraith himself.

As she lies in the Houses of Healing, on the verge of death, Éomer comes to realize how little he has understood his sister, and how much he (and Théoden, who is now dead) has taken her for granted. Aragorn, who has come to try to heal Éowyn of the near-fatal wounds she received in battling the ringwraith, declares that she suffers from a far deeper "malady," an illness that predates his first acquaintance of her (*LOTR*, 866). Upon hearing this claim, Éomer is puzzled. He readily acknowledges that she was saddened by Aragorn's inability to return her love, but he does not recognize the true nature and depth of her suffering. Gandalf, who is also present, explains that the "poison" offered by Théoden's chief counselor, Wormtongue (in service to Saruman), affected Théoden and Éowyn both. Though "born in the body of a maid," Gandalf tells Éomer, Éowyn has "a spirit and courage *at least the match of yours*" (*LOTR*, 867; emphasis added). This comment is intended, it would seem, to spur Éomer to imagine how he would have responded, had he been in Éowyn's position. Gandalf tells Éomer that, though both he and Éowyn have suffered in watching Théoden fall into what seemed "a mean dishonoured dotage," Éomer has had outlets for his innate "spirit and courage," such as "horses, and deeds of arms, and the free fields," whereas Éowyn has had none but has had to face "the bitter watches of the night" in solitude (*LOTR*, 867). "Her part," Gandalf informs Éomer, "seemed to her more ignoble than that of the staff [Théoden] leaned on" (*LOTR*, 867). Echoing Éowyn's own words to Aragorn about her fear of being confined in a womanly "cage," Gandalf describes how Éowyn reached the point of despair: "all her life seemed shrinking, and the walls of her bower closing in about her, a hutch to trammel some wild thing in" (*LOTR*, 867). Deeply moved by Gandalf's words, and understanding at last his own blindness, Éomer gazes silently upon his sister, "as if pondering anew all the days of their past life together" (*LOTR*, 867). Éomer finally comes to understand and appreciate his sister, yet it is not he who plays the most significant role in helping her to overcome her "malady." Such a happy role belongs to another.

Upon awakening in the Houses of Healing, Éowyn recovers relatively quickly from the injuries she sustained on the battlefield, but she is not yet prepared to embrace any possibility of hope. Though she has gained great honor—"her deed," in Aragorn's words, having "set her among the queens of great renown" (*LOTR*, 867)—such fame is not sufficient, she finds, to satisfy her restless yearnings. The turning point for her comes through her encounter with Faramir. Like her, he has been gravely injured and must also remain in the Houses of Healing, awaiting news from the front.

Faramir, Tolkien indicates, is someone uniquely situated both to understand and assist her. During his fateful meeting with Frodo and Sam in Ithilien, Faramir speaks of the culture of Rohan, offering both praise and criticism, in a way that mirrors what is worthy of both praise and criticism in Éowyn. Saying that the Rohirrim "remind us [the Gondorians] of the youth of Men" (*LOTR*, 678), Faramir refers to their eagerness, vitality, and unfailing loyalty but also, more subtly, to their relative immaturity regarding the cultivation of virtues other than courage. Faramir tells Frodo and Sam that, as a result of the long alliance between the Rohirrim and the Gondorians, each has taken on some of the qualities of the other. The Rohirrim have benefited from their interaction with the Gondorians, insofar as they have become "enhanced in arts and gentleness" (*LOTR*, 679). The Gondorians have benefited greatly from the "fierce valour" of the Rohirrim, who "have ever proved true to us, aiding us at need" (*LOTR*, 678), but they have also, regrettably, become more like the Rohirrim in that they "now love war and valour as things good in themselves, both a sport and an end" (*LOTR*, 679). Like the Rohirrim, the Gondorians now also "esteem a warrior . . . above men of other crafts" (*LOTR*, 679). When Faramir finally learns the nature of Frodo's quest, and Frodo's willing acceptance of it, he is amazed. Wondering whether the folk of the Shire are all like Frodo—willing to take up a noble but virtually hopeless task, and thus to exercise, one might say, the most extreme form of "valour without renown"— Faramir remarks that, if so, the Shire must be "a realm of peace and content, and there must *gardeners* be in *high honour*" (*LOTR*, 681; emphasis added). His point is not that warriors should not be honored, or that war is not at times necessary, but rather that the best society would be one in which "gardeners," those adept at bringing forth and cultivating life in all its fullness, would be even more highly esteemed than "warriors," those adept at defending society against its enemies.[40]

Faramir's assessment of the respective qualities of the Rohirrim and the Gondorians reverberates, in many respects, in his interaction with Éowyn. When he gently refuses her request to be released and sent back into battle, she is taken aback, assuming that, from his point of view, she probably appears to be "like a child" who does not possess "the firmness of mind to go on with a dull task to the end" (*LOTR*, 959–60). Seeing herself through his eyes, she begins—in almost Socratic fashion—to acknowledge her deficiencies and to question her seemingly certain judgments. "For the first time," Tolkien writes, "she doubted herself" (*LOTR*, 959). Intrigued by her, and moved to pity her, Faramir seeks out her company. In him, she finds a companion who, even though her equal in "spirit and courage," is also—as she is both perceptive and honest enough to admit—her superior in wisdom. As together they "endure with patience the hours of waiting" (*LOTR*, 960), Éowyn grows, as never before, in self-understanding.

When she hesitates to accept his offer of love, he discerns that her uncertainty is rooted in her confusion over her feelings for Aragorn, and in her belief that Faramir's feelings for her stem from mere pity. With regard to Aragorn, Faramir tells her, gently but firmly, that in both her naive love for Aragorn and her response to Aragorn's inability to return such love, she has displayed immaturity of judgment. Likening her attraction to Aragorn to that of "a young soldier" who admires "a great captain," Faramir explains that her feelings for Aragorn grew out of her mistaken desire for honor alone. Because she "wished to have renown and glory and be lifted far above the mean things that crawl on the earth," she believed herself in love with the "high and puissant" Aragorn (*LOTR*, 964). When Aragorn failed to return her love, Faramir argues, she made her most grave mistake, desiring then "to have *nothing*, unless a brave death in battle" (*LOTR*, 964; emphasis added).

Faramir recognizes that, as with Denethor, such despair had brought Éowyn to the brink of death. However, unlike Denethor, who sought to hasten both his own death and that of his son, Éowyn has abandoned hope, but not love. Her ability to stand against the ringwraith is due, at least in part, to her great love for Théoden. Perhaps for this reason, she is spared from the ultimate consequence of despair and given another chance at life.

With regard to his own feelings, Faramir admits that he initially pitied her, but he loves her now. When he looks at her, he no longer sees a woman who should be pitied but "a lady high and valiant," one who has "won renown that shall not be forgotten," and who shall always have his love, whatever her circumstances might be, even should she become "the blissful Queen of Gondor" (*LOTR*, 964). As she ponders these words, Tolkien writes, "the heart of Éowyn changed, or else at last she understood it" (*LOTR*, 964). In accepting Faramir's love, and in offering her love to him in return, she speaks about herself in a way that is reminiscent of Faramir's words to Frodo and Sam in Ithilien. Recognizing now that some things are even more worthy of pursuit than the "renown" gained through "valour in battle," she no longer wishes to be a warrior who "[takes] joy only in the songs of slaying" (*LOTR*, 965). Rather, echoing Faramir's earlier words to Frodo and Sam about how good it would be to live in a society that honors gardeners, she says that she now intends to become "a healer," to "love all things that grow and are not barren" (*LOTR*, 965). Faramir, in joyful response, tells her that they shall "dwell in fair Ithilien and there make a garden" (*LOTR*, 965).

WISDOM AND ULTIMATE JUSTICE

For Tolkien, the ability to exercise wise judgment is tied to a steadfast belief in the ultimate justice of the cosmos, even in the face of circumstances that seem hopeless. In no image within the *legendarium* is this more powerfully conveyed than in the scene of Aragorn's death, which is told in "The Tale of Aragorn and Arwen." According to Plato, Homer's model for death is Achilles, who learns that the only sound response to death is despair. Tolkien's model, in contrast, is Aragorn. After a long and successful reign as king of Gondor, Aragorn decides to exercise the ancient prerogative of the Númenórean rulers, freely giving up his life before the onset of senility and debility, and handing on the kingship to his son.[41] Faced with his beloved wife's, Arwen, anguished pleading for him to delay his death, Aragorn concedes that death is a cause for "sorrow" but not for "despair," since he believes that "we are not bound forever to the circles of the world, and beyond them is more than memory" (*LOTR*, 1063).

It is telling that, at the moment he embraces his death, Arwen calls him by his childhood name, Estel. As Tolkien conveys in "The Converse of Finrod and Andreth," *Estel* is the Quenya word for "hope," or, more accurately, "trust." One kind of hope, *Amdir*, implies "an expectation of good, which though uncertain has some foundation in what is known" (*MR*, 320). *Estel*, however, implies a deeper kind of hope, a hope that "is not defeated by the ways of the world, for it does not come from experience" but rests upon "trust" that the creator "will not suffer Himself to be deprived of His own, not by any Enemy, not even by ourselves" (*MR*, 320). In calling upon Estel, Arwen thereby relies not only upon her beloved husband but also upon the one thing that is needed, Tolkien suggests, to prevent her from being "overthrown at the final test" (*LOTR*, 1063). The wisdom of Aragorn's final words to Arwen is suggested through the depiction of what happens to his body after death. In a scene that contrasts sharply with the death of Saruman, Aragorn's corpse undergoes a transformation that reflects the essential goodness of his soul, confirming the truth of that true *Estel* on which he has based his life: "A great beauty was revealed in him," so that all who looked upon him saw "that the grace of his youth, and the valour of his manhood, and the wisdom and majesty of his age were blended together" (*LOTR*, 1063).

In examining Tolkien's *legendarium* as a "response" to Plato's critique of poetry, we see that one could not readily charge Tolkien with presenting "lies" masquerading as truth, or with undermining moral virtue. On the contrary, Tolkien provides a vision of the whole while simultaneously communicating the limitations of that vision. Rather than encouraging his readers to regard his poetry as providing them with direct and comprehensive knowledge of the truth in its fullness, Tolkien intends that his *legendarium* both spark wonder and defend the enduring value of the experience of wonder. Furthermore, rather than undermining moral virtue, Tolkien provides a compelling defense of the dignity of virtue and the misery of vice. Though Plato expresses doubt as to whether poetry can adequately portray genuine human goodness and wise judgment, Tolkien's vivid and compelling array of character types does precisely that.

NOTES

1. The word has two connotations. In one sense, it means to make in a broad, general way, and can be used in reference to a variety of human endeavors. In another, narrower sense, it means the characteristic activity of the poet— the making of literary art. Clearly Tolkien, well aware of the dual meaning of *poiesis*, uses it in both ways. The former connotation is reflected, for example, in Tolkien's depiction of the Noldor, who, in comparison with the other elvish clans, are the greatest "makers" with respect to the vast range of scientific and artistic endeavors. The latter connotation is reflected, for example, in Tolkien's depiction of the Noldor's great gift specifically for language and literature, and his references, in his academic essays, to the art of the *Beowulf* poet, e.g., "Beowulf: The Monsters and the Critics," 5–6.

2. All references designated *S* are to Tolkien, *The Silmarillion*.

3. Tolkien wrote this poem in a letter to C. S. Lewis, seeking to persuade him of the truth of Christianity. He used part of it later in his essay "On Fairy-Stories," 74.

4. It might be said that Tolkien goes further than the ancient Greeks, claiming that the writer of fairy story, of "fantasy," is the quintessential poet, since fantasy, given that it is most fully detached from the particular facts of the world, is the "most nearly pure form" of poetic creativity ("On Fairy-Stories," 69).

5. The ancient Greek word *poiein* means "to make." From it is derived the word *poiesis*, which means "maker" and, more specifically, "poet." See note 1.

6. I rely primarily on the translation provided by Bloom, *Republic*.

7. Socrates conveys four statements made by poets about philosophers: "yelping bitch shrieking at her master"; "great in the empty eloquence of fools"; "the mob of overwise men holding sway"; and "the refined thinkers who are really poor" (607b–c). Bloom states that the sources of these quotations are unknown (Bloom, *Republic*, 471n7).

8. The use of this word has become so common among scholars that it is often used as a direct transliteration, without italics.

9. Griswold explains that Socrates, in arguing as if all imitative poetry had earlier been banned, mischaracterizes the discussion from book 3, where it

was decided that some, but not all, imitative poetry would be banned. Accord-ing to Griswold, Socrates "recasts the critique in very different terms" in book 10, because of the "intervening discussion" of "the 'theory of the Forms'" ("Plato on Rhetoric and Poetry").

10. Commenting on this passage, Rosen remarks, "At least since Proclus, readers have suspected that the reference to a form of nature (in the special sense of a Platonic Idea) of the bed is a sign of the ironical intention of Plato. It is at least dubious whether there are Platonic Ideas of artifacts" (*Quarrel be-tween Philosophy and Poetry*, 7).

11. Bloom, *Republic*, 429. Rosen remarks that this is an "inaccurate, even obtuse, description of the 'mimetic' nature of poetry" (*Quarrel between Philoso-phy and Poetry*, 7).

12. As Bloom argues, "Both Homer and Socrates in some way possess this [comprehensive] kind of knowledge; they both have a view of the whole" (*Re-public*, 430).

13. Plato makes a similar suggestion in the *Ion*, where he subjects Ion's claim to be "wonderfully wise . . . about Homer" to philosophic questioning (541a1). Unable to provide any explanation of Homer's poetry, let alone an ar-gument on behalf of Homer's wisdom, Ion ends by agreeing with Socrates' "saving assumption" that the source of Homer's poetry is not Homer's own wisdom, but divine inspiration (534b3–d1).

14. As Pieper argues, "only he who knows the 'idea,' that is to say, the de-sign of a reality, fully knows this reality; only he who knows the 'idea' of a thing knows this thing as intensively as it can possibly be known at all; he alone 'com-prehends' the thing in the strict sense of the word. . . . But such knowledge is not possible for the human mind" (*Enthusiasm and Divine Madness*, 76).

15. Rosen, *Quarrel between Philosophy and Poetry*, 15. Rosen goes on to provide an extended discussion of this issue in reference to the *Republic* and the *Philebus*.

16. Pieper, *Enthusiasm and Divine Madness*, 77.

17. As Rosen argues, Plato shows that "it is not mimesis alone that leads poetry to corrupt the *dianoia* [thoughts], but rather mimesis that is ruled by de-sire instead of by intellect (*nous*) and judgment (*phronēsis*)" (*Quarrel between Philosophy and Poetry*, 21).

18. For an excellent account of Aristotle's understanding of poetry that places it within his philosophy as a whole, see Davis, *Poetry of Philosophy*. Davis argues that for Aristotle, "Philosophy is not possible apart from a willingness to wonder about the seemingly ordinary. Poetry uses various means of bringing out the strange in the ordinary" (147). Yet differences between poetry and phi-losophy remain: "Although philosophy has a poetic element, it is not the same as poetry. The problems to which philosophy seeks solutions would be invisible without poetry, but poetry does not by itself provide solutions" (148).

19. Tolkien, *Letters*, 144.

20. See his foreword to Tolkien, *War of the Jewels*. Shippey also follows Christopher Tolkien in distinguishing between "The Silmarillion" and *The Silmarillion*, in *The Road to Middle-earth*, 223.

21. All references designated *MR* are to Tolkien, *Morgoth's Ring*. In "Notes on Motives in the Silmarillion," Tolkien writes, "It has to be remembered that the 'mythology' is represented as being two stages removed from a true record: it is based first upon elvish records about lore and about the Valar and their own dealings with them; and these have reached us (fragmentarily) only through relics of Númenórean (human) traditions, derived from the Eldar, in the earlier parts, though for later times supplemented by anthropocentric histories and tales. These, it is true, came down through the 'Faithful' and their descendants in Middle-earth, but could not altogether escape the darkening of the picture due to the hostility of the rebellious Númenóreans to the Valar" (*MR*, 401–2).

22. Even if Tolkien had succeeded in refashioning the texts devoted to the earlier history of the elves before his death, and thereby left a more coherent and unified saga, he nevertheless would have retained, in some form, these aspects of his work.

23. On this point, see Wood, *Gospel according to Tolkien*, 31–38.

24. According to "Quendi and Eldar," Pengolodh had mixed Noldorin and Sindarin ancestry, having lived in Gondolin from the time of its foundation and then eventually surviving its destruction (Tolkien, *War of the Jewels*, 396).

25. All references designated *LOTR* are to Tolkien, *Lord of the Rings*.

26. Rosen, *Quarrel between Philosophy and Poetry*, 13.

27. According to Gadamer, Homeric poetry depicted "arête [virtue] without *phronēsis* [prudence]," which proved incapable of defending itself against the sophistry dominant during Socrates' life. Plato, Gadamer argues, points directly to this flaw in the Myth of Er: "He who in an earlier life shared in virtue through 'custom without philosophy' . . . chooses the life of a tyrant in the new allotment of lives! (619bff.)" ("Plato and the Poets," 61–62n9).

28. *Odyssey*, 11:489–91. This quotation also appears at the beginning of book 3 of the *Republic*, 386c, used by Socrates to justify censorship of the poets.

29. As Rutledge states, "As has often been remarked, Milton's Satan (in *Paradise Lost*) is so glamorous that we forget he is evil. We will have no such problem here" (*Battle for Middle-earth*, 107).

30. Although the elves are often referred to as being immortal, this is not necessarily the case. The Valar and Maiar, created as pure spirits, are immortal, but the ultimate fate of the elves is uncertain. It would seem that, though extremely long, the lifespan of the elves is not unending. Because they have real, physical bodies, their natural lifespan coincides with that of the created world, which will, at some point, however distant, come to an end. For Tolkien's most direct commentary on the ultimate fate of the elves, see *Athrabeth Finrod ah*

Andreth ("The Converse of Finrod and Andreth") in *MR*, esp. 311–12, 319–20; see also Tolkien, *Letters*, 285–86, 325.

31. See the prologue to *LOTR*, 2–7. The last of the three hobbit clans to settle in the Shire, the Stoors made their dwelling in the Eastfarthing, mainly in Buckland and the Marish, the regions along the Brandywine River. It may be of interest to note that Bilbo, Frodo, Merry, and Pippin all have ancestry among both of the other hobbit clans, i.e., the Harfoots and the Fallowhides, but Frodo and Merry also have ancestry among the Stoors. See *LOTR*, appendix C, 1104.

32. For a similar argument, see Wood, *Gospel According to Tolkien*, 55–56.

33. According to Pieper, Plato suggests that the human inclination and capacity for wickedness cannot be explained apart from the fact that the human mind is finite. Pieper links this Platonic suggestion with Thomas Aquinas's argument that the human inclination to evil cannot be wholly explained apart from "its origin from nothingness" (*Enthusiasm and Divine Madness*, 78).

34. *Deinotes* in ancient Greek, *astutia* in Latin. See, e.g., Aristotle, *Nicomachean Ethics*, 1144a23–37, and Thomas Aquinas, *Summa Theologica*, IIa-IIae, 55, 3–5. As Pieper states, cunning or cleverness is "the most characteristic form of false prudence" (*Four Cardinal Virtues*, 19).

35. All references designated *NE* are to Aristotle's *Nicomachean Ethics*.

36. For example, in learning that Aragorn, Gimli, and Legolas only recently parted from the Lady Galadriel in Lothlórien, Éomer asks whether they are like Galadriel in being "net-weavers and sorcerers" (*LOTR*, 432). Also, in reference to Aragorn's decision to leave the Rohirrim and take the Paths of the Dead, Éomer remarks, "Alas that a fey mood should fall on a man so greathearted in this hour of need! Are there not evil things enough abroad without seeking them under the earth?" (*LOTR*, 781).

37. At the time of their parents' death, Éomer was about twelve years old, and Éowyn, about seven years old (*LOTR*, appendix A, 1070).

38. Théoden's wife died in childbirth, and he never remarried. Théodred was about twenty-four years old when Éomer and Éowyn's parents died and they came to live within the royal household (*LOTR*, appendix A, 1070).

39. Her despair is most vividly conveyed in the reaction that Merry has in seeing her, whom he believes to be Dernhelm: glancing at her, Merry sees "the face of one without hope who goes in search of death" (*LOTR*, 803).

40. Faramir's comments are reminiscent of Aristotle's assessment of the Spartans, who cultivated and honored the virtue of courage above all others. This made them capable of preserving themselves "as long as they were at war," but it was disastrous in times of peace, since they did not know "how to be at leisure" (*Politics*, 1271b2–3).

41. Regarding this prerogative as a "grace" by which he can freely "give back the gift" (*LOTR*, 1037), Aragorn provides an example of an attitude toward death that contrasts sharply with that of the ancient Númenórean kings, who

eventually refused to exercise this prerogative, in a foolish and ultimately ruinous attempt "to escape death in their own day, not waiting upon hope" (*S*, 265–66). This attitude, Aragorn surely knows, is one to which those of Númenórean ancestry are, to their great detriment, continually prone. As Faramir relates to Frodo and Sam, Gondor's decline is due largely to the Númenórean tendency to "[hunger] after endless life unchanging," which has led those in authority to neglect their responsibilities (*LOTR*, 678).

BIBLIOGRAPHY

Aristotle. *Aristotle's Nicomachean Ethics*. Translated with commentary by Hippocrates G. Apostle. Grinnell, IA: Peripatetic, 1985.
———. *The Politics*. Translated with introduction, notes, and glossary by Carnes Lord. Chicago: University of Chicago Press, 1984.
Davis, Michael. *The Poetry of Philosophy: On Aristotle's "Poetics."* South Bend, IN: St. Augustine's, 1992.
Gadamer, Hans-Georg. "Plato and the Poets." In *Dialogue and Dialectic: Eight Hermeneutical Studies on Plato*, translated with an introduction by P. Christopher Smith. New Haven, CT: Yale University Press, 1980.
Griswold, Charles. "Plato on Rhetoric and Poetry." In *The Stanford Encyclopedia of Philosophy*. Spring 2004 ed. http://plato.stanford.edu/archives/spr2004/entries/plato-rhetoric/.
Pieper, Josef. *Enthusiasm and Divine Madness: On the Platonic Dialogue "Phaedrus."* South Bend, IN: St. Augustine's, 2000.
———. *The Four Cardinal Virtues*. Notre Dame, IN: University of Notre Dame Press, 1966.
Plato. *The Republic of Plato*. Translated with notes and an interpretive essay by Allan Bloom. New York: Basic, 1968.
Rosen, Stanley. *The Quarrel between Philosophy and Poetry*. New York: Routledge, 1988.
Rutledge, Fleming. *The Battle for Middle-earth: Tolkien's Divine Design in "The Lord of the Rings."* Grand Rapids, MI: Eerdmans, 2004.
Shippey, Thomas. *The Road to Middle-Earth: How J. R. R. Tolkien Created a New Mythology*. New York: Houghton Mifflin, 2003.
Tolkien, J. R. R. "Beowulf: The Monsters and the Critics." In *The Monsters and the Critics and Other Essays*, edited by Christopher Tolkien, 5–48. London: HarperCollins, 1983.
———. *The Letters of J. R. R. Tolkien*. Edited by Humphrey Carpenter with the assistance of Christopher Tolkien. Boston: Houghton Mifflin, 2000.
———. *The Lord of the Rings*. 50th anniversary ed. Boston: Mariner, 2012.

————. *Morgoth's Ring*. Edited by Christopher Tolkien. Boston: Houghton Mifflin, 1993.

————. "On Fairy-Stories." In *The Tolkien Reader*. New York: Ballantine, 1966.

————. *The Silmarillion*. Edited by Christopher Tolkien. New York: Houghton Mifflin, 2001.

————. *The War of the Jewels*. Edited by Christopher Tolkien. New York: Houghton Mifflin, 1994.

Wood, Ralph C. *The Gospel According to Tolkien: Visions of the Kingdom in Middle-earth*. Louisville, KY: Westminster John Knox, 2003.

CHAPTER 2

ON FATE, PROVIDENCE, AND FREE WILL IN *THE SILMARILLION*

Helen Lasseter Freeh

Amid the ruins of World War I lay the nineteenth-century's promise of progressivism. Science and rationalism had replaced religious faith in providence for defining the course of world history; yet, in the wake of the war's devastation, progressivism faltered and a more ancient and perennial understanding of fate controlling human life reemerged in England. Most writers and thinkers came to believe that human efforts were ultimately meaningless and human beings inescapably subject to chaotic or mechanistic forces within a purposeless universe. The Christian concept of providence was not only something most nineteenth- and twentieth-century English writers and poets had already dismissed, but something that seemed absurd in the face of the war's horrors. Yet counter to this growing resignation to fate within the artistic culture of England, J. R. R. Tolkien created a fictional world providentially governed by a gracious deity.

Tom Shippey names Tolkien the "author of the century" because Tolkien's work confronts "the origin and nature of evil."[1] I would suggest that Tolkien addresses the nature of evil by examining a deeper question: What is the principle of order defining a world in which radical evil and suffering continue to flourish? The answer to this question is integral for understanding a person's place in the world. Tolkien's great contribution to twentieth-century cultural and religious life was to offer an answer to the despair of materialism and determinism. Tolkien is the author of the century because he gives a response to the hopelessness caused by a sense of fated entrapment—the helplessness of the self no less than its environing community—that much of twentieth-century literature presents but to which it does not provide an answer.

Through the mediation of a fictional secondary world in *The Silmarillion*, Tolkien returns his modern audience to the ancient yet extremely relevant conflict between and among fate, providence, and free will. Tolkien presents this controversy to his modern audiences in a way that enables them at least to consider it, if not accept it. Tolkien uses mythic and poetic devices, rather than direct philosophical or theological discourse, as his means for presenting anew the universal problem of human freedom in the face of deterministic forces. He sets his fictional world on a providential foundation while also acknowledging his characters' sense of fatedness in the world. Tolkien frames his fictional world providentially, but he employs an elvish (and thus non-Christian) narrator to tell its history. And because this narrator struggles to credit such a providential order amid the lived experience of a seemingly fated world, Tolkien is able to address similar concerns that his modern audience shares over humanity's plight before externally imposed powers. Three central myths of *Silmarillion*, "The Music of the Ainur," "Of Túrin Turambar," and "Of Beren and Lúthien," illustrate the conflict within the world order of Middle-earth between free will and forced external circumstances.

THE LIMITED PERSPECTIVE OF THE ELVISH NARRATOR

Tolkien uses the immortal life of the elves to provide a narrator who can survey the entire course of history over centuries, even millennia. The elvish narrator's perspective on history is such that he should be *better* equipped to see providential patterns within events, if such patterns exist. However, though the elvish narrator may recount the whole story, he is never sufficiently able to remove himself from his temporal perspective in order to observe the whole course of events, as an eternal perspective would allow. Tolkien's analysis of the elvish perspective indicates why his elvish narrator is more inclined to interpret history as fatalistic or random rather than providentially designed. He says that the elves must "endure with and within the created world, while its story lasts. When 'killed,' by the injury or destruction of their incarnate form, they do not escape from time, but remain *in* the world, either discarnate, or being re-born. This becomes a great burden as the ages lengthen, especially in a world in which there is malice and destruction."[2] Tolkien emphasizes that the elves are "immortal" but not "eternal." The elves fully experience the ravages of time not in their own body but in the decay, loss, and death of the world around them. Ralph Wood's argument on the dangerous temptation to immortality the Ring offers also applies to the elvish experience of immortality in a mortal world:

> For fallen creatures to go on living endlessly would be a terror to the world and a torment to themselves. . . . if we had no prospect of dying, we would commit the two evils that undermine the good— pride and despair: pride that we will always have time to do the things that we ought to have done; despair that we will never cease doing the things we ought not to have done.[3]

The elvish tendency in *Silmarillion* seems to incline towards despair rather than pride, as the elves regret the destructive actions that have led and that keep leading to ruin.

As an interpreter of history for his audience, the elvish narrator has difficulty seeing events that necessarily bring change and destruction as lying within a providential order. He also has difficulty accepting that *both* elves and humans retain the power of free will. Tolkien's original version of the *Ainulindalë*, or "The Music of the Ainur," describes the elvish perspective on their place within a wider world order.[4] In *The Book of Lost Tales*, Rúmil indicates that elves believe a type of fate binds them as it does not bind humans. Rúmil quotes Ilúvatar as saying, "to Men I will give a new gift, and a greater." Rúmil goes on to indicate the nature of this gift:

[Ilúvatar] devised that Men should have a free virtue whereby within the limits of the powers and substances and chances of the world they might fashion and design their life beyond even the original Music of the Ainur that is as fate to all things else. . . . Even we Eldar have found to our sorrow that Men have a strange power for good or ill and for turning things despite Gods and Fairies to their mood in the world; so that we say: "Fate may not conquer the Children of Men, but yet are they strangely blind, whereas their joy should be great."[5]

Rúmil, as one bound by fate, does not understand why mortals do not recognize and rejoice over their freedom and power. In Rúmil's view, elves do not have the same freedom as humans to counter fate's demands, even though "fate" in this depiction is understood as the Valar's beneficent design for the world. Even so, two of Tolkien's stories serve to question the accuracy of the elvish perspective by showing in reverse the dichotomy between elvish fatedness and human freedom. The Beren and Lúthien story directly counters the elvish assumption that they are fated, and the Túrin tale explores the possible constraints that fate places upon human free will.

AINULINDALË

The *Ainulindalë* differs from the other tales in the *legendarium* because, within the context of the mythology, the elves believe that the chief vala, Manwë, revealed it directly to them. In only this one story does the elvish narrator stand as an amanuensis for the Valar, the angelic beings directly below the one god, Ilúvatar, who created and sent them to guide and protect the world. Manwë reveals to the elves a story with an explicitly providential perspective on creation, not the temporal perspective that limits the elvish worldview. The *Ainulindalë* myth demonstrates three central aspects of a providential world order in Middle-earth: a divine design to all temporal events, love as the basis of all creation and creative activity, and, finally, the importance of free will within the divine design. These three aspects are shown initially in the tale of Beren and Lúthien but find full expression in *The Lord of the Rings*.

First, the *Ainulindalë* establishes a divine design to the universe, including Middle-earth. The narrator says that Ilúvatar gives the Ainur a glimpse of his design: "They saw a new World made visible before them, and it was globed amid the Void, and it was sustained therein, but was not of it. And as they looked and wondered this World began to unfold its history, and it seemed to them that it lived and grew."[6] Ilúvatar, however, does not act alone in creating the world; the lesser "deities," the Ainur (later named the Valar), also assist him.

Tolkien uses the medieval metaphor of the "music of the spheres" to disclose that, though the universe's creation is communal in nature, the creation "song" is guided and shaped by a single conductor, Ilúvatar. The Ainur's song begins melodiously but ends discordantly because Melkor refuses to sing in accord with the other Valar. He places himself and his talents apart from the community, and, as a result, the music becomes cacophonous, harsh, and contrary to Ilúvatar's symphonic design. Ilúvatar must twice stop the music to urge Melkor to follow divine guidance. Yet when Ilúvatar and the Ainur begin the music anew, Melkor continues his steadfast refusal to create in harmony with them.

At the third discordant song, Ilúvatar becomes angry with Melkor's repeated rebellion. He stops the dissonant music and chastises Melkor. Though Ilúvatar does not violate Melkor's freedom by forcing him to follow the divine harmony, he warns the rebel vala against the futility of taking the creative process away from Ilúvatar's control. Melkor may believe he is forming a new creation according to his own design, but Ilúvatar makes clear that Melkor's power remains well within the larger divine order: "No theme may be played that hath not its uttermost source in me, nor can any alter the music in my despite. For he that attempteth this shall prove but mine instrument in the devising of things more wonderful, which he himself hath not imagined."[7] Ilúvatar will not simply change evil into good but will instead weave everything that Melkor mars into something surprisingly more beautiful and good. Every rebellious act that Melkor commits, though intended only for his own selfish benefit, leads eventually to the greater glory of Ilúvatar. The narrator conveys this promise for Middle-earth in the opening tale of *Silmarillion*—a promise of ultimate providential power despite opposing forces.

The second aspect of providential order that the myth reveals is the centrality of love in Ilúvatar's creative action. The ability to love and to accept love is directly related to the ability to embrace the world as either fated or providential. If the world is providentially ordered, then one should embrace the love of the creator who creates not only the world but everything within it. The person's response to this primal and final love is either rejection or acceptance, pride or humility. If the world is understood as fated, by contrast, there is no necessity for the person to respond to any initiating and culminating love, but one need only resist the antagonistic powers intent on destroying the person or the person's beloved. The majority of the Ainur reciprocate Ilúvatar's initial love for them, but Melkor rejects it because he will not submit to any power over him. He seeks instead to dominate others and to be worshipped by them out of fear, not love. Although some characters, such as Túrin, repeat Melkor's behavior in rejecting love, others, like Beren and Lúthien, break this pattern in their embrace of sacrificial love.

The third aspect of Middle-earth's providential nature that "Music of the Ainur" reveals is the importance of created beings' freedom working in consort with divine intent. Because Ilúvatar loves his creation, he refuses to override its freedom. One of the fundamental descriptions of providence that the creation myth offers is the interplay of free will between Ilúvatar and his creation. In describing the Ainur's role in shaping and forming the universe, Ilúvatar affirms not only his ordering of the universe but also his creatures' indispensable participation within the divine design. Ilúvatar does not crush their creative freedom but rather desires for them to remain within the community of creator and creatures, using their freedom for the advancement of the good. As the narrator states, Ilúvatar "declared to [the Ainur] a mighty theme, unfolding to them things greater and more wonderful than he had yet revealed; and the glory of its beginning and the splendour of its end amazed the

Ainur." Integral to the design is the Ainur's free involvement with it: "I have kindled you with the Flame Imperishable, ye shall show forth your powers in adorning this theme, each with his own thoughts and devices, if he will. But I will sit and hearken, and be glad that through you great beauty has been wakened into song."[8] He reveals to them a brief glimpse of his overarching vision, whose realization requires the Ainur's contributions, even if this must also include Melkor's selfish counterdesigns. He says: "Behold your Music! . . . each of you shall find contained herein, amid the design that I set before you, all those things which it may seem that he himself devised or added. And thou, Melkor, wilt discover all the secret thoughts of thy mind, and wilt perceive that they are but a part of the whole and tributary to its glory."[9]

The opening creation myth depicts evil as the domination of others, an image Tolkien repeats throughout *Silmarillion* and *Lord of the Rings*. In writing of the nature of evil in *Lord of the Rings*, Matthew Dickerson argues that Sauron's Ruling Ring dominates others by denying them free will.[10] Domination reflects the Augustinian understanding of evil as *privatio boni*, the denial and absence of the good, indeed its very non-being. Because evil refuses to acknowledge the wondrous being of others, it attempts to dominate them by denying full being to them. In the *Ainulindalë*, the narrator reveals that the One, Ilúvatar, deliberately refuses such domination. He creates the Ainur and his "Children"—elves and men—to have free will to realize or else to refuse the perfect intention of Ilúvatar. He works in consort with the wills of his creatures, and they, in turn, work in unity with Ilúvatar's loving guidance of his creation, not his forceful domination. Hence his refusal to destroy Melkor, though the rebel vala persists in his disobedience. Ilúvatar certainly *has* the power to stop or prevent evil, but he does not do so because of his greater love for his creation's freedom. He wants his creatures to enact the good by their own free will in cooperation with his own purposes. Ilúvatar's actions thus prove to be the model for others to follow or be judged against: one creature's will should not preclude, deny, or enslave another's will. Yet Tolkien is by no means endorsing anything akin to J. S. Mill's celebrated "harm" principle—the notion, namely, that one is free to do as one wills so long as one does no harm to others. One inevitably harms others when one violates the will of Ilúvatar, thus one's freedom must also include a willingness to resist those who cause such harm.

TÚRIN TURAMBAR

The elvish narrator's presentation of the mortal Túrin Turambar's story complicates the question of providential order in Tolkien's mythological cosmos by suggesting that *both* fate and free will are responsible for Túrin's destruction. But although the narrator does not acknowledge any providential hand at work in the world, neither does the tale incarnate the grim logic of an entirely fated world, for it shows Túrin to be partially responsible for his final ruin because of his wrong choices. As if to make matters even more complicated, the narrator's portrayal of Turambar's life also shows how circumstances do indeed entrap him and how malevolent forces do in fact overpower him, thus apparently contradicting the elvish belief that humans have the unique gift of escaping fate.

Melkor's Curse upon Túrin as a Form of Fate

The 1977 edition *Silmarillion*'s inclusion "Of Túrin Turambar" belongs to a longer tale, the *Narn i Hîn Húrin*, or "Tale of the Children of Húrin," in *Unfinished Tales*. Both versions tell of Melkor's curse, but the *Narn* version makes the role of Morgoth's curse more explicit than the 1977 edition account. In the longer description, the narrator presents a dialogue between Morgoth (another name for Melkor) and Húrin, Túrin's father, regarding fate and providence. Morgoth declares that he has dominion over all events and people within Arda, and Húrin expresses faith in Ilúvatar's promise that a larger providential design controls even Morgoth and his deeds. Despite being imprisoned and tortured by Morgoth, Húrin denies his supreme authority. In response, Morgoth declares he will reveal his dominion by destroying Húrin's family:

The shadow of my purpose lies upon Arda, and all that is in it bends slowly and surely to my will. But upon all whom you love my thought shall weigh as a cloud of Doom, and it shall bring them down into darkness and despair. Wherever they go, evil shall arise. Whenever they speak, their words shall bring ill counsel. Whatsoever they do shall turn against them. They shall die without hope, cursing both life and death.[11]

Placed in the context of Morgoth and Húrin's debate over fate and providence, Túrin's disastrous life seems, therefore, to be nothing other than the curse's fulfillment, thus proving Morgoth's claim to be "Master of the fates of Arda."

The more one attributes power to the curse in determining the course of Túrin's life, the less one can uphold the free nature of his will. If Melkor's curse virtually overwhelms Túrin's freedom, then he bears hardly any blame for his mistaken actions. Regarding the curse's presence from the tale's outset, Paul Kocher observes:

In reflecting upon this grim tragedy of incest and suicide the reader is likely to ask sooner or later whether it is consistent with the doctrine underlying the whole of *The Silmarillion*, that Elves and Men have been created with wills free to choose between right and wrong. This is to ask whether Morgoth's curse upon Húrin and his children succeeded, and this in turn is to ask whether Morgoth or Ilúvatar by his Providence governed the course of their lives.[12]

Kocher points us to the central dilemma that the elvish narrator is attempting to resolve. If within the context of Tolkien's world such curses as Melkor's do have binding power, then is Túrin subject to the determinism of Melkor's curse and thus bound to act in the destructive manner that he does? In other words, to what extent, if any, is Túrin's will free?

To accept the supremacy of fate over free will is to remove responsibility for one's actions and thus the subsequent consequences of those actions. When Túrin declares, "Morgoth has laid a curse upon [Húrin] and all his kin,"[13] he demonstrates his own conviction about the curse's power, thus excusing his own responsibility for his choices. Commenting on the *Narn* version of the story, Shippey maintains that the real blame for Túrin's future lies with his mother, Morwen, who decided to send him away as a child: "She is given very clear advice by her husband before he leaves, '*Do not be afraid!*' and '*Do not wait!*' She remembers this, but she ignores it, because 'she would not yet humble her pride to be an alms-guest,' even of Thingol. . . . All this comes from Morwen's mistaken decision to separate from her son, and one of its roots is pride."[14] Shippey argues that human freedom, not simply impersonal fate, helps move events, but he does hold that external circumstances ultimately beyond Túrin's control force him towards a determined, ruinous future. If Shippey is correct about Morwen's responsibility for her son's tragic life, then fate continues to be the power behind Túrin's life, because an external agent limits his freedom by predetermining his life's course.

The Dragon's Power over Túrin as a Power of Fate

In recounting Túrin's story, the narrator not only reveals the authority of Morgoth's curse over Túrin's life, but also that an evil superhuman creature can dominate a mortal's weaker body and mind— just as *Lord of the Rings* demonstrates Sauron's similar dominance of others. In the mythology of *Silmarillion*, the dragons are the most evil and powerful of Melkor's corrupted servants, and neither elves nor humans can successfully resist them. In the Túrin episode, the dragon Glaurung quickly overwhelms the elvish defenses when he attacks the realm of Nargothrond; and when Túrin attempts to fight against Glaurung, the dragon easily casts a paralyzing spell over him: "Without fear Túrin looked into [Glaurung's serpent-eyes] as he raised up the sword; and straightway he fell under the binding spell of the lidless eyes of the dragon, and was halted moveless."[15] The narrator makes clear that the dragon completely overwhelms Túrin's body; however, whether the spell also binds Túrin's mind is not as clear. Tolkien grants his dragons immense physical and psychological power over other creatures, including humans. They thus exercise a strong persuasive mastery in their deceits.

The spell's domination of Túrin calls into question the freedom of his later decisions. Túrin is entranced, for example, but Glaurung deceitfully lays out to him two choices, both of which have bad results. Paralleling the dilemmas so characteristic of Norse sagas, the bewitched Túrin is caught in the vise that Bertha Phillpotts calls the "awful choice between two evils."[16] Glaurung claims that Túrin can rescue either the elf-maiden Finduilas or his mother and sister, whom Glaurung deceitfully declares to be in mortal danger. Rescuing one party will result in the other's death, claims the dragon. Túrin personally witnessed the orcs' capture of Finduilas, but he hears only from Glaurung that his family is in jeopardy. Though an evil consequence will result from either choice, Túrin believes Glaurung's lies and chooses to abandon Finduilas in order to rescue his family. Only when he belatedly discovers the dragon's deceit is Glaurung's sorcerous hold over Túrin broken: "Then Túrin's eyes were opened, and the last threads of Glaurung's spell were loosed." The narrator then indicates that Túrin belatedly and angrily understands "the lies that had deluded him."[17] He sees the fullness of the truth and the depth of his deception—and thus the wrongness of his original choice—only after it is too late for him to save Finduilas from her immediate danger.

The narrator suggests that the dragon's spell limits Túrin's ability to choose properly, but the narrator also implicitly blames Túrin both for his pride in thinking he could defeat a dragon and for his foolishness in believing the dragon. Túrin saw with his own eyes that the orcs had taken Finduilas captive, along with the other women of the fallen elvish city, but he trusted Glaurung's false report about his family. In deciding to rescue his family, Túrin believes an enemy while rejecting the wisdom of a friend, Gwindor, who had prophesied that Finduilas "alone stands between thee and thy doom. If thou fail her, it shall not fail to find thee."[18] Túrin does fail her; and, as a consequence of his choice, Túrin saves neither group of women, thus enabling the doom that Gwindor had prophesied to approach its fulfillment.[19]

Túrin's failure before the dragon's greater strength reveals the limits of human resistance to evil. Paul Kocher points out a certain parallel between Túrin's actions in the dragon episode and his later actions in the marriage to his sister: when Túrin has the ability to choose rightly, he does not, and his choices lead to circumstances that then bind his will. Kocher asserts that although Túrin has no will power sufficient to overcome the dragon, he did have the ability to avoid the original encounter and should have done so: "Before and after the trances, . . . free choices are made by Túrin which develop his situation in a direction leading toward his suicide."[20] One significant free choice Túrin makes is to ignore the advice of the vala Ulmo, who urgently told Túrin and the elves to guard against the dragon's approach by tearing down the bridge into the city. By disregarding the authority of a vala and choosing instead to rely on his own wisdom and strength, Túrin unchains events that end, alas, in his incestuous marriage and suicide. Though external circumstances may affect and even bind the characters' minds and wills, they still retain a certain limited freedom. As Kocher makes clear, the Middle-earth of *Silmarillion* is not a fated realm, though freely made choices often produce fatalistic consequences. Even so, the apparently fated outcome could have been favorable had people chosen rightly.

Another more serious example of apparently fated circumstances checking Túrin's freedom can be discerned in his incestuous marriage to his sister, Nienor. The narrator creates a particularly acute tension between fate and free will in the examination of this relationship and the responsibility the participants bear for its development. Unavoidable circumstances seem to force Túrin's life in a specific way, circumventing his free will such that he and Nienor, who did not know each other as siblings, meet and fall in love. Nienor, disobeying the order to remain in the safety of Doriath, chooses to search for her long-lost brother. She is captured by orcs, escapes from them, but eventually loses her sanity. A crazed woman, she runs naked into the woods where Túrin finds her but does not know her to be his sister. Critics have noted the Kullervo story from the *Kalevala* as the model for the Túrin story,[21] but the narrator gives a significant twist to the Finnish account. Following the pattern of Kullervo, the tale of Túrin also shows that uncontrollable external circumstances bring Túrin and Nienor together. Yet, unlike Kullervo, who forces himself sexually upon a maiden, Túrin strictly follows chivalric behavior towards the vulnerable woman. He rescues her from death, takes her under his protection, and only later do they fall in love, marry, and conceive a child. They commit incest in complete ignorance of their blood relationship while following a noble code of conduct. Yet once they meet, they have no real control over their love, since they know of no reason why they should not love each other. Thus are they responsible for the choices that led to their original meeting, but they have no moral culpability for the incestuous marriage itself, as fate seems to have directed their lives toward disaster.

Despite not being culpable for marrying his sister, Túrin holds himself liable, as do others. This presentation of accountability follows F. Anne Payne's description of *wyrd*, understood here as "fate," in the life of an Anglo-Saxon hero. She argues that the hero meets his *wyrd* when he has transgressed, unknowingly but irreversibly, the boundaries of *wyrd*. Though she is analyzing the power of fate in *Beowulf*, Payne's argument is applicable to the events of Túrin's life:

> *Wyrd* is the force that eventually destroys the lives of the violators of unknowable universal order in the world of Beowulf. It is the agent in the most terrible experience of the day of death. It is the opponent of man in the strange area of the most intense perception and consciousness. Though it may hold off for a while, the individual in the end makes an error in choice and releases forces whose consequences at the moment of crisis he controls no longer and *Wyrd* is victorious.[22]

Thus does the Túrin episode follow the pattern of *wyrd* in one of its expressions—merciless fate that condemns a person for transgressing laws of which he has no knowledge. Túrin makes a choice to marry Nienor, but it is a decision based on ignorance. Subsequently yet unknowingly, he violates a universal law against incest, thus releasing still further forces he cannot control. Túrin despairs at the situation in which fated circumstances have placed him, condemning himself for the destruction he has caused. Fully accepting fate's power over him, Túrin abandons hope of mercy for himself and makes the final choice to take his own life.

Free Will Incurs Fate

The marriage of Túrin to Nienor offers a clear example of the wheels of fate catching up unwilling persons, but the circumstances leading to the marriage are the result of several previous choices Túrin has made. Though he is not morally responsible for the act of incest itself, Túrin's earlier wrong choices set up circumstances from which he and his sister cannot later escape. For instance, he chose to refuse Beleg's request on behalf of Thingol to return to Doriath and, as a consequence, he is not reunited there with his mother and sister. Yet it is not simply one bad choice alone that creates an unbreakable chain of cause and effect, for Túrin constantly rejects the chances to choose rightly and thus to alter, however slightly, the otherwise inexorable workings of fate. Thingol repeatedly offers Túrin mercy, but Túrin pridefully rebuffs him on each occasion. Túrin is also given the chance to avoid his later fate by returning the love of Finduilas, but he both rejects her love and betrays her trust when he abandons her to a horrible end with the orcs. Had he accepted and returned her love, he never would have entered into the "doomed" marriage with his sister. Túrin also has the chance to choose rightly by heeding Ulmo's advice and tearing down the bridge into Nargothrond, but he willfully refuses to obey the wisdom of another, even a vala.

In the Túrin episode, the narrator sets Túrin in a complicated situation that discloses the interlocking forces of fate and freedom. On the one hand, the narrator tells the story as illustrating and fulfilling Melkor's curse. Yet, on the other hand, the story repeatedly shows the protagonist making bad choices that result in evil consequences. His repeated refusals of the good escalate in significance, resulting in ever greater, more devastating consequences to his life and the lives of those around him. What makes Túrin's final self-destruction so poignant is the combined nature of both fateful circumstances and his own free choices. Though fate appears extremely strong and active in forcing Túrin's life in a specific direction, it does not preclude his responsibility for what happens to him or to those connected with him. Rather than being simply a story of an innocent, helpless man caught up in the maelstrom of fate, the Túrin tale reveals a figure who repeatedly chooses and acts according to his overwhelming pride (the Anglo-Saxon concept of *ofermod*). Hence his ultimate act of pride in the rejection of life itself, suicide.

The different narrators of *Silmarillion* show free will used wrongly, in discord with the beneficent providential design of the cosmos, as flawed characters willfully choose to deny the good, even as they are also beset by forces that make the consequences of these denials result in inevitable, fatalistic effects. However, as the next episode will show, the tale of Beren and Lúthien stands in contrast to that of Túrin, because it presents the protagonists properly using free will in cooperation with Ilúvatar's initial promise of providential power in history.

BEREN AND LÚTHIEN

The elvish chroniclers of *Silmarillion* struggle to reconcile the elves' creation myth, and its stress on providential design, with subsequent events of elvish history. The narrator of the Túrin Turambar tale deals with the clash of fate and freedom without reference to any larger overarching providential order; the Beren and Lúthien story, by contrast, is recounted by one who understands the same conflict from a transtemporal perspective. The story reveals a two-fold element of providential activity: the open and unfixed nature of the future, and the free human cooperation with providence in realizing a beneficent outcome.

Though a web of circumstances seems to ensnare Beren and Lúthien, the two lovers exercise their free will properly, positively responding to love and using their free will for the sake of others. Túrin names himself "Master of Fate," but neither Beren nor Lúthien has such high self-regard. In recognizing their weakness before forces beyond their control, they unintentionally find strength. In his analysis of the Beren and Lúthien tale, Tolkien comments on the accidental discovery of strength through the confession of weakness, a clear reference to St. Paul's claim that "power is made perfect through weakness" (2 Cor. 12:9):

we meet, among other things, the first example of the motive (to become dominant in Hobbits) that the great policies of world history,
"the wheels of the world," are often turned not by the Lords and
Governors, even gods, but by the seemingly unknown and weak—
owing to the secret life in creation, and the part unknowable to all
wisdom but One, that resides in the intrusions of the Children of
God into the Drama.[23]

The elves call this story the "Lay of Leithian," which means "release
from bondage," for in the end, Lúthien escapes from the confines
of the world by choosing the ultimate expression of weakness—
mortality and death. Her embrace of Beren's mortal condition becomes the means by which Lúthien overcomes fate. The elvish narrators, recognizing the transcendent quality of her decision, honor
her for it. Instead of being an account of fated destruction and ruin,
like the majority of *Silmarillion* tales, the Beren and Lúthien tale
moves to a favorable end that is poignantly joyful for the two central
characters—and the audience.

Some critics would disagree that the tale is one of victory,
however. Tolkien himself points out the disastrous consequences of
Beren and Lúthien's "successful" quest: "the capture of the Silmaril,
a supreme victory, leads to disaster. The oath of the sons of Fëanor
becomes operative, and lust for the Silmarils brings all the kingdoms
of the Elves to ruin."[24] Though the silmarils' recapture brings disaster on the elvish kingdoms, the downfall is not due to Beren and
Lúthien's choices but to the mistaken actions of others—Fëanor and
his sons—in their mad attempt to retrieve the silmarils at all costs.
The earlier "sins" of the Noldor continue to have devastating consequences, but the "reparation" that Beren, Lúthien, and others subsequently make also initiates a series of beneficial consequences. Tolkien does not make these explicit, but Richard C. West notes them:
"With irony typical of Tolkien, this victory leads not only to the
death of King Thingol and the destruction of his kingdom of Doriath but also, later, to the successful voyage of Eärendil the Mariner
to plead with the Valar . . . for the aid that ultimately overthrows
Morgoth. And the repercussions continue throughout the history of

Middle-earth."²⁵ The meritorious consequences of Beren and Lúthien's actions continue even into the Third Age, the end of which
Lord of the Rings concerns.

Free Will Countering Fatalism

The world order that the narrator presents in "Of Beren and Lúthien" stands in stark contrast with the fatalistic quality of the Túrin
tale. Shippey accurately points out the difference: "A case could be
made for seeing Tolkien's other major 'human story,' the tale of
Beren and Lúthien, as the philosophical antithesis to Túrin. It is a
story of love across the species of elf and human, rather than a tale of
incest; . . . Lúthien masters fate and death in a way that Túrin cannot
even aspire to."²⁶ The story of the two lovers contains certain deterministic elements, yet it more strongly presents the nature of providential activity within Middle-earth—the important cooperation
between creaturely freedom and providential power within an underlying historical design.

The narrator expresses this sense of cooperation by repeatedly
using the passive voice, implying that characters are as much acted
upon as acting, a technique Tolkien uses throughout *Lord of the
Rings*. For instance, the narrator describes Beren's quest for the realm
of Doriath in passive terms: "It was put into his heart that he would
go down into the Hidden Kingdom, where no mortal foot had yet
trodden." This unstated force could be the "doom"—a word having,
in Tolkien's work, the triple significance of judgment, decree, and
destiny—about which Melian speaks and which Beren calls "fate."
Yet, though the narrator suggests that an unnamed mover has placed
a questing desire into Beren's heart, Beren still *responds* to this desire
by seeking and finding a path into Doriath despite the clear danger to
himself. The land through which Beren travels is particularly dangerous because the opposing powers of two maias clash there. As the
narrator says, Doriath is the region "where the sorcery of Sauron and
the power of Melian came together, and horror and madness walked."
This journey, the narrator says, "is not accounted least among the
great deeds of Beren, but he spoke of it to no one after, lest the horror

return into his mind." The narrator highlights Beren's unique decision to risk the dangerous path by stating that "none know how he found a way, and so came by paths that no Man nor Elf else ever dared to tread to the borders of Doriath."[27] An unnamed power directs Beren along ways he could not have found alone, but he also clearly cooperates with its intention. In another use of the passive voice, again suggesting cooperation of wills, the narrator says that "Beren looking up beheld the eyes of Lúthien, and his glance went also to the face of Melian; and it seemed to him that words *were put* into his mouth. Fear left him, and the pride of the eldest house of Men returned to him."[28] The narrator describes Beren as speaking with another's voice. Whether it is Melian or some unseen power who inspires Beren's speech, in either case Beren still chooses to hazard death by asking for Lúthien's hand in marriage from Thingol.

In the Beren and Lúthien tale, the narrator presents two alternating suggestions regarding the constraints of fate and the extent of providence. On the one hand, he tells a story in which the ill effects of a badly used free will—Fëanor's oath binding the Noldor elves to pursue Melkor after he stole the silmarils—continue to constrain innocents, thus diminishing the extent of their free will. Yet on the other hand, he suggests the possibility of altering those consequences, of escaping the constraints of fate, through properly used freedom. Thus does the story display the ways whereby freedom may be used both to resist and further the effects of fate. Verlyn Flieger recognizes this tension between liberty and necessity and ultimately concludes that freedom is constrained: "The interactions of fate and free will are more tellingly presented here than in any other episode of *The Silmarillion*. Thingol's actions are bound by the Music. Beren's are not. Who then is free, and who bound when their paths and actions intersect? Thingol's response to Beren's declaration of love for Lúthien fixes Thingol's own doom and that of his kingdom."[29]

Flieger accepts the elvish belief that elves are bound by the music of the Ainur, whereas men are not. If Flieger (and the elves) are correct that fate, or the "music," binds Thingol to choose as he does simply because he is elvish, then his daughter, Lúthien, must also be bound by the same fate. The text itself counters such a conclusion by showing that Lúthien has two clear moments of free choice: the first when she chooses to accompany Beren into Morgoth's realm, and the more important second moment when she chooses mortality—a decision running directly counter to the very "music" of the Ainur, which shaped the world and its natural laws, including the course of both men's and elves' lives, following Ilúvatar's purpose for each race. In neither choice does the narrator imply that an external power, such as fate, or a vala, or even Ilúvatar himself, forces Lúthien to a specific end. She chooses freely.

Because both an elf and a mortal *can* choose rightly, their proper actions highlight the abuse of free will by other characters of both races—in particular Thingol, Fëanor, and Túrin. Though the narrator shows the continued effects of Fëanor's initial choices regarding the silmarils, he does not present simply a story of inescapable destructive consequences. The agency of others negatively affects Beren and Lúthien, but it does not negate their freedom to escape the deterministic cycle of a fated world order. They are not inexorably ensnared in circumstances, but, by their own choices and actions in accordance with Ilúvatar's will, they are able to turn evil conditions into partial good. For instance, Beren and Lúthien transform Thingol's evil desire for Beren's death into a good he neither intended nor foresaw; they reclaim one of the silmarils from Melkor, an action whose consequences lead eventually to the Valar's permanent ejection of Melkor from Middle-earth.

The conflict between freedom and fate becomes ever more dramatic as the characters themselves gradually realize the potential consequences of their choices. At the edge of Morgoth's realm, for example, Beren discerns that his promise to seize the stolen silmaril from Melkor must surely lead to his own death. Not for fear of his own life but for that of Lúthien, he recoils; indeed, he considers forsaking his sworn oath by abandoning the quest. Unlike Fëanor and his sons, who refuse to recant their oath even in the face of its obviously evil outcome, Beren shows that he is not constrained by a single act of his will, the earlier oath. His oath has its own unalterable consequences, but Beren still remains free to exercise his will in response to new circumstances and to the consequences of old choices. Standing on the edge of the enemy's realm, Beren is again free to choose to go forward or not.

Huan, the "hound of Valinor," voices the power that Beren still possesses, describing a limited freedom similar to the one that Norse poets offer to their protagonists—"the awful choice between two evils."[30] Huan says, "You can turn from your fate and lead [Lúthien] into exile, seeking peace in vain while your life lasts. But if you will not deny your doom, then either Lúthien, being forsaken, must assuredly die alone, or she must with you challenge the fate that lies before you—hopeless, yet not certain."[31] Though he speaks prophetically, Huan shares the narrator's lack of omniscience—he admits that part of the future is dark to him. Though perhaps not recognizing his own wisdom, Huan introduces a new element into the pagan formula of doomed choice: hope, hope that lies beyond destruction, hope that an invisible power may intervene to assist the protagonist. Unable himself to envision such transcendent intervention, Huan sees only two paths open to Beren, both of which have bad ends: Beren can turn away from his apparently certain death in Morgoth's realm, thus ensuring that he will never again enjoy inward peace. If on the other hand he chooses to fare forward into the evil realm of Angband, then he must either abandon Lúthien, who may die without him, or else he must allow her to accompany him to what seems their sure and mutual death.

Though Huan offers a moment of choice to Beren, Lúthien also exercises her own free will in choosing to remain with her beloved, will he or nill he. Beren is not an isolated hero, therefore; Lúthien is also a companion in Beren's choice. Recognizing her determination, Beren "sought no longer to dissuade her." Richard West emphasizes that Lúthien's decisions and actions result in the quest's success, arguing that Lúthien "does far more to achieve the quest of the Silmaril than does Beren, even urging him on when he is ready to abandon it rather than put her at risk."[32] Lúthien's contributions are indispensable, but she achieves the quest only through working in consort with Beren. Mutually strengthened by the love and companionship of the other, they *both* show the resolve and courage to venture into the heart of Morgoth's realm. The episode thus illustrates the virtue of "northern courage" that Tolkien defined in his essay on *Beowulf* as "the creed of unyielding will"[33]—heroes refusing to retreat even in the face of death. Yet, such northern sources as *Beowulf* typically do not present any reward for the hero's proper action beyond that of *lof*, which is fame after death. The Beren and Lúthien myth, by contrast, does suggest such a reward—though a complex one, not a simple "payment" for their self-sacrificing lives.

It is a reward linked to the intrusion of transcendent agency twice in the story. First, when Beren and Lúthien encounter the monstrous wolf, Carcharoth, at the gates of Angband, the narrator declares that "suddenly some power, descended from of old from divine race, possessed Lúthien, and casting back her foul raiment she stood forth, small before the might of Carcharoth, but radiant and terrible." With the aid of this unexpected intervention Lúthien casts Carcharoth into a deep sleep.[34] Lúthien descends in part from the Maiar, the beings slightly lower than the Valar in the hierarchy of creation. Thus, the power to which the narrator alludes could be an internal, elvish might hidden from Lúthien herself prior to her encounter with the wolf, or it could be the supernal divine power of the Valar themselves. In either case—whether it is an internally awakened power or an externally interventive power—something intercedes to enable Lúthien's victory over Carcharoth. The narrator neither shows Lúthien acting autonomously against a more powerful foe nor suggests a third party pushing her aside to defeat the enemy. Rather do we witness the essential character of providence at work within Middle-earth—a force enabling and cooperating with Lúthien's own strength. A higher, transcendent power never violates Lúthien's freedom but rather works through her abilities to overpower the great wolf.

Although not being able to articulate fully the role of providence as originally described in the creation myth, the narrator tells of a second example of providential involvement in the story—the direct transcendent rescue of Beren and Lúthien from death. Beren, having cut one of the silmarils from Morgoth's crown, foolishly decides to excise another; and in doing so, his knife snaps, slicing the sleeping Morgoth and breaking the spell that Lúthien's song had cast on him.

"The hosts of Morgoth were awakened," we learn, and Beren and Lúthien flee before them. Lúthien's elven power now spent, Beren seeks to guard her from the second assault of the now-awakened Carcharoth, but the wolf bites off his hand, still clutching the silmaril. Though the wolf flees in berserk horror from the pain caused by the powerful jewel inside its stomach, Beren and Lúthien are too weak and wounded to defend themselves against the coming hosts of Morgoth. As the narrator states, "Thus the quest of the Silmaril was like to have ended in ruin and despair; but in that hour above the wall of the valley three mighty birds appeared, flying northward with wings swifter than the wind. . . . they lifted up Lúthien and Beren from the earth, and bore them aloft into the clouds."[35] Since the eagles serve here as a *deus ex machina*, the rescue of Beren and Lúthien raises many questions about the nature of such beneficial "coincidences." Is it random chance that the eagles happen to be present just when Beren and Lúthien flounder in mortal danger? Were the eagles sent to look for them by someone who knew they would need rescuing? The narrator does not explicitly identify Manwë's assistance in this episode, but the eagles are known to be under his provenance (though *not* his domination), and their appearance suggests the vala's involvement in saving Beren and Lúthien. The eagles save Beren and Lúthien, as they also will save Frodo and Sam after the Ring's destruction, though questions pertaining to the eagles' prompting or motivation remain unanswered.

The tale of Beren and Lúthien moves inevitably toward Beren's death, Lúthien's bereavement at their parting, and her great moment of choice between an elvish and a human "doom." From the elvish translation of the title, "Release from Bondage," the narrator suggests that, by choosing to follow Beren in mortality, Lúthien finds a release from the elvish bondage to the temporal realm. Yet it is not merely death itself that enables Lúthien's deliverance, for many elves die in battle, but their violent deaths are not accorded the same honor as Lúthien's. The key difference is that Lúthien knowingly *chooses* to surrender her immortality in order to join her mortal Beren in life but also in death.

Tolkien's mythology inverts the innate desire of mortals for immortality as presented in the mythologies of nearly all human cultures. Instead, Tolkien presents a race of immortals desiring mortality. Pengolodh, another elvish narrator who recounts a different version of the *Ainulindalë*, declares that "the sons of Men die indeed, and leave the World; wherefore they are called the Guests, or the Strangers. Death is their fate, the gift of Ilúvatar unto them, which as Time wears even the Powers shall envy."[36] The narrator's treatment of death in the Beren and Lúthien saga shows the elvish perplexity over the mystery that an apparent evil such as death, which causes such great grief, can also be a special gift—one that the elves both fear and desire.

After Beren's death, Lúthien pleads that the Valar might bring him back to life. She sings a song of such poignant beauty that Mandos desires to grant her request. Pitying her, Mandos appeals to Manwë, the highest of the Valar, to bring Beren back from the dead and to make him immortal like Lúthien. Though Mandos is similar to a god of the afterlife, Manwë replies that neither he nor any vala has the power to "change the fates of the Children of Ilúvatar. . . . For it was not permitted to the Valar to withhold Death from [Beren], which is the gift of Ilúvatar to Men." The Valar are also bound by the laws that they themselves established for the world, and the laws Ilúvatar instituted for his own children. Yet the narrator indicates that Manwë sought counsel from Ilúvatar concerning this petition, declaring that Lúthien "might return to Middle-earth, and take with her Beren, there to dwell again, but without certitude of life or joy. Then she would become mortal, and subject to a second death, even as he."[37] Given his earlier assertion that the Valar have no power to alter the "fate" of the elves, Manwë's permission of Beren to return to life must mean that Ilúvatar, answering the Valar's petitions, granted such approval. Tolkien makes this precise point in his *Letters*: "Immortality and Mortality being the special gifts of God to the *Eruhíni* ["Children of Eru"] . . . it must be assumed that no alteration of their fundamental kind could be effected by the Valar even in one case: the cases of

Lúthien (and Túor) and the position of their descendants was a direct act of God."[38]

Having been given the authority to alter the fates of the *Eruhíni*, Manwë then presents Lúthien with two difficult choices in response to her poignant plea. These two choices, unlike the earlier options that Huan presented to Beren, do not follow the pagan pattern that Phillpotts indicates, for either choice will issue in joy tinted with the necessary sadness of sacrifice and suffering. Unlike Beren's dilemma of mutually inimical alternatives, Lúthien will find blessings within whichever path she chooses. In this way, Tolkien integrates the pattern associated with a fated world order into a more providential view. Lúthien may either choose to live in Valinor until the end of time, so that her love for Beren will be finally but completely removed from her memory, thus enabling her to experience no grief at her separation from him; or else Lúthien can give up her own immortality—thus accepting her own future death—and have Beren sent back to Middle-earth for a brief extension of his life. In the first choice, she will live forever without final sorrow but also, by necessity, without her love for and memory of Beren. In the second, she must surrender her own immortality, accepting mortality in order to be reunited with Beren, if only for a short time. This second choice, as Manwë clearly states, does not guarantee a second life of unabated joy without suffering. Lúthien chooses the riskier second path of mortality, returning to Middle-earth to join Beren as a fellow mortal.

Her motivation for such an apparently foolish, short-term decision supports the story's antipagan theme. She freely chooses to abandon immortality out of love for another rather than herself. Such a loving choice implies a deep trust. The story is clear that, even though Lúthien chooses a life that will have death as its inevitable consequence, she is not guaranteed consequential happiness for making it. As in Huan's warning to Beren, so is Lúthien's future as a mortal uncertain, yet not hopeless. Her choice suggests her underlying hope and faith in Ilúvatar's promise—that mortality *is* his gift. Elves have no idea how this may be so or what happens to men after death, but Lúthien is willing to rely on Ilúvatar's promise and thus to experience death. She chooses mortality without sure knowledge of the future either within or beyond life, but she chooses out of trust, hope, and love—the essence of faith.

Though a providential vision is at the heart of Tolkien's formation of Middle-earth, those who live within the design cannot always discern it. The myth as told by the elves in *Silmarillion* reveals the limitations of a time-bound perspective. Shippey appropriately points out that "in spite of Eärendil," the mariner who persuades the Valar to return to Middle-earth and thus to rout Melkor, "the later-published work [*Silmarillion*] feels blacker and grimmer than the earlier [*Lord of the Rings*]; the sense that 'chance' or 'luck' may contain a providential element is not so strong."[39] This is certainly the case, but the problem may not be that providence is absent from *Silmarillion*, but that the narrators of the *legendarium* cannot comprehend the divine design in which—so they have been told—they play a crucial role. The narrator of the story of Beren and Lúthien comes closest to reconciling Ilúvatar's providential promises with the experience of living in a flawed world amid hostile powers. Yet it is not until *Lord of the Rings* that Tolkien's human narrator becomes capable of more fully reconciling the apparent clash of faith and doubt, freedom and fate, and thus of more fully conveying the providential design of Middle-earth to a contemporary audience.

NOTES

1. Shippey, *J. R. R. Tolkien*, ix; see also *Road to Middle-earth*, 329.
2. Tolkien, *Letters*, 236.
3. Wood, *Gospel according to Tolkien*, 114.
4. According to Christopher Tolkien, the original version of "The Music of Ainur" is not very different from the later versions that his father wrote during his lifetime and the version that Christopher used for the published work. The central vision, or core, of the myth remains intact throughout the various versions; for, rather than changing the story, Tolkien simply expanded it (cf. Tolkien, *Book of Lost Tales*, 61–62). Christopher states that, in the early version, his father formally expresses the "different fates of Elves and Men" (ibid., 62–63), but the published version does not include this discussion of the two races.

Again, Christopher does not make clear his reasons for excluding this rather important extended description of the nature of elvish and human beings.

5. Tolkien, *Silmarillion*, 59.

6. Ibid., 17.

7. Ibid.

8. Ibid., 15.

9. Ibid., 17.

10. Dickerson, *Following Gandalf*, 95.

11. Tolkien, *Unfinished Tales*, 67.

12. Kocher, *Reader's Guide*, 174.

13. Tolkien, *Silmarillion*, 209.

14. Shippey, *J. R. R. Tolkien*, 252–53.

15. Tolkien, *Silmarillion*, 213.

16. Phillpotts, "Wyrd and Providence in Anglo-Saxon Thought," 5.

17. Tolkien, *Silmarillion*, 215.

18. Ibid., 213.

19. Note that in *The Two Towers*, Aragorn chooses to save Merry and Pippin, who have been captured by orcs. Though Aragorn, too, faces an evil dilemma, the peril of Merry and Pippin is actual, whereas Frodo's danger remains potential. Frodo is more "deserving" of protection, given that he bears the Ring, which must be destroyed; but Merry and Pippin are the weak ones in clear and present danger. Aragorn chooses rightly in seeking to rescue the two young hobbits because he chooses the good at hand rather than a supposed and distant good.

20. Kocher, *Reader's Guide*, 174.

21. See Shippey, *J. R. R. Tolkien*, 250, and *Road to Middle-Earth*, 261–62. There is also a distant resemblance, of course, to the Oedipus story.

22. Payne, "Three Aspects of Wyrd in Beowulf," 16.

23. Tolkien, *Letters*, 149.

24. Ibid.

25. West, "Real-World in a Secondary World," 260.

26. Shippey, *Road to Middle-earth*, 254.

27. Tolkien, *Silmarillion*, 164.

28. Ibid., 166; emphasis added.

29. Flieger, *Splintered Light*, 137.

30. Phillpotts, "Wyrd and Providence in Anglo-Saxon Thought," 5.

31. Tolkien, *Silmarillion*, 179.

32. West, "Real-World in a Secondary World," 265.

33. Tolkien, "Beowulf," 21.

34. Tolkien, *Silmarillion*, 180.

35. Ibid., 182.

36. Tolkien, *Morgoth's Ring*, 21.

37. Tolkien, *Silmarillion*, 187.

38. Tolkien, *Letters*, 194.
39. Shippey, *Road to Middle-earth*, 253.

BIBLIOGRAPHY

Dickerson, Matthew T. *Following Gandalf: Epic Battles and Moral Victory in "The Lord of the Rings."* Grand Rapids, MI: Brazos, 2003.

Flieger, Verlyn. *Splintered Light: Logos and Language in Tolkien's World.* Grand Rapids, MI: Eerdmans, 1983.

Kocher, Paul H. *A Reader's Guide to "The Silmarillion."* Boston: Houghton Mifflin, 1980.

Payne, F. A. "Three Aspects of Wyrd in Beowulf." In *Old English Studies in Honour of John C. Pope*, edited by Robert B. Burlin, Edward B. Irving, Jr., and Marie Borroff, 15–35. Toronto: University of Toronto Press, 1974.

Phillpotts, Bertha. "Wyrd and Providence in Anglo-Saxon Thought." In *Interpretations of "Beowulf": A Critical Anthology*, edited by R. D. Fulk, 1–13. Bloomington: Indiana University Press, 1991.

Shippey, Thomas. *J. R. R. Tolkien: Author of the Century.* Boston: Houghton Mifflin, 2000.

———. *The Road to Middle-earth.* Rev. ed. Boston: Houghton Mifflin, 2003.

Tolkien, J. R. R. *Book of Lost Tales.* Vol. 1 of *The History of Middle-earth.* Edited by Christopher Tolkien. Boston: Houghton Mifflin, 1984.

———. *The Letters of J. R. R. Tolkien.* Edited by Humphrey Carpenter with the assistance of Christopher Tolkien. Boston: Houghton Mifflin, 1981.

———. *Morgoth's Ring.* Vol. 10 of *The History of Middle-earth.* Edited by Christopher Tolkien. Boston: Houghton Mifflin, 1993.

———. *The Silmarillion.* Edited by Christopher Tolkien. Boston: Houghton Mifflin, 1977; 1998.

West, Richard C. "Real-World Myth in a Secondary World: Mythological Aspects in the Story of Beren and Lúthien." In *Tolkien the Medievalist*, edited by Jane Chance, 259–67. New York: Routledge, 2003.

Wood, Ralph C. *The Gospel according to Tolkien: Visions of the Kingdom in Middle-earth.* Louisville: Westminster John Knox, 2003.

UNLIKELY KNIGHTS, IMPROBABLE HEROES

Inverse, Antimodernist Paradigms
in Tolkien and Cervantes

Michael D. Thomas

What do Miguel de Cervantes Saavedra (1547–1616) and John Ronald Reuel Tolkien (1892–1973) have in common? Many, perhaps most, scholars would say, "Not much" (which explains why nothing has yet been written comparing the two). It is true that these two authors wrote in different languages and in different ages, using distinctive styles and narrative techniques, but they do, I contend, share some remarkable similarities. Reading *El Ingenioso Hidalgo Don Quijote de la Mancha* and *The Lord of the Rings*, one begins to note certain parallels in fictional worlds and characterizations and a common paradigm of virtues. For this reason, I believe that we can productively place their masterworks side by side and learn something new and fresh about both writers.

Their novels both exceed a thousand pages, were published in parts, and boast hundreds of characters together with many intricate subplots and twists and turns in their stories. A comprehensive comparison/contrast would be formidable. Here I propose to consider three striking parallels between these two world-renowned and widely read authors: (1) both create fictionalized visions of unconventional, even "improbable" heroes, (2) both stress the development

of traditional virtues—especially courage and "knightly" character—
and (3) through their novels, both protest the progressively modern
ages in which they write, especially the funding and development of
"war machines" at the expense of basic human needs (from "ar-
madas" to artillery) and the subsequent loss of life on a previously
unimagined scale. As we shall see, both Tolkien and Cervantes offer
imaginative readings of their current social milieu that stand at vari-
ance with the prevailing ideas of their age.

Both authors give literary embodiment to a moral vision that
features inverse heroic models, characters who depart from and con-
test traditional conceptions of the hero. In their masterworks, Tolkien and Cervantes articulate unusual images of heroism, leadership,
and knighthood in which unlikely and seemingly unqualified characters grow into roles traditionally reserved for those more obviously
competent. Since the valiant leader is conventionally construed as
relatively young, strong, "knightly," and of noble lineage, we certainly do not expect such qualities to be assigned to the weak, the
small, the peasant, and the old and frail. In each work, these latter
characters evolve in their sense of mission as they also progress in
their ability to fulfill it. They move from "doing" heroic acts to "becoming" heroic men (and hobbits) of virtue.

Cervantes launches his unlikely knight into a cynical, corrupt
early modern age ruled by monarchs zealous in geographical conquest, wealthy from imported gold, powerful in military armaments;
these Spanish kings, obtuse or indifferent to the most basic needs of
their people, also left their country desolate and impoverished. Tolkien takes on the claims of modernity by creating characters who call
into question the industrial or technological gains that have also produced the escalating devastation of two world wars. In the final
analysis, he seems to suggest that modernity is not worth the price of
its violence and destructiveness.

The biographies of both authors are also somewhat similar. That
they could have, in their later years, produced such wildly popular
works of literature, best sellers translated into many languages and
read worldwide, seems exceedingly implausible, given that Cervantes
was for decades a failed dramatist, poet, and fiction writer, and

Tolkien was an Oxford philologist specializing in esoteric ancient languages. Both might have been considered unlikely world-class writers and improbable creators of world-class novels. Even though a span of 450 years separates their careers, both of them experienced poverty, many family hardships, and the ill fortunes of war. Cervantes lost the use of his left hand in the naval Battle of Lepanto, Tolkien fought on the western front during World War I, including the Battle of the Somme, where he was grievously sickened by trench fever. They had both undoubtedly observed heroic actions in combat carried out not only by high-profile commanders and generals but also by common soldiers, those considered the least likely to be "heroic" and thus the least honored for their valor. Finally, both men were Catholic Christians with a peculiar vision of nobility and knighthood that hearkened back to medieval times.

It seems highly likely that Tolkien had read *Don Quixote*, though there is no real proof that the Oxford professor had mastered the Spanish classic thoroughly or was attempting to model his novel after Cervantes's book. Tolkien once characterized Cervantes as a "weedkiller to romance," an assessment that, given his low opinion of chivalric romance, may be more positive than negative.[1] Humphrey Carpenter does note that throughout his life Tolkien showed a deep and abiding interest in the Spanish language. Young Ronald was fascinated by "the collection of Spanish books in Father Francis's room. His guardian spoke Spanish fluently, and Ronald had often begged to be taught the language." He also "began work on an invented language . . . [that] showed a great deal of Spanish influence." In the closing days of World War I, Tolkien convalesced in a hospital and dedicated himself, among other things, to "improving his Spanish."[2]

PHILOSOPHICAL AND LITERARY DIFFERENCES

Despite these important convergences, there are also contrasts and potentially problematic points that center on each author's estimate of chivalric romance. Tolkien had near contempt for the genre, preferring Saxon heroic traditions over later Norman imports. Cervantes begins his novel by announcing that he is doing nothing more than ridiculing the extravagant novels of chivalry that obsessed so many Spanish readers of his time. By part 2, however, he has shifted his focus to contrasting rare chivalric virtue with widespread social vice. Thus both authors may have scorned the chivalric form of the genre, but in the end they praised the ethos and traditional values that chivalry embodied. Cervantes used romance as a model for his parody; Tolkien sought to avoid the romance genre altogether. Arwen, for instance, is Aragorn's "lady," but he does not serve her, rescue her, or invoke her name in the quixotic or even the chivalric sense.[3] Don Quixote, by contrast, "serves" the lady of his choice, Aldonza Lorenzo, whom he romantically renames Dulcinea del Toboso. He pays her tribute in every mission, acts in her name, and even tries to rescue her from what he believes to be an evil curse. In addition, Don Quixote has made himself into a "knight-errant," but the word "knight" never appears in *Lord of the Rings*. In Tolkien's creation, wizards and other mythical beings serve as evil foes. In *Don Quixote*, by contrast, such malicious creatures exist only in the mind and delusions of the knight himself and in the novels he has read. Cervantes presents no real magic except that of the imagination.

Another area of significant difference lies in the idea of the cooperative social or feudal contract. Don Quixote, in practice, does not submit himself to any sovereign nor does he belong to a cadre of questers such as we encounter in *Lord of the Rings*. The Manchegan hidalgo is a sort of maverick or lone wolf, a single cavalier seeking to bring light to the darkness. He is a roving doer of good deeds who also believes that he is confronting vast supernatural forces of evil that are conspiring to defeat him. In Tolkien, by contrast, the Company of Nine Walkers is allied as they do battle with demonic powers of darkness that are attempting to enslave Middle-earth. Not only does Don Quixote confront a comically lesser order of evil than the Fellowship faces, he also lacks the larger fellowship that Tolkien regards as essential to all worthy endeavors.[4] For in Tolkien's world, it is only by communal participation and interdependence—not by solitary knight-errantry alone—that evil can be defeated.

A final point of contrast lies in their use of humor. Tolkien sets the humor of *Lord of the Rings* against the backdrop of a serious mission to save the Middle-earth. Don Quixote's battles, by contrast, are mockery and parody: a doddering old man wanders about in rusty armor on a broken-down nag and frightens people, sometimes with threats and sometimes with actual attacks. When he feels he must act in order to fulfill his mission, he fails, or else succeeds only accidentally. Much of Cervantes's humor is slapstick, springing initially from the ineptness of his protagonist and later from the mockery of a cruel world. In part 1, when the knight attempts to "save" a perceived victim, he often ends up injuring himself and many other hapless persons, who end far worse than if he had never "rescued" them. In part 2, bored aristocrats decide to amuse themselves at the knight's expense. The resulting make-believe kingdom and cruel jokes are neither encouraging nor hopeful; rather, the nobles' sadistically conceived "events" cause Don Quixote and Sancho Panza to suffer both physically and emotionally. Even so, Cervantes portrays the deluded knight as much saner than the world's alleged sanity and far nobler than the world's so-called nobility

WHAT IS THE IDEAL KNIGHT?

Don Quixote repeatedly cites historical and literary examples of brave knights who serve as his reference and role models—they were all valiant, most often invincible warriors whose list of deeds and adventures were still "sung" and celebrated. Obviously, the aged gentleman can never begin to resemble any of these legendary figures or duplicate their feats. Don Quixote's models, for example, include Rodrigo Díaz de Vivar (known popularly as the "Cid," a historical warrior fictionalized in a famous epic poem), but also the "Knight of the Burning Sword," a giant-killer whom he had first encountered in a novel about chivalry. The crazed, would-be knight-errant looks for inspiration to several other epic heroes from history, myth, and folklore, including Bernardo del Carpio, Amadis of Gaul, Roland, Rinaldo de Montalbán, and Galalón.[5]

Tolkien, on the other hand, presents Gandalf and Aragorn as models of courageous and powerful "knights": both are strong, fearless fighters and formidable swordsmen. In the grand heroic epic tradition, Gandalf rides a horse with a mysterious name, Shadowfax. Yet even these ideal warriors find themselves in need of transformation by way of their quest to destroy Sauron's Ruling Ring, just as do the unlikely heroes whom we shall examine shortly. The wizard, for example, ascends from Gandalf the Grey to become Gandalf the White. He is leader and savior of the Company, but he is also embarked on a mysterious life-journey that is conducted on a higher plane, a preternatural pilgrimage that intersects with the storyline only occasionally. He progresses in his journey by passing repeated tests of courage without ever seeming to falter. In his encounter with the evil Balrog, Gandalf fights heroically and courageously, much like the fictional characters whom Don Quixote had read about and whom he so much admired. When Gandalf returns from his strange passage beyond space and time, he announces that he has "ascended" to the rank of "White Wizard," creating a clear sense of his progress in courageously battling ever more evil and powerful opponents. He later confronts the Black Captain of the ringwraiths and leads the deadly assault on the Black Gate of Mordor, further proving his unflinching courage in many dangerous conflicts with armies of evil creatures.

Once Strider emerges as Aragorn, the rightfully returning king of Gondor, he leaps into the breach of battle, as would a powerful and fearless knight. Like Gandalf, he passes a series of stringent "tests" without wavering. Aragorn epitomizes the decisiveness and daring that befits an ideal heroic warrior and a king. He travels to Minas Tirith, for example, via a dark and dangerous route, the Paths of the Dead. As Aragorn forges ahead, Gimli asks of him, "Does he feel no fear?" (*LOTR*, 769).[6] In addition, Aragorn confronts Sauron through the palantír, claiming that he has mastered the power of the stone. Ironically, this encounter filled Sauron with doubt and fear, since none other had ever been able to use the palantír with such command. Aragorn is thus the perfect example of an invincible warrior, a superlative hero who has passed all tests for bravery and who has earned the respect of all and the right to lead others into battle.

Both of these heroic figures make potent and admirable leaders, the most qualified and likely to fight the ultimate battle with ultimate evil, that is, they fight the orcs and their "war machines" with swords and raw courage. Both clearly parallel the ideal knights of ancient lore, and in most traditions they would be the central characters and heroes of the story, the ones chosen by destiny or providence to defeat evil and thus save their realm from destruction. As Aragorn and Gandalf both increase in valor and fortitude, readers might well expect a dramatic doomsday confrontation with the maleficent forces. Yet, surprisingly, providence has entrusted Frodo, a lowly inhabitant of Hobbiton who is terribly unsure of himself, with the most vital role in the saving of Middle-earth; this assignment falls to a highly unlikely "knight-hero," an obscure and unimpressive hobbit.

UNLIKELY KNIGHTS AND IMPROBABLE HEROES

The most salient point of similarity between these two masterworks involves the central characters, Don Quixote and Frodo, and their sidekicks, Sancho Panza and Sam Gamgee. In these models of Tolkien and Cervantes we see the clearest inversion of social, narrative, and heroic paradigms. Don Quixote, for example, is roughly fifty when he begins his mission; Frodo is fifty, middle-aged in hobbit years. The former is a rickety old man driven insane from reading too much fantastic literature. As a result of his excessive indulgence in novels of chivalry that "dry out his brain" (*DQ*, 58), he decides to embark on a mission to save his world through a series of battles and adventures. Tolkien's hero, on the other hand, is a hobbit who has heard stories of monolithic clashes between good and evil but who does not consider himself qualified to undertake any heroic mission, much less to save the whole of Middle-earth.

Don Quixote chooses as his squire a squat peasant named Sancho Panza. Though no more suited to a chivalric mission than his master, the squire remains loyal to his knight all the way through. So does Sam, a gardener lacking the qualities of either knight or squire, accompany Frodo and remain faithful to him until the very end.

Sancho, the peasant and self-proclaimed coward, eventually becomes the governor of an island, and a rather good governor at that, much to the surprise of those who arranged for his promotion as a joke. In similar fashion, Frodo's boon companion Sam heroically distinguishes himself in the battle against Shelob, the giant spider. Though not the ruler of an island, Sam is destined eventually to become mayor of Hobbiton.

Don Quixote and Squire Sancho obviously do not measure up to heroic ideals in any sense. The wobbly old gentleman is perhaps the most unlikely warrior-knight imaginable, yet he is the only true hero of Cervantes's story, the only one even remotely successful in attempting to live out a commitment to chivalric virtues. Frodo and Sam, who are far more limited in social stature, remain nonetheless entrusted with the most crucial of all missions, a quest for which men, elves, wizards, or even dwarves would seem far more qualified. Though they do indeed falter in various ways, they also endure and, in the process, grow in character. Like Don Quixote and Sancho, they become the real heroes of the story, even with their shortcomings, delusions of grandeur, physical limitations, and personal failures.

DOING VERSUS BECOMING

In part 1, Don Quixote conceives his quest as a series of adventures and encounters, practicing and imitating the deeds of famous knights:

> He believed that it was necessary, both for his own honor and for service of the state, that he should become a knight-errant, roaming through the world with his horse and armor in quest of adventures and practicing all that had been performed by the knights-errant of whom he had read. He would follow their life, redressing all manner of wrongs and exposing himself to continual dangers. (*DQ*, 58)

Having characterized this mission as "the oddest fancy that ever entered a madman's brain" (*DQ*, 59), the narrator describes the frail old gentleman's ludicrous attempts to look like a knight: rusty armor, a pasteboard visor, and a broken-down nag for a "steed." His conception of knighthood initially requires a checklist of what he must do and what gear he must wear.

Frodo likewise imagines his calling as consisting in something he must do, but unlike Don Quixote, he feels unable to do it. He believes himself completely incompetent to bear the Ring back to the Cracks of Doom and thus initially resists his calling. The Council of Elrond debates the fate of the Ring, seeking wisdom about how to respond to the threat of Mordor. Frodo, still reluctant to accept his destiny (or perhaps eager to give it up), blurts out to Aragorn, the rightful heir to the Sword that was Broken: "Then [the Ring] belongs to you, and not to me at all!" (*LOTR*, 240). Frodo strongly protests that Aragorn is the ideal Ringbearer, an experienced warrior who should be entrusted with the most dangerous dimension of the quest, the actual destruction of the One Ruling Ring. Yet he gradually begins to understand and accept his calling, eventually overcoming his dread: "I will take the Ring . . . though I do not know the way" (*LOTR*, 264). Fearing that he lacks sufficient strength or fortitude to undertake so immense a mission, Frodo cannot yet comprehend that the very hardships and dangers of the quest will forge a surpassing courage within him.

Early in part 2, Don Quixote further defines his mission as a restoration or revival of the noblest virtues: "I am only striving to convince the world of its errors in not reviving that most fortunate age in which the order of chivalry flourished. . . . Today sloth triumphs over industry, idleness over labor, vice over virtue, arrogance over bravery, and theory over the practice of arms" (*DQ*, 535). This statement greatly surpasses the naive checklist he had formulated when his quest began in part 1. In his evolving conception of chivalric ideals, Don Quixote affirms that knighthood does not depend on an inventory of tasks and equipment, nor even a bold itinerary. Rather, in this new articulation of his mission, he sees that he is engaged in a struggle to turn a cultural tide. He is one man seeking to restore such virtues as bravery and industry in an age where they seem to have been abandoned, perhaps entirely forgotten. He hopes to revitalize the spiritual inertia of his "modern" age with spiritual energy from the past—to replace the lust for quick riches, power, and empire with a zeal for justice, humility, and charity.

The comic quality of the Don's revitalizing of chivalric virtue becomes evident in part 2, chapter 17, where he has a brief encounter with a lion. Finding the beast caged in a cart, the knight demands that the keeper open the small pen door and thus free the lion for combat. Happily, the lion proves to be bored rather than hungry. He yawns, sticks his head out, looks around, turns, and saunters back in. The aging knight stands and faces the lion without fear in a scene that recalls a similar incident wherein the renowned Spanish knight, El Cid, shames his pet lion back into its cage. Proud of his new-won "courage," Don Quixote denominates himself the "Knight of the Lions." In his mind, he has faced off the lion and thereby passed a significant test of courage. Notwithstanding the tongue-in-cheek tone of this incident, Don Quixote triumphantly asks, "Are any enchantments able to prevail against true valor? The enchanters may be able to rob me of good luck, but of courage they cannot" (*DQ*, 645). This statement that synthesizes Don Quixote's philosophy of engagement with evil could also serve as a summary of the central theme of *Lord of the Rings*. The final triumph in Tolkien depends far less on weapons than on the character of the swordbearers and Ring-bearers, that is, not on magical enchantments but on courageous decisions to persevere against a powerful enemy even in the most hopeless of circumstances.

Yet Cervantes is more than a satirist of chivalric delusions. In part 2, chapter 42, Sancho is preparing to govern his island (a prank arranged by a duke and duchess). His master gives him spiritual advice for governing that centers on what he perceives to be the traditional qualities of knights: prudence, humility, nobility of character, and the cultivation of virtue (*DQ*, 824–25). He tells Sancho first to "fear God, for to fear Him is wisdom, and if you are wise, you cannot err" (*DQ*, 824). He also counsels his companion to take pride in his humble origins, for "if you make virtue your rule in life, and if you pride yourself on acting always in accordance with such a precept, you will have no cause to envy princes and lords, for blood is inherited, but virtue is acquired, and virtue in itself is worth more than noble birth" (*DQ*, 825). Sancho does well as a governor, much to the surprise of his wealthy sponsors, who desired only to laugh at a buffoon. Instead, he quickly gains a reputation for "Solomonic wisdom" (*DQ*, 847).

Sam, Frodo's loyal "squire," bears significant resemblance to Sancho. He answers a similar call to daring deeds and in the process surpasses all expectations. Just as Aragorn and even Gandalf undergo tremendous moral enhancement, so also does Sam grow into his own proper role. He engages Shelob in sword-to-spider combat while Frodo lies paralyzed, seemingly dead. Sam does not think about heroic tests of courage; he acts on moral instinct rather than abstract ideals: "Sam did not wonder what was to be done, or whether he was brave, or loyal, or filled with rage. He sprang forward with a yell" (*LOTR*, 711). Small Sam attacks the bloated spider and slashes her "with a dreadful gash" (ibid.). In spite of his obvious weaknesses—his diminutive size, his lack of experience and skill—the humble hobbit gardener becomes a servant hero who plays an indispensable role in Frodo's escaping Shelob's lair and eventually reaching the Cracks of Doom.

Sam and Sancho both lack the seemingly essential credentials for fulfilling the roles to which they have been summoned: social standing, wealth, or fame. In a sense, both are "men of the earth" who till the soil and bring forth fruit. Yet both instinctively reveal attributes of genuine and lasting worth: in Sancho's case, proverbial wisdom and loyalty to his master through all kinds of tribulation and persecution; and in Sam's case, courage and loyalty to his master in the terror of battle and the fearful progress up Mount Doom. The war against Sauron and his forces having finally been won, Aragorn honors the valorous hobbits, setting them on his throne, even though Frodo does not feel in the least heroic. Later, in "The Scouring of the Shire," when the Shirrifs challenge the returning hobbits, the little creatures bravely draw their swords. The timid creatures who first set out on the Quest of Mount Doom have become fearless warriors. Even so, they are not bloodthirsty. In his final confrontation with Saruman, for example, Frodo refuses to allow the evil wizard—who surely deserves death—to be slain by hobbits. Frodo has emerged as something even greater than a warrior, a knight of mercy rather than wrath.

By the end of part 2, Don Quixote has also grown in stature, but more as a tragic than a heroic figure, as the idealistic dreamer has finally been beaten by the cynical world he sought to change. He has lived out his ideals nobly, only to be defeated in a sort of mock combat by the lawyer Sansón Carrasco. Having failed in a previous attempt, this friend of the family is bent on forcing the Knight of the Woeful Countenance to return home. Carrasco thus appears as the "Knight of the White Moon," arrogantly challenging the downcast cavalier to a joust. The defeated knight must return home for the space of a year. Carrasco easily brings Don Quixote to the ground but without mortally wounding him. The aged knight, defeated physically and spiritually, bruised and stunned, describes himself as weak and unfortunate. But though he has failed in the obvious sense, Don Quixote has triumphed in a larger and deeper sense. For he does not regard himself as a mere victim of the world's cruelty but rather as a knight who, despite his divinely commissioned quest, lacked the necessary virtue of prudence: "Nothing that happens here below, whether of good or evil, comes by chance, but by the special disposition of Providence. . . . I did not act with all the prudence necessary, my presumptions have brought me to my shame" (*DQ*, 999). Not long after this scene, Don Quixote again becomes Alonso Quijano the Good, and dies in his bed.

Both novels demonstrate the ways in which adventure and perseverance in hardship may produce courage and define character. In Cervantes's more pessimistic version of events, the unlikely hero makes a commitment to high virtues and noble endeavors, but he is overwhelmed and defeated by a brutal and cynical world. In Tolkien's more optimistic version of these same questions, providence ensures that evil is defeated and that all the pilgrims progress in character and virtue, despite their evident failures.

CRITICIZING MODERNITY

In 1492, Columbus "discovered" America, but not before Ferdinand and Isabella had unified Christian Spain and driven out the Moors. The Catholic king and queen had finally unified a disparate collection of small Christian kingdoms and established a centralized monarchy able to defeat the Moors and then, in the sixteenth century, to become a worldwide empire. In the first half of the sixteenth century, Charles I ruled not only Spain but also the Holy Roman Empire. In this larger role, he felt obliged to lead Spain into war against two peoples whom he considered as threats to Christendom: Protestants in northern Europe and Muslims advancing in the east. His son, Philip II, continued the father's program of conquest through the last half of the century, attempting to stabilize this unwieldy worldwide domain. Driven by a missionary zeal for Christian converts, but also by a lust for conquest and greed for gold, the Spaniards completely subjugated two advanced native American civilizations as they extended their power over most of two western continents. The riches from America aided the hiring of mercenaries and the amassing of military firepower and armor. Despite the evident successes of this enterprise, there were also colossal and lamentable failures, most notably the English defeat of the "Invincible Armada" in 1588, an imperial effort for which, after the victorious Battle of Lepanto, Cervantes was forced to become a roving commissary.

Spain's global advances never really benefited the common people, who remained in abject poverty in the city or in the country. Don Quixote's travels take place mostly in rural areas, with only one visit to the great port city of Barcelona. Most of the novel occurs in rural Spain where the poverty is plainly visible, but where also the wealth of the few is patently obvious.[7] Thus do the knight and his companion face the cruelty of a bored and wealthy aristocracy obsessed with elaborate entertainments to relieve its own ennui. The Duke and Duchess, having invited the knight and his squire to their castle, hire actors and create "special effects" in order to ridicule the pair. One actor plays the Devil and another acts the role of Merlin the Magician. Don Quixote and Sancho are thus made the butt of many sadistic and physically painful jokes. That Cervantes had contempt for these complacent aristocrats goes virtually without saying.

Tolkien also wrote in the face of evils he abhorred. Michael White observes that the "*The Hobbit* arrived in a troubled world. . . . That spring, [1937] Guernica in Spain had been obliterated by the Fascists, and in September, the Japanese leveled Shanghai."[8] *Lord of the Rings* appeared eighteen years later, in 1954, amidst the aftermath of World War II and the dawn of the atomic age. The Allies had defeated fascism but were unable to contain either the spread of totalitarianism in Russia and China or the threat of atomic annihilation nearer at hand. Tolkien stresses the value of a simple life that envisions humanity in harmony with nature, but he also calls for an aggressive, organized resistance to encroaching evil. He underscores the need for company and cooperation, each member making a unique contribution to the larger providential pattern of history. Frodo's pressure and stress are "real," but Don Quixote's are mainly imagined, though he also suffers from the cruelty of others and his own recklessness. Whereas Frodo returns to the Shire victorious but too weary to enjoy the fruits of victory, Don Quixote is utterly defeated, conquered both spiritually and physically. Yet though he dies in defeat, his vision lives on through Sancho Panza. By contrast, Frodo does not die but rather sails with Gandalf to the Grey Havens that lie over the western seas, there to find the reward of his pilgrimage far beyond the Shire and Middle-earth.

Despite the differences in their narrative techniques, tone, and style, Tolkien and Cervantes share a common desire to expose the perils and horrors of advancing modernity. Each author proposes a return to traditional values and cardinal virtues, such as courage, and each highlights the importance of those who are clearly unqualified yet courageous enough to resist the evils at hand. Both authors set forth such virtues as prudence, unwillingness to compromise with evil, and the common sense of conventional wisdom. Both novels also elevate an understanding of "knighthood" that may involve literal weapons but does not chiefly depend on them. Both writers offer an uncompromising call to stand firm in the face of danger—in Cervantes's words, with "the valor of [a] dauntless heart" (*DQ*, 496).

Michael White observes that Tolkien's trilogy "struck a chord with a new generation of young people who were then just getting into drugs and what was soon to be called the hippie culture."[9] This undulating pattern is common to human history. The present generation often detects a loss of the virtues that an earlier age had enshrined. Perhaps *Don Quixote* and *Lord of the Rings* have enduring appeal precisely because they make admirable the transcendent virtue and heroism that the modern age has largely lost. Thus there should be no great surprise that Tolkien's work quickly became a global phenomenon, its current popularity enhanced not only by its enduring moral appeal but also by the visual power of Peter Jackson's films. Cervantes's novel is a perennial favorite, boasting more editions, translations, and copies than any other book except the Bible. It has profoundly influenced some of the world's greatest writers and thinkers, including Einstein, Twain, Dickens, Melville, Dostoevsky, Tolstoy, and Kierkegaard. The masterworks of Tolkien and Cervantes will retain their eminence for a single and simple reason: they both discern the ethical and religious poverty often endemic to modernity, offering over against it the rich moral vision embodied by such unlikely heroes as Don Quixote and Sancho Panza, Frodo Baggins and Samwise Gamgee.

NOTES

1. White, *Tolkien*, 220.
2. Carpenter, *J. R. R. Tolkien*, 45, 106.
3. For additional information on their "love story," see Tolkien, *Lord of the Rings*, 1032–38.
4. His "company" is limited to Sancho Panza, who invites comparison with Frodo's companion, Sam. Sancho, however, is never a combatant, but Sam becomes one at a crucial juncture in the story.
5. Cervantes, *Don Quixote*, 58–60. All future quotes from this translation will be found in parentheses as *DQ*.
6. *LOTR* shall designate Tolkien, *Lord of the Rings*.

7. For many of these social and historical perspectives, I am indebted to an essay by Ife, "Historical and Social Context."

8. White, *Tolkien*, 161.

9. Ibid., 224.

BIBLIOGRAPHY

Carpenter, Humphrey. *J. R. R. Tolkien: A Biography.* Boston: Houghton Mifflin, 1987.

Cervantes, Miguel de. *Don Quixote.* Translated by Walter Starkie. New York: New American Library, 1979.

Ife, B. W. "The Historical and Social Context." In *The Cambridge Companion to Cervantes*, edited by Anthony J. Cascardi, 11–31. Cambridge: Cambridge University Press, 2002.

Tolkien, J. R. R. *The Lord of the Rings.* Boston: Houghton Mifflin, 1987.

White, Michael. *Tolkien: A Biography.* New York: New American Library, 2001.

CHAPTER 4

TOLKIEN OR NIETZSCHE; PHILOLOGY AND NIHILISM

Peter M. Candler, Jr.

In memory of Stratford Caldecott

He who wants to partake of *all* good things
must know how to be small at times.
—Nietzsche, *Human, All Too Human*

THE ORIGINS OF AN ALLUSION

There seems to be no evidence that J. R. R. Tolkien ever read Friedrich Nietzsche; in fact, as commentators are often rather pleased to point out (playing upon a kind of myth Tolkien himself played no small part in constructing), it seems that Tolkien read very little from his own century, except for the works of his fellow convivators at the Eagle and Child.[1] It is perhaps no accident that Tolkien's reading seemed to comport with his drinking. One might even argue that there's something basically very religious about beer, and that this explains in part why the works of Tolkien bear a certain theologic-ity born of friendships nurtured in the public-house. Nietzsche, by contrast, was a notorious teetotaler and said that "coffee spreads darkness," an ascetic troglodyte ever in search of pure air, an anti-Christ who once bemoaned "how much beer there is in the German intellect!"[2] It is hard to imagine, however, that the name of the Hermit of

Sils Maria was never invoked during those sessions at the Eagle and Child in St. Giles' Street.

What, if any, manner of direct experience Tolkien had with Nietzsche, it is impossible to say. It is difficult to believe, however, that his influence was not felt in some indirect way. In 1913, just two years after the last of Nietzsche's untranslated works, *Ecce Homo*, made its appearance in English, Charles Sareola wrote, "A searching estimate of Nietzsche in English still remains to be written. And there is only one man that could write it, and that man is Gilbert K. Chesterton."³ Chesterton never wrote such a "searching estimate," but he did write about Nietzsche, largely negatively, if somewhat superficially, already in *Heretics*, published in 1905. Five years later, in 1910, Chesterton dealt with Nietzsche a good deal more seriously by having his fictional protagonists confront a Nietzschean figure with the ironic name of Morrice Wimpey. He offers them hospitality only if they assent to his belief that the entire universe operates according to the *Wille zur Macht*: "Here you can fall back on that naked and awful arbitration which is the only living thing that balances the stars—a still, continuous violence. *Vae Victis*! Down, down, down with the defeated! Victory is the only ultimate fact. Carthage *was* destroyed, the Red Indians are being exterminated: that is the single certainty."⁴ One might be justified in inferring then a kind of Chesterton-mediated Nietzsche as influencing Tolkien, but as it stands this must remain a conjecture, however likely.

Nevertheless, the interest of this essay is not the direct or indirect influence of Friedrich Nietzsche upon the work of Tolkien, much less the question of whether *The Lord of the Rings* can be seen as in any way influenced by Nietzschean themes. Rather am I interested in what must remain a kind of allusive affinity between the two thinkers. After all, they are both, by profession and by their own admission, philologists, and both are in some way or another suspicious of the mechanization of European culture. Nonetheless, both Tolkien and Nietzsche shared a problematic, if not caustic, relationship to modernity as a philosophical-cultural problem. In what sense, then, does their shared profession of philology inform their respective "responses" or "critiques" of modernity? Moreover, in what sense does philology, for each, offer a kind of redemptive alternative understanding that modernity, however conceived, cannot deliver?

The answers to these questions are not at all straightforward. Even so, I contend that for Tolkien, philology (understood broadly as "the love of words") returns one to the inescapably linguistic character of all revelation and truth, pointing to a certain conception of the human being as fundamentally sacramental in its created participation in the life of the Trinity. Thus will I argue that philology, for Tolkien, is a fundamentally positive science, insofar as it discloses the innate fecundity of "natural" human formulations and products—a naturality itself bespeaking a transcendence that cannot be reduced to any material cause. At the same time, I will argue that Tolkien's taxonomy of culture(s) reveals a certain kind of Thomist conception of human making that renders even pagan culture not as Christianity's antagonistic "other," but instead as its surprising friend. For *poiesis* is itself profoundly disclosive of the divine—understood, of course, from the perspective of Catholic Christianity. Tolkien's "response" to modernity is therefore to reenshrine narrative, particularly the "fairy tale," as the medium of Christian persuasion to beauty. That is, it is not apodictically that Tolkien seeks to make a case for Christianity; rather he "argues" for Christianity by making an appeal to the beautiful in the form of the story, more particularly, in the form of his characters. Even in their pre-Christian forms, they anticipate the Christ, who is the consummate form of the beautiful, the good, and the true. After modernity (or at least, within its death-throes) the Christian appeal is made, with a certain element of charm (if not "glamour"), to a *mythos* that is in some way more attractive because more beautiful, and more beautiful because more truthful.

Nietzsche, too, understands modernity as tending towards a kind of nihilism that permits no easy dismissal. For Nietzsche, as for Tolkien, one must appeal to a different conception of the human being in terms of a new narrative, or a different *mythos*—an alternative form of being and beauty. Nietzsche similarly refuses the demonstrative in favor, first, of the aphoristic, and, later, of the poetic. For him philology renders the limits of intelligibility or credibility of a concept. In other words, Nietzsche's critique of Christianity is "philological" at the point where he argues that, if one were to "get at the root" of things, to find out what the "original" meaning or concept is behind all the various deceptive masks, one would then come either to some retrievable idea or, ultimately, to nothing. Philology is thus an essentially *negative* science insofar as it undoes or "deconstructs" the real, disclosing it as fundamental *chaos*. Yet what remains after the dismantling accomplished by philology is, again, the need for the creative reconstruction of *mythos*. The truthfulness of Nietzsche's account is thus proportional to the beauty of his form, which is ultimately that of Zarathustra. Nowhere is the contrast between Nietzsche and Tolkien starker than in the forms of their two chief poetic creations, Zarathustra and Frodo Baggins.

THE SACRAMENTALITY OF SUBCREATION

Our chief concern here must be with what Thomas Aquinas called *recta ratio factibilium*, "right reason about things to be made." In article 57 of the *Prima Secundae* of the *Summa Theologiae*, Thomas famously distinguishes *art* from *prudence*. Art "has the nature of a virtue" but, properly speaking, remains an "operative habit."[5] Art is "right reason about things to be made," but prudence is "right reason about things to be done." Nevertheless art "is called a virtue" because it has a relation to the good. Yet it is not a perfect virtue "because it does not make its possessor to use it well."[6] The correlative distinction between making and doing, or *poiesis* and *praxis*, is as old as Aristotle's *Metaphysics* and *Nicomachean Ethics*: *poiesis* is an activity that extends to an external object; *praxis* is an activity that remains within the agent. Thus art is not a perfect virtue, because, as *poiesis*, its activity passes into an external object and does not, like prudence, concern the good of the artist, but only the good of the thing made. For Aquinas, "art does not presuppose rectitude of the appetite" since prudence concerns *praxis*. Nonetheless, art has to do with the goodness of the thing made—and even the imprudent can produce good art. "The fact that a man is a poisoner," Oscar Wilde rightly remarked, "has nothing to do with his prose."

Aquinas is notoriously evasive when it comes to any explicit account of beauty. Despite being one of the transcendentals, beauty did not become a discrete object of study until the eighteenth century. Nonetheless, there is indeed a peculiarly Thomistic "aesthetics," as evidenced by Umberto Eco and others, though this must be gleaned from his work, since he nowhere treats it in the same way he treats "the good" and "the true."[7] Even so, although Tolkien is not straightforwardly "Thomist," he is quite clearly, like Flannery O'Connor, at least "a Thomist thrice-removed."[8] This is evident in the way in which he understands the human activity of *poiesis* to be explicitly bound up with creation, particularly in the sense that all human making reflects the gratuity of creation itself, forming not a discrete set of activities of an agency having a purely human propriety, but rather participating in the divine creation itself.

In question 44 of the *Prima Pars* of the *Summa Theologiae*, Thomas Aquinas says,

> some things . . . are both agent and patient at the same time: these are imperfect agents, and to these it belongs to intend, even while acting, the acquisition of something. But it does not belong to the First Agent, Who is agent only, to act for the acquisition of some end; He intends only to communicate His perfection, which is His goodness; while every creature intends to acquire its own perfection, which is the likeness of the divine perfection and goodness.[9]

The centerpiece of Thomas's account of human making is the divine gratuity, in which human beings analogically participate in any act of making. The act of creation belongs to God alone, and bodies cannot, strictly speaking, "create," because their making always acts upon already-existing matter, to which they give "accidental" form.[10] Hence to create is "not proper to any one Person, but is common to the whole Trinity."[11] Human beings cannot create, but they can compose.[12] Thomas alludes here to the notion of *concreation*—although his discussion seems to tend specifically to nature, one can speak of the human agent as "concreating" with God in any human making. Any act of human *poiesis* is therefore a participation in the creative agency of God—an act that is nevertheless "creation" by analogy, insofar as human beings are, analogically speaking, "self-subsistent beings." Denys Turner makes this crucial point clear:

> Thomas . . . argues that anything at all in the sensible world is a sign of something sacred, and so in a general sense is a "sacrament" even if, other than in the cases of the seven sacraments of the Christian dispensation, they lack the character of a sacrament in the strict sense, for only those seven are "causes" of our sanctification. . . . The connection of thoughts between creation's power to disclose God and its possessing in a general sense the form of the sacramental is in Thomas incontestable.[13]

Thus in an analogous sense, all art, as *signum*, "re-presents," rendering its object "really present" under the form of paint, or verse, or other media. As created things, these objects are intelligible and beautiful in so far as they are "laid up," offered as oblations to God. Hence the claim of Aquinas that "all things desire God as their end, when they desire some good thing, whether this be intellectual or sensible or natural, i.e., without knowledge; because nothing is good and desirable except forasmuch as it participates in the likeness to God."[14]

Yet these "offerings" are not our own, but are received as gifts. Not simply gifts *for us*, but gifts to themselves and to the rest of creation. In other words, the things of this world exist not simply for our use but have a kind of subsistence in themselves that does not require any kind of human legitimation of their existence. As Tolkien suggests, the created order is utterly gratuitous, in a way that grants to the objects of the world their proper dignity and freedom as unique singulars in their own right:

> As for "other things" their value resides in themselves: they ARE, they would exist even if we did not. But since we do exist one of their functions is to be contemplated by us. If we go up the scale of being to "other living things," such as, say, some small plant, it presents shape and organization: a "pattern" recognizable (with vari-

ation) in its kin and offspring; and that is deeply interesting, because these things are "other" and we did not make them, and they
seem to proceed from a fountain of invention incalculably richer
than our own.[15]

The implication of all this is that without the doctrine of the creation,
understood as the generous and gratuitous bringing into being of
all that is and all that appears, we lose the world. This is not a question of the created order over and against God, as it is in Nietzsche
(get rid of God, recover man), but rather a matter of the sacramental
order of creation, without which the things of this world themselves
lose their inherent dignity as irreducible singulars. When Aquinas
says that "all things desire God," he means not just rational creatures,
but quite literally *all things*. Tolkien might add that this includes our
own subcreations: for is not God "the Lord, of angels, and of men—
and of elves"?[16] What makes human beings unique in the order of
creatures is that they "collaborate with God in making."[17] This is not
to arrogate to the human creature some idolatrous status but rather
to fulfill the evangelical exhortation to: "Let your works shine before
men, that they may see your good deeds and glorify your Father Who
is in heaven."[18] Or, to cite St. Augustine's celebrated dictum: "become
what you are."[19]

How does this account of human sign-making help us to understand Tolkien's own treatment of a similar theme, that of storytelling,
specifically the "fairy story"? In the first instance, Tolkien says that
"the mind that thought of *light*, *heavy*, *grey*, *yellow*, *still*, *swift*, also
conceived of magic that would make heavy things light and able to
fly, turn grey into gold, and the still rock into swift water."[20] Such ad-
jectives ("there is no spell or incantation in Faërie more potent") are
irreducibly human artifacts, and like all human products, they go out
from their makers and assume a rich and extended sense that surpasses even the intentions of the inventor.[21] As such they are *remembered* concepts whose life is sustained by their constant use, however
various. This use remains bound to certain "rules," and it is of the
nature of Faërie to suspend those rules. Yet in that suspension they
image the concreative character of human making.

The human subcreative power is to mix and transpose these predicates to different objects: "we can take green from grass, blue from heaven, and red from blood" and transfer those descriptors to things with which they are not "naturally" associated, such as putting "a deadly green on a man's face" and thereby producing a "horror." Yet the ability to wield such an "enchanter's power" does not mean that it will always be well exercised. One can exercise the art of enchantment for evil no less than for good ends. Regardless, when one exercises this ability, one nonetheless partakes of something distinctly human—one makes signs. As Tolkien says, "in such 'fantasy,' as it is called, new form is made; Faërie begins; Man becomes a subcreator."[22] The imagination of such poetic forms is that "aspect of 'mythology'" proper to fallen humanity that Tolkien names "subcreation," as opposed to "either representation or symbolic interpretation of the beauties and terrors of the world."[23]

THE GLAMOUR OF *POESIS*

In "Beowulf: The Monsters and the Critics," Tolkien argues that most contemporary critics of the poem, besotted by its ostensible "historical" value as a source of information for the Anglo-Saxon age, have missed the fact that, as he writes, "the illusion of historical truth" in *Beowulf* is "largely a product of Art."[24] It seems that Tolkien here means "illusion" not in the modern, pejorative sense that is also given to "myth," but rather in its etymological origin from *in-ludere*, to be "in-play."[25] This "illusion of historical truth" in *Beowulf* is not simply a matter of peeling back the disguising husk in order to espy the historical kernel, but is in fact one of those "peculiar poetic virtues" of the poem itself. A crude historicism actually robs history of its own inherently illusory quality, rendering to it a *less* trustworthy status as history. The "illusion of historical truth" is therefore dangerous because it may disclose a truth that is *more than* historical, and even history, for Tolkien, "often resembles 'Myth,' because they are both ultimately of the same stuff."[26]

Tolkien remained suspicious of historical-critical methods in philological literary criticism that assume that there is some "essence" to which one could reduce a poem. The danger in such methods is that they treat a poetic creation as an instrument, a thing that can be mined or reduced to *some other thing*, or a story that can be turned into mere use. Such tactics are ultimately a rejection of the work of art as an irreducible event in itself, which is its own end. In a profound sense, such a version of philology takes the "fun" out of literature because it removes from it the fundamental element of play. Strictly speaking, play is like contemplation in serving no purpose external to itself. Thus Tolkien concludes, "the lovers of poetry can safely study the art, but the seekers after history must beware lest *the glamour of Poesis* overcome them."[27]

In "On Fairy-Stories" Tolkien also invokes the notion of "the glamour of Elfland," which has been transformed into "mere finesse" in so much of the "flower-and-butterfly" daintiness of elves in Disneyesque postrationalist literature. What is it about Elfland that is so "glamourous"? Tom Shippey writes, "the quality [Tolkien] evidently valued more than anything in literature was that shimmer of suggestion which never quite becomes clear sight but always hints at something deeper further on." Faërie, for Tolkien, is characterized as a kind of "primal desire": "the realisation, independent of the conceiving mind, of imagined wonder,"[28] "the desire of men to hold communion with other living things."[29] Surely reflecting on his own childhood, Tolkien declares that the successful fairy story is one that awakens such desire.[30] It is precisely this sense of "glamour," as alluring playfulness or merriment, that characterizes Faërie as the site in which the possibility of "communion with other living things" becomes reality. Such an eschatological hope in the restoration of creation is "escapist" only in the sense of an escape from imprisonment. It is escape only if one means something akin to "liberation"—a deliverance not *from* but *into* reality.

In contrast to Coleridge's dictum that literary art requires a "willing suspension of disbelief," Faërie makes possible a kind of "literary" or "secondary belief." This suggests that the world of

Faërie is not "false" but "true," in the sense that it operates according to rules of play that, when violated, return one to the "Primary World." Only then can Faërie be entertained in suspended disbelief, because there emerges a boundary across which one looks into the "Secondary World"—one is no longer "within" the enchanted Secondary World. This is analogous to what Johan Huizinga has to say about play:

> The player who trespasses against the rules or ignores them is a "spoil-sport." The spoil-sport is not the same as the false player, the cheat; for the latter pretends to be playing the game and, on the face of it, still acknowledges the magic circle. It is curious to note how much more lenient society is to the cheat than to the spoil-sport. This is because the spoil-sport shatters the play-world itself.[31]

Such are the unhappy results when one "pretends" at Faërie: disbelief destroys the world of Faërie itself, causing it to fail.[32]

It follows that the world of fairy stories is true, but not simply in a "metaphorical" sense. The denigration of the "secondary" linguistic world of Faërie is analogous to a modern depreciation of metaphor as mere ornamentation. As Janet Soskice has shown, what in the wake of such historicism has come to be called "metaphorical truth" is not simply a chimera or mere fancy. For example, she writes, "We may warn someone, 'Watch out! That's a live wire,' but even if we think wires are not literally 'live' we do not add 'but of course that is only metaphorically true.'"[33] The same principle seems to apply to fairy stories. They cannot be told with such a caveat without violating the rules of Faërie from the outset. In other words, it adds nothing to say of elves that they are true *in a sense*, any more than it does to say of this world that it exists *in a sense*. For both claims are true, but not because they simply correspond to a reality "out there." Rather is the existence of Faërie analogical in precisely the same sense as the existence of the "primary world." Being itself, as David Burrell and others have shown, is not univocal but analogical.[34]

Because of the analogical structure of creation itself, the things of this world are "consonant" with each other. The metaphor is apt, since Tolkien confessed to W. H. Auden that he intended *Lord of the Rings* not to "fit with formalized Christian theology" but rather to render it "consonant with Christian thought and belief."[35] It is worth remembering here, from *The Silmarillion*, the crucial image of creation as originating in music. This sense of "consonance" explains why the pagan world of *Beowulf* is not Christianity's "other." For Tolkien, the author of *Beowulf* is groping after the truth that in itself can never be possessed. The noble but frustrated human longing characteristic of pagan antiquity is the occasion, if not quite for pity, then at least for mourning. Because the creation—which includes all human subcreations and all works of nature—is created by God and sustained by its participation in God, the creation is therefore imbued with a graced musicality that, for all its cacophonous disharmony, is capable of intimations of a transcendent harmonic likeness. As Tolkien writes, "It is this deeper likeness which makes things, that are either the inevitabilities of human poetry or the accidental congruences of all tales, ring alike."[36] So *Beowulf* is truly enchanting, in its fantastical elements, because it calls forth a likeness, a kind of recognition in the reader of something that cannot easily be thematized, but that nevertheless concerns the *telos* of all human lives. As Tolkien writes in a letter to Deborah Webster, "far greater things may colour the mind in dealing with the lesser things of a fairy-story."[37]

For Tolkien, philology is an essentially "reconstructive" science that deals with the re-covery or dis-covery of what Shippey calls "asterisk-reality," a world now lost to us but in a sense available through philological "re-creation": "this activity of re-creation— creation from philology—lies at the heart of Tolkien's 'invention' (though maybe not of his 'inspiration'); it was an activity which he kept up throughout his life."[38] Hence his lament over the demotion of this "noblest of sciences" from its historical preeminence:

Philology has been dethroned from the high place it once had in this court of inquiry. Max Müller's view of mythology as a "disease of language" can be abandoned without regret. Mythology is not a disease at all, though it may like all human things become diseased.

You might as well say that thinking is a disease of the mind. It would be more near the truth to say that languages, especially modern European languages, are a disease of mythology. But Language cannot, all the same, be dismissed. The incarnate mind, the tongue, and the tale are in our world coeval.[39]

In a famous letter to his American publisher, Tolkien wrote of his own compositions that "a name comes first and the story follows."[40] Is this not precisely the logic of creation? Before all, God creates the world in Genesis by giving it a name. By divine *fiat* God's creating is the same as his naming. In naming "light," God calls it into being. So do the plants and animals truly come into being as Adam names them. (This pattern is impressively reflected in Tolkien's own *enarratio* of Genesis in *Silmarillion*.) This is equally true of ordinary human existence: we do not choose our own names any more than we choose our own stories. Because we cannot simply "make up" our own accounts of ourselves, we remain creatures who compose but do not create, operating within the limits of what is given to us.

The theologian, as David Hart suggests, must attend to surfaces, which are, after all, "where all things come to pass."[41] Tolkien's philological appeal to fairy stories in a sense partakes of this same attention to surfaces as a counter to the characteristically modern claim that pure "essences" can be known without linguistic mediation—a claim for which Nietzsche too has no small amount of scorn. For Tolkien, there can be no possibility of a Cartesian *mathesis universalis* or of a Leibnizian *characteristica universalis* intelligible to all rational subjects.[42] Truth itself is storied, and thus not reducible to an atomic moment or concept. It follows that for Tolkien truth is ultimately—and not just ultimately, but before everything else—triune. It is not enough simply to say that the world is created *ex nihilo* by an eternal "simplicity," but by a Holy Trinity who in its primordial fecundity is not threatened by any kind of "original" violence, strife, or chaos. For this reason Tolkien's "creation myth" in *Silmarillion* depicts a prior, though learned, harmony among the Ainur.[43] Truth thus resists even any puerile conflation with "being," understood as pure eternal *stasis*, a fixed and timeless thing. Rather is truth (because identical with the "being" of God) an eternal self-offering, self-receiving charity that renders it immune to colonization or conquest by any single notion of truth as power or violence.

HOW TO PHILOLOGIZE WITH A HAMMER

It is noteworthy that Friedrich Nietzsche was not a professional philosopher. He never held a position in philosophy; in fact, in 1871 he made an unsuccessful bid to take up the chair of philosophy at the University of Basel vacated by Gustav Teichmüller late in the previous year.[44] After 1879, when Nietzsche officially resigned his professorship of classical philology in Basel, he never again held an academic position, but he began a decade of extraordinary literary production.[45] Though Nietzsche's activity from 1879 to 1889 was not conducted in the rôle of an academic philologist, his late work illustrates how his own understanding of philology is both broader and narrower than the classical conception of the discipline.

During his own lifetime, Nietzsche's relationship to the institutional philological establishment became somewhat acerbic, because Nietzsche, like some others before him,[46] came to question the very foundations of philological science. He argued that philology is a modern product whose possibility is ultimately grounded in nothing but itself. In this protest he was railing against the form of academic philology that sought to "reconstruct" an illusory antiquity that it could then claim to have "discovered."[47] It is not difficult to understand how Nietzsche could see that behind such a practice lay a philological will to power.

Yet Nietzsche's argument to this point is itself philological, in the sense that his exposure of the illusory pretensions to authenticity among contemporary philologists was itself philological. Philology, in other words, disclosed philology's own hidden presuppositions. In this sense, the discipline is much broader for Nietzsche than technical etymological genealogy or linguistic reconstruction; it is something more like *Kulturkritik*, "the apprehension of a cultural error" or "a mode of cultural mystification."[48] In that sense, Nietzsche's later work, as James Porter argues, is in keeping with this conception of philology, and his critique of Christianity is the preeminent example of the genealogical unveiling (what later Nietzscheans would rightly label "de-construction") of a "corruption." Consider, for example, the following account from *Daybreak*, written in 1881:

> *The philology of Christianity.*—How little Christianity educates the sense of honesty and justice can be gauged fairly well from the character of its scholars' writings: they present their conjectures as boldly as if they were dogmas and are rarely in any honest perplexity over the interpretation of a passage in the Bible. Again and again they say "I am right, for it is written—" and then follows an interpretation of such impudent arbitrariness that a philologist who hears it is caught between rage and laughter and asks himself: is it possible? Is this honourable? Is it even decent?—How much dishonesty in this matter is still practised in Protestant pulpits, how grossly the preacher exploits the advantage that no one is going to interrupt him here, how the Bible is pummeled and punched and the art of reading badly is in all due form imparted to the people: only he who never goes to church or never goes anywhere else will underestimate that.[49]

For Nietzsche, the philological axe, having been laid to the root of the tree of Christianity, fells it by making belief itself unbelievable. To put it another way, philology exposes Christianity as a "fairy tale." *Contra* Tolkien, "fairy-tales" represent, for Nietzsche, the world of childish illusion, and philology can expose Christianity for what it really is—make-believe:

> It may be hoped man will raise himself so high that the things previously highest to him, e.g., the belief in God he has held up to now, appear childlike, childish, and touching: indeed, that he will *do again* what he did with all the myths—turn them into children's stories and fairy-tales.[50]

For Nietzsche, "a good philologist (and indeed any philologically trained scholar) is repulsed by false textual interpretations (e.g., those made by the Protestant preachers in the pulpits—which is why the learned professions no longer go to church."[51] At the same time, Nietzsche eloquently acclaims philology as "that venerable art which demands of its votaries one thing above all: to go aside, to take time, to become still, to become slow—it is a goldsmith's art and connoisseurship of the *word* which has nothing but delicate, cautious work to do and achieves nothing if it does not achieve it *lento.*"[52] A noble asceticism attends Nietzsche's practice of philology, which for him is very nearly a kind of spiritual discipline. However, such "delicate, cautious work" hardly characterizes one who intends to "philosophize with a hammer." It is above all to the smashing of idols that the hammer is put,[53] and no one is a better practitioner of "the hardness of the hammer, the *joy even in destroying*"[54] than the prophet of the *Übermensch* and the eternal recurrence: Zarathustra.

In Nietzsche's case, all philological reconstructions are expressions of will to power, and one must begin by destroying these false idols. The central imperative of this call to arms is to destroy Christianity in order to erect hyperborean self-overcoming in its place. This is the fundamental logic of Zarathustra: *destroy in order to create*. At the same time, as Stanley Rosen has shown, Nietzsche presents his reader with a noble lie in his exhortation to a creativity that can exist only in an order in which there can be nothing new, but only "the illusory or phenomenal manifestation of the actual or noumenal fluctuations of chaos (i.e., intrinsically random motions of points of force)."[55] In other words, Nietzsche's is a world in which "there is no creation at all."[56]

In 1888, Nietzsche described *Zarathustra* to Karl Knortz as "the profoundest work in the German tongue, and the most perfect in its language."[57] Whether he was right about this rather delirious claim, the figure of Zarathustra is his stratospheric answer to the "life-denying" form of life promoted by Christianity. Zarathustra is the will to power incarnate, a prophet of the eternal recurrence of the same, and the figure in whom Nietzsche's philosophy as a whole finds its fullest expression.

It is interesting to note that Zarathustra is also a response to the nihilism of modernity, insofar as out of the ruins of the modern project must emerge a positive, "Yes-saying" figure, the embodiment of the Dionysian spirit who will offer a way beyond such negations. Yet negation is central to the mission of Zarathustra. As Nietzsche writes of Zarathustra in *Ecce Homo*, "The imperative, 'become hard!', the most fundamental certainty *that all creators are hard*, is the distinctive mark of a Dionysian nature."[58] It is also curious that Nietzsche would choose the name of Zarathustra for his greatest poetic creation, since Zoroaster was the founder of a pre-Christian dualistic religion that sprang up in Persia in the seventh and sixth centuries BC. The Zoroastrian universe is a virtually proto-gnostic world of inherent strife between a god of light and a deity of darkness. In creating the figure of Zarathustra, Nietzsche appeals to Zarathustrian "charm" as a persuasive form. One of the reasons why Christianity is so uncompelling, according to Zarathustra, is that its human "shape" is so unpersuasive: "They would have to sing better songs to make me believe in their redeemer: his disciples would have to look more redeemed!"[59]

Herein lies the alleged truthfulness of Zarathustra: he is the anti-Christ in the precise sense that he is the unequivocal aesthetic anti-form of Christ. Whereas Christ, according to Nietzsche, offers the gift of eternal life, Zarathustra offers the gift of eternal recurrence. The Zarathustrian gospel is that of creative will that first destroys in order to create. Nietzsche is quite conscious that he is writing a new gospel that lays claim to the true story of being, now understood as chaos. It is no accident that Nietzsche's sworn enemy is Christianity; for whatever the quality of his understanding of Christianity, he recognizes that his own *mythos* was entirely "other" to the Christian story. In so doing, he at least registers the sense in which Christianity does indeed represent a *skandalon* to every pagan account of being as strife and of human virtue as heroism. In this light, therefore, Nietzsche rightly establishes the notion of the eternal recurrence as *the* only worthy alternative to the Christian *kerygma*.[60]

The *locus classicus* of the expression of eternal recurrence is found in *Thus Spoke Zarathustra* 3, "Of the Vision and the Riddle," in which Zarathustra speaks, oddly enough, to a dwarf:

> "Behold this moment!" I went on. "From this gateway Moment a long, eternal lane runs *back*: an eternity lies behind us.
> "Must not all things that *can* run have already run along this lane? Must not all things that *can* happen *have* already happened, been done, run past?
> "And if all things have been here before: what do you think of this moment, dwarf? Must not this gateway, too, have been here—before?"[61]

For Nietzsche as for Tolkien, the "road goes ever on and on," but for Nietzsche it is the road of identical repetition of the same, forever. One can see how this teaching of Zarathustra is related to his call for the poetic creation. Nietzsche declares in *The Twilight of the Idols*, "I fear we are not getting rid of God because we still believe in grammar."[62] Nietzsche is not worried that there remains a discernible order or pattern in languages that bespeaks some kind of intelligence at work in the human species—as a kind of implicit proof of God's existence or philological natural theology.[63] Rather is he rendering negatively what is rendered positively in Tolkien's account: the irreducibly linguistic *shape* of truth, the mythological *form* of being.

Nietzsche attempts, paradoxically, to articulate the "goal" of human life so as to repeat identically the Dionysian in the form of Zarathustra. As such, the form of Zarathustra is entirely univocal—it can be infinitely repeated only in the same way, without real difference:

> "I shall return, with this sun, with this earth, with this eagle, this serpent—*not* to a new life or a better life or a similar life:
> "I shall return eternally to this identical and self-same life, in the greatest things and in the smallest, to teach once more the eternal recurrence of all things."[64]

To become like Zarathustra is to reproduce a single way of being at every instant: destroy, create. The form of Zarathustra, unlike the form of Christ, is impatient of variation; one can only be like *this*; the form of Dionysus can only eternally recur—identically, always.

In the figure of Zarathustra, Nietzsche offers an alternative poetic form of life to the form of the Christ of Christianity (which Nietzsche understood as an invention of St. Paul). The crucial point here is that Nietzsche's confrontation with Christianity is conducted entirely on aesthetic grounds, and that his critique of it operates at the level of "taste." For that reason, he says, "the critic of Christianity cannot be spared the task of making Christianity *contemptible*."[65] As Hart writes, Nietzsche "understood that Christian truth depends first upon a story, and so to meet his critique of Christianity tellingly, one must engage it on the field of rhetoric, persuasion, and aesthetic evaluation first, and not that of 'historical science' or the discourses of 'disinterested' reason."[66] It is interesting to note that Nietzsche's mythopoetic invention is, like Tolkien's, premised upon the centrality of *mythos* for the *polis*, and both figures are concerned about the sufficiency and availability of the mythological apparatus in their respective cultures. One the one hand, Tolkien ventured to bequeath to England a mythological treasury it lacked; on the other, Nietzsche saw the reinstauration of a similarly German *mythos* as essential to the renewal of the "German spirit." Both therefore recognized the inseparability of politics from myth, but for different reasons and with very different outcomes.

A NEW MYTH FOR ENGLAND?

In *The Birth of Tragedy*, Nietzsche had written of the need for the purification of the German spirit, through the return to its mythology of itself:

> We think so highly of the pure and vigorous core of the German character that we dare to expect of it above all others this elimination of the forcibly implanted foreign elements, and consider it

possible that the German spirit will return to itself. . . . But let him never believe that he could fight . . . without the gods of his house, or his mythical home, without "bringing back" all German things! And if the German should hesitantly look around for a leader who might bring him back again into his long lost home whose ways and paths he scarcely knows anymore, let him merely listen to the ecstatically luring call of the Dionysian bird that hovers above him and wants to point the way for him.[67]

In the same passage, he speaks of the "solemnly exuberant procession of Dionysian revelers . . . to whom we are indebted to German music—and to whom we shall be indebted for *the rebirth of German myth*.[68] Whatever Nietzsche's intentions, it is clear that *Also sprach Zarathustra* did in fact become "a new myth for Germany"—at least a "Germany" mythologically ill-conceived—when, in 1935, "a handsomely bound copy of *Thus Spake Zarathustra* . . . had been solemnly placed, alongside *Mein Kampf* and Alfred Rosenberg's *Myth of the Twentieth Century*, in the vault of the Tannenberg Memorial (commemorating the Germans' decisive victory over the Russians in the autumn of 1914) as one of the three ideological pillars of Germany's *Third Reich*."[69]

It is difficult to imagine Tolkien's "new myth for England" inspiring anything like an empire (much less a *Reich*), since *Lord of the Rings* is animated by a deliberately anti-imperial spirit that celebrates all of those virtues Nietzsche found so hideous: pity, mercy, charity. At the very least, Tolkien's creation is, albeit unlike most fairy tales, a story of failure. It is an account of the irretrievability of a lost past whose loss threatens every present. Tolkien regarded "Britain" as a conceptual Leviathan whose imperial pretensions would mean the dissolution of everything peculiarly English. As Nicholas Boyle argues, *Lord of the Rings* stands as a critique of British cultural *amnesia*:

> And a critique it must be, for a historical parallel to the success of Frodo's quest could only be, not the triumph of Britain, but its self-immolation—the dissolution of the empire and of everything built

on the act over four centuries old by which England ceased to be Catholic and became Britain, a willed rejection of all the features of modernity that made mid-twentieth-century British society possible.[70]

Modern Britain, argues Boyle, is "defined by what it has forgotten"—an example of the displacement of analogical *anamnesis* as the central constitutive activity of the *polis*.

It is entirely noteworthy in this context that the story of *Lord of the Rings* begins and ends in the same place: the Shire.[71] The story, like *The Hobbit*, is an account of a journey and a return, an *exitus* and a *reditus*, but in a very important way, *Lord of the Rings* narrates, very differently than does *The Hobbit*, the nature of the return and the place to which one returns. The Shire of "The Long-Expected Party" is not at all the same as the scoured Shire to which the hobbits come back. Now bereft of the Party Tree, neither the Shire nor Frodo is the same as when the Fellowship first departed. The Party Tree proves to be the central token of Hobbiton's memory. One might wonder here to what extent Tolkien signals the loss of genuine festivity as the dangerous consummation of a modernity that threatens our future: "*The Lord of the Rings* is not just the story of hobbits venturing out to discover the greater world to which the Shire belongs. It is also the story of the greater world breaking in on The Shire, potentially with annihilating consequences."[72] The hobbits return to the Shire to find it changed forever, irreparably damaged and effaced and threatened with the loss of its own memory—not as nostalgia, but as *anamnesis*, that (analogous) activity that renders all human activity significant because is the possibility of the past returning to us again and again, ever new: "The Shire, like Middle Earth in its state of decline, and indeed like modern England, is defined by what it has forgotten, and the hobbits' great expedition into the world to which the Shire belongs is a reawakening that will redefine the home from which they started."[73]

It is impossible to know whether or not Tolkien had Nietzsche in mind when constructing Middle-earth, but it is clear that Tolkien's world is every bit as anti-Zarathustrian as Nietzsche's is anti-Christian. For in Tolkien's work there is a particularly Christian vision that illuminates an entirely pagan world, though one not bereft of an intimation of something *more than pagan*. Tolkien, curiously, draws attention to the appeal of Christian imagination by subcreating a world in which there is no mention of Christ whatsoever, much less any presence of overt religiosity. It is, oddly enough, by depicting paganism, so to speak, *sub specie aeternitatis*, that he is able to appeal to the "glamour" of Christ. In other words, Christianity is here reimagined, not "under the form of paint," but "under the form of hobbits," and it is to the aesthetic "shape" of such creatures that we must now turn.

THE VIRTUES OF HOBBITON

In contrast to the univocal identity that eternal recurrence is condemned to repeat, Tolkien's Middle-earth survives the terrorism of Mordor because of the efforts of varied and sundry forms: men, elves, ents, dwarves, wizards, and hobbits. No single form of life is adequate as a representation of virtue—the moral shape of Middle-earth is not simply identical with that of the hobbits but remains a function of a particular Fellowship. The form of Christ is not identical with any single human life but is productive of an endless variety of lives whose different shapes constitute the "communion of saints" (and this is perhaps at least an indication of why the lives of the saints are so essential to Christian self-understanding). So in a sense there is a valid opposition: Zarathustra *or* the lives of the saints. They are both poetic forms, in the imitation of which consists (or does not) our good as human beings. Zarathustra can of course be disputed on the philosophical coherence of his doctrines, but this is not why Nietzsche presents him as he does. What I have been calling his "form" is the irreducible quality or shape of his life as an object of aesthetic delight and persuasion. On those grounds he cannot simply be rejected but must, as it were, be "out-narrated."

Similarly, the lives of the folk of Middle-earth are not "allegorical" in the sense Tolkien always derided, as if the men simply *stood for* "courage" or the wizards for "wisdom" or some such univocal representational scheme. There are indeed virtues peculiar to each, and even some virtues that may be higher than others, but the characters are not hypostases of such virtues. At the same time, there is something peculiar to hobbits that makes them particularly well suited to the mission to destroy the Ring, and there is ample reason to suspect it lies in their playfulness, in the fact that, as John Milbank points out, they "are both brave and cunning *because* they prize naïve festivity above the dwarfish interest in accumulation and preservation."[74] In some ways, what makes the hobbits, for Tolkien, worthy of imitation (and also at times prone to deception) is their ludic virtuosity, their dexterity in play.

This is why the ending of *The Return of the King* is so remarkable: Sam returns home with a self-deflating ironic announcement: "I'm back." But of course a hot meal is already prepared and waiting for him. The Party Tree has been replanted and is already showing promising growth, and yet the Shire is not at all the same. He *is* back because he recognizes that the new situation does not call for nostalgic recovery but for *anamnesic* re-creation, in which the Shire is "raised" again—not just as it was, but differently. In fact, it is not yet what it will be. And for Sam, the meal goes ever on before him, patient of his delight.

Curiously, Nietzsche's critique of Christianity has made possible such a reimagination of its own story, and Tolkien's may be one such instance of this strange back-formation. Indeed, he has "bequeathed Christian thought a most beautiful gift, a needed anamnesis of itself—of its strangeness."[75] The poetic form of Zarathustra recalls the truly unclassifiable quality of the form of Christ and how his entire "shape"—the indissoluble totality of the whole: his begetting from the Father before all worlds, his birth, infancy, ministry, death, resurrection, and ascension, none of which is isolable as a concept but available only as a story told and retold—confounds the pagan tale of everlasting chaos. Tolkien's own pagan subcreations perform a similar anamnesic recollection of Christianity's peculiarity in the form of hobbits—creatures who do not exactly fit into any preexisting list, not even the entish catalogue of beings (*LOTR*, 453).[76] On the other hand, hobbit festivity is really the only form of virtue that stands the slightest chance of resisting the will of Sauron. Men, even wizards, are prey to the temptations to *use* the Ring, to attempt to reorient it to a utility to which the Ring itself refuses to submit. It is an evil object because it represents the abolition of play, the conscription of all being to usefulness, particularly in the way in which those who try to use the Ring end up being used *by it*. Yet the hobbits, more than anyone else, recognize that it is used at one's peril and, above all, that the Ring is so sinister because it is a thing that *cannot be enjoyed*.

What is the One Ring but an image of Zarathustrian eternal recurrence? Unlike the other rings made by the elves, the One Ring is unadorned with any gemstone. It is a perfect unbroken circle, unaffected by the accidents of heat or external force, impervious even to the will of its bearer. It is, moreover, an image of false eternity—the identical repetition of all things with no beginning and no end. At the same time, as a symbol of evil, the Ring circumscribes a nonspace, a pure privation. The essence of the Ring is its nothingness. This is why, at the end of *Return of the King*, the Ring must be destroyed in the fires of Mount Doom, its source and origin. The Ring must return to its origin—thus effecting a *reditus* to its source that is a parody of the divine cosmological *reditus* of creation in the sense that the source and end of the Ring is consuming fire. But even this fire is mortal and will one day flame out to embers, so that the Ring is, paradoxically, defeated by that which it cannot promise to anyone: death.

As eternal recurrence, the Ring is so diabolical not because it promises immortality but because it cancels mortality itself, and in canceling death it obviates life. The One Ring is the consummate token of nihilistic discourse in that, though it makes death a nothing, it also makes it disappear. The worst thing about the Ring is that it can't even kill, because it has already taken away death itself.[77] As Gandalf says to Frodo of the Great Rings:

"A mortal, Frodo, who keeps one of the Great Rings, does not die, he does not grow or obtain more life, he merely continues, until at last every minute is a weariness. And if he often uses the Ring to make himself invisible, he *fades*: he becomes in the end invisible permanently, and walks in the twilight under the eye of the dark power that rules the Rings. Yes, sooner or later, if he is strong or well-meaning to begin with, but neither strength nor good purpose will last—sooner or later the dark power will devour him." (*LOTR*, 46)

This is preeminently true of the One Ring of Power. Its great danger—which appears to be its great virtue, at least in its utility to Frodo—is that it makes its bearer invisible. Sauron himself is the ultimate example of this invisibility. He can never be seen because evil has entirely evacuated him of substance, reduced him to nothing but an all-seeing eye. If there were ever a metaphor for modern philosophy as Tolkien must have understood it, it is the disembodied, panoptic eye of Sauron.[78] And this is emblematic of a modern disposition, which is not, the desire to see the world *sub specie aeternitatis*, but rather to view it from the aspect of *nowhere*. This is the true bondage of *hubris*: not to see from eternity but to see from no-place, to simply *gaze*, to repeat univocally, the same gesture *ad infinitum*.

The Christian story is otherwise. The world can be seen, heard, tasted only *sub specie aeternitatis* because that is the only aspect from which anything could appear. This is not the same as an Archimedean point of "objectivity," which sees merely appearances as all identical. Rather, to see "from the aspect of eternity" is to see appearances for what they are: surfaces bearing a likeness to one another because they all share in an ontological peacefulness that they do not own or manufacture but receive as gift. They can therefore be like one another but truly different from one another because they are created by the One God, who in His eternal tri-unity, creates the world from nothing. As David Jones says, "the works of man, unless they are of 'now' and of 'this place,' can have no 'for ever.'"[79] In the Christian account, to see the creation *sub specie aeternitatis*, therefore, is not to erect an optic tower of Babel from which the neutral gaze could reduce all appearances to mere flatness (as happens when one, for example, reads a map), but rather to recognize that the aspect of eternity has not retreated from every act of vision to an inaccessible private realm (i.e., the Cartesian mind as the prototype of this pseudo-eternity). In this sense it is the prime act of *hubris* to *refuse* to see in this way, insofar as it amounts to a rejection of the truth that in all our seeing we give as much as we receive, and of the claim that our understanding is never entirely our own property, but partakes of the divine generosity, without which nothing at all could be seen.

In the epilogue to "On Fairy-Stories," Tolkien speaks of "the Christian Story" as the preeminent fairy story, not simply because its ending is a happy one. It is Faërie *properly speaking*, and all other true fairy stories are only so by analogy to this one. It is in the perfect coincidence of the form of the Christian Gospel with "reality" in Tolkien's primary sense that its uniqueness lies. Tolkien is not saying that Christianity is a "fairy story" because it is like "fairy stories"; he is saying that the reason "fairy stories" are persuasive is because they are *like* the Christian story. This is because Faërie is not here, as it is in all other literary subcreations, an "other world." Rather, "this story has entered History and the primary world; the desire and aspiration of sub-creation has been raised to the fulfillment of Creation."[80] In this story "Legend and History have met and fused."[81] It is *true*, moreover, because its form is Christ, who is the form of beauty. For that reason "the Art of it has the supremely convincing tone of primary Art, that is, of Creation."[82] The Gospel is true Faërie—its timbre is not of a happiness conferred by a simple resolution but the joy of a present that is pregnant with a promised future.

What does this say about other stories, including pagan ones? There is no doubt that the figure of Zarathustra is quite simply anti-Christian, both in its creator's explicit intention and in his aesthetic form. Nor is there any doubt that the form of Christ represents a comprehensive "revaluation of all values" of pagan antiquity. As Hart has shown, Nietzsche's opposition, set forth in *The Anti-Christ*—namely, *Dionysus versus the Crucified*—is a true one, perhaps the only one. In Zarathustra, "one gospel meets another."[83]

Zarathustra's gospel is in fact as old as Heraclitus, as Nietzsche himself acknowledges; it cannot but be, if all things eternally recur. The Christian revelation, in stark contrast, marks the truly revolutionary advent of the new in human culture. One must concede that Nietzsche is exactly right on this point: Christianity does inaugurate an account of beauty—as disclosed in the creating, the crucified, and the risen Incarnate Word—that upsets all previous notions of beauty. At the same time, from the side of Christianity, the pagan world can be seen only as the *Beowulf* poet saw it: as also created, and thus as desiring of God. This means that all stories, including pagan ones, are in the end *anathemata*—"things offered up"—because even ours has no final purchase on the truth. To see *sub specie aeternitatis* is to grant to those stories their proper integrity as "subcreations," whether now true or false. As Hart writes, "whereas the story of violence simply excludes the story of peace, the Christian story can encompass, and indeed heal, the city that rejects it: because that city too belongs to the peace of creation, the beauty of the infinite, and only its narrative and its desires blind it to a glory that everywhere pours upon it."[84] Put another way, narratively speaking at least, there is no salvation outside the Church because the Church has no outside.

Slavoj Žižek argues:

> The message of Christianity . . . is that of infinite joy beneath the deceptive surface of guilt and renunciation: "The outer ring of Christianity is a rigid guard of ethical abnegation and professional priests; but inside that inhuman guard you will find the old human life dancing like children, and drinking wine like men; for Christianity is the only frame for pagan freedom."
>
> Is not Tolkien's *Lord of the Rings* the ultimate proof of this paradox? Only a devout Christian could have imagined such a magnificent pagan universe, thereby confirming that *paganism is the ultimate Christian dream*.[85]

Tolkien, in turn, declares that "all tales may come true; and yet, at the last, redeemed, they may be as like and as unlike the forms that we give them as Man, finally redeemed, will be like and unlike the fallen that we know."[86] All tales may yet come true because, as David Jones declares, "There is only one tale to tell." But as Jones also adds, most importantly, "the telling is patient of endless development and ingenuity and can take on a million variant forms."[87] There is only one tale to tell, and it is what Tolkien calls the *eucatastrophe* of the Christian evangel. But because creation partakes of the divine *logos*, it is capable of potentially infinite variations and modulations upon a single theme, at whose heart is the story of ontological peace.

All other stories may be tales of violence (hence they are the true "fairy stories," in Nietzsche's sense), but they may come true—redeemed into a form whose appearance now may be unlike what its author expected or anticipated. Perhaps this is because, as Tolkien adds in a footnote, the "Art" of the Christian story is "in the story itself rather than in the telling; for the Author of the story was not the evangelists."[88] So perhaps Žižek would be more correct in saying that "Christianity is the ultimate dream of paganism," because only Christianity preserves paganism as paganism, because the former can conceive difference as harmonious and nonviolent in a way that pagan imagination cannot.[89]

Truth ever eludes us because it ever draws towards its inexhaustibility. If truth is elusive, this is because it is ever "glamorous" and playful, in the fullest sense of *e-ludere*. The life of the Trinity is endless play, because it is peaceful, self-giving *caritas* that has no "outside." God never ceases from creating the world, and all of our making is but a partaking of that creativity. Sin emerges, therefore, as a refusal of divine generosity, and, as the scriptures attest from Genesis to Luke-Acts, is an attempt to hoard what is from beginning to end sheer gratuity. Thus are the virtues of Hobbiton, lying as they do in the hobbits' aesthetic distaste of such possessiveness, worthy of imitation.

TOLKIEN OR NIETZSCHE?

Proverbial wisdom holds that "all that glitters is not gold." In what could be a summary of Tolkien's aesthetics, however, the refrain throughout *Lord of the Rings* reverses the syntax on this little bit of traditional wisdom. For as Tolkien has it, "All that is gold does not glitter," to which he adds,

> Not all those who wander are lost;
> The old that is strong does not wither,
> Deep roots are not reached by the frost.
> From the ashes a fire shall be woken,
> A light from the shadows shall spring;
> Renewed shall be blade that was broken,
> The crownless again shall be king. (*LOTR*, 167)

There is, it seems to me, a substantial, though subtle difference in the two adages. The traditional formulation amounts to saying something like, "Don't be fooled by appearances because they are inherently deceptive." Tolkien's version seems to suggest something different: "Attend more closely to appearances, for the truth has yet to arrive." This is particularly true given the "eschatological" thrust of the song's concluding line—"the crownless again shall be king"— which points to a fullness of meaning awaiting us. Put another way, in the former case, the "not" negates the gold, while in the latter, it negates the glittering. What is important in the first instance is the "not gold"; in the latter, the "does not glitter." Tolkien's revision of this traditional axiom emphasizes that the un-gold-like appearance of gold points to an excess in which it is, for that very reason, *more than* gold. Tolkien may be seen here as adverting to what Maurice Blondel called a "plenitude of the object," in the sense that what an object is is really *more than* it is.[90] Moreover, it seems to suggest that beauty is not simply epiphenomenal but attached to the very ontological nature of beautiful things, which may not at all appear so. In other words, Tolkien discerns that beauty is not simply a function of the senses or of perception. This is, after all, the demography of Faërie, whose inhabitants "do not always look like what they are."[91]

To make matters more interesting, the precise formulation appears, with surprising aptness, in Nietzsche's *Human, All Too*

Human: "*Alles, was Gold ist, glänzt nicht.*" Section 340 of "The Wanderer and His Shadow," in R. J. Hollingdale's translation, reads: "*Gold.*—All that is gold does not glisten. A gentle radiance pertains to the noblest metal."[92] Nietzsche spins this differently. In saying, "A gentle radiance pertains to the noblest metal," does he not suggest that what sets gold apart as gold is precisely its gold-ly appearance? Does this not mean that gold is the "noblest metal" *because* a "gentle radiance" pertains to it? Or, perhaps, the implication might be, in a more Nietzschean fashion, that the gentle radiance is really all there is to the gold. What it is, is simply, and no more than, its appearance.

It may be pagan wisdom to say that "all that glitters is not gold," but it is Christian wisdom to say that "all that is gold does not glitter." Even Nietzsche was capable of such an intimation. But the form of Christ is capable of "transubstantiating" all moments of human *poiesis*. The Word who is before all worlds, who creates all worlds, who was made flesh and dwelt among us—does not all creation speak, in an infinite variety of tones, keys, timbres, and tongues, of that Word? Does not the Word made flesh render all flesh in some sense *articulate*? As Jones puts it, "There is no escape from incarnation. It's like a shunting train."[93] This is because, as Maurice de la Taille says, in a line David Jones is fond of quoting, "He placed Himself under the order of signs."[94]

Tolkien's vision of creation centers on genuine newness, in which destruction is not necessary to creation. It is the hope of the return of the past in a nonidentical newness. Only then can the Shire be received back, as it is given up in the quest to destroy the Ring. Sam's words at the end of the cycle, "I'm back," are true in a genuinely naive sense: the casual nonchalance of the ending seems incommensurate with what has happened, yet at the same time, Sam is more "home" now than when he left. The Shire, though now threatened with the loss of the memory of festive past—a memory *absolutely central* to the life of the hobbits, and to the success of the mission— must begin the long work of *anamnesis*, of rendering "really present" those who are now absent, especially Frodo. The Shire will thus never be the same; it will always be different from what it was and bear the wounds of loss. But the hobbit hope, like the Christian hope, is not nostalgia for a "recovery" of a vanished past—after all, it is Gollum who is obsessed with "roots and beginnings" (*LOTR*, 51); instead, it is the hope for the return of the past *to us*, albeit with a drastic difference. At the same time, that hope gives us back our deaths; indeed, it gives back all deaths and restores them in the promise that the bodies of the dead will be resurrected—they will be returned, not as they were, but glorified.[95] The replanting of the Party Tree is the necessary element of recalling the presence of the lost, the departed and the not-yet, which will restore the Shire once again, for without them, the Shire quite literally *is* not.

NOTES

1. See the beginning of the essay, Tolkien, "Beowulf: The Monsters and the Critics," and Letter 294, to Charlotte and Denis Plimmer, February 8, 1967, in *Letters*, 377: "I seldom find any modern books that hold my attention." See also Shippey, *Road to Middle-earth*, 6.

2. Nietzsche, "What the Germans Lack," in *Twilight of the Idols*, 72. Regarding beverages of a different cask, I am entirely in sympathy with David Hart's suggestion that "a theological answer to Nietzsche could be developed entirely in terms of the typology of wine." See Hart, *Beauty of the Infinite*, 108 ff. There may be more than just bombast to Nietzsche's claim that "to believe that wine *exhilarates* I should have to be a Christian—believing what for me is an absurdity" (*Ecce Homo*, 694).

3. Charles Sareola, "Nietzsche," *Everyman*, May 16, 1913, 136; quoted in Thatcher, *Nietzsche in England*, 207.

4. Chesterton, *Ball and the Cross*, 53.

5. Aquinas, *Summa Theologiae*, Ia, IIae, 57, 3, *resp.* Hereafter *ST*.

6. Ibid., *ad* 1.

7. Cf. Eco, *Aesthetics of Thomas Aquinas*.

8. The most formative elder influence on Tolkien's boyhood was Fr. Francis Morgan, a priest of the Birmingham Oratory, founded by John Henry Newman in 1849. One can only speculate on the influence of a figure such as Aquinas on Tolkien, but there can be little doubt that some kind of mediated Thomism was certainly in the air that Tolkien breathed—whether at the Oratory school or delivered, perhaps, through the pipe-bowl.

9. Aquinas, *ST*, Ia, 44, 4, *resp.*

10. Ibid., 45, 5, *resp.*

11. Ibid., 45, 6, *resp.*

12. See Eco, *Aesthetics of Thomas Aquinas*, 173–79.

13. Turner, *Faith, Reason and the Existence of God*, 224–25.

14. Aquinas, *ST*, Ia, 44, 4, *ad* 3.

15. Tolkien, Letter 340, to Camilla Unwin, May 20, 1969, in *Letters*, 399.

16. Tolkien, "On Fairy-Stories," 156. It matters little whether or not elves "actually exist." To ask such a question might already reveal a crude materialism at work in one's notion of "existence," not to mention what counts as "actuality."

17. Jones, "Art and Democracy," in *Epoch and Artist*, 88.

18. Matt. 5:16, as Augustine cites it in *City of God*, 5:14, 215.

19. A gloss on this same passage of scripture.

20. Tolkien, "On Fairy-Stories," 122.

21. Ibid.

22. Ibid.

23. Ibid.

24. Tolkien, *Monsters and the Critics*, 5.

25. See Huizinga, *Homo Ludens*, 11. See also Rahner, *Man at Play*.

26. Tolkien, "On Fairy-Stories," 127.

27. Ibid.

28. Ibid., 116.

29. Ibid., 117.

30. Ibid., 134.

31. Huizinga, *Homo Ludens*, 11.

32. Ibid. It must be said here that what Huizinga means by "play" and what Tolkien means by Faërie are not at all the same as "a frivolous indulgence in pointless triviality," but rather constitute a fundamental characteristic of humanity as such. In Tolkien's case, fairy stories are "a natural human taste (though not necessarily a universal one)" ("On Fairy-Stories," 136).

33. Soskice, *Metaphor and Religious Language*, 70.

34. See Burrell, "From the Analogy of 'Being' to the Analogy of Being," 113–26; Hart, *Beauty of the Infinite*, 241 ff; Cunningham, *Genealogy of Nihilism*, 181–89.

35. Letter 269, to W. H. Auden, May 12, 1965, in *Letters*, 355.

36. Tolkien, "Beowulf," 24.

37. Letter 213, to Deborah Webster, October 25, 1958, in *Letters*, 288.

38. Shippey, *Road to Middle-earth*, 57.

39. Tolkien, "On Fairy-Stories," 121–22.

40. Letter 165, to the Houghton Mifflin Co., in *Letters*, 219.

41. Hart, *Beauty of the Infinite*, 28.

42. See Toulmin, *Cosmopolis*.

43. Tolkien, *Silmarillion*, 15.

44. Cf. Cate, *Friedrich Nietzsche*, 122–25.

45. During this period he wrote *The Wanderer and His Shadow, Daybreak, The Gay Science, Thus Spake Zarathustra, Beyond Good and Evil, On the Genealogy of Morals*, two books on Wagner, *The Twilight of the Idols, The Anti-Christ*, and *Ecce Homo*.

46. Cf. Porter, *Nietzsche and the Philology of the Future*, 8.

47. Ibid., 6.

48. Ibid., 4.

49. Nietzsche, *Daybreak*, sec. 84, 49.

50. Nietzsche, *Writings from the Late Notebooks*, sec. 39[17], 41.

51. Ibid., sec. 34[48], 3.

52. Nietzsche, Preface to *Daybreak*, sec. 5, 5.

53. Nietzsche, Foreword to *Twilight of the Idols*, 32.

54. Nietzsche, "*Thus Spoke Zarathustra*: A Book for All and None," in *Ecce Homo*, sec. 8, 765.

55. Rosen, *Mask of Enlightenment*, 13.

56. Ibid.

57. Nietzsche, Letter 171, to Karl Knortz, June 21,1888, in Middleton, *Selected Letters of Friedrich Nietzsche*, 299.

58. Nietzsche, *Ecce Homo*, 765.

59. Nietzsche, *Thus Spoke Zarathustra*, 116.

60. Cf. Candler, "Theology at Midnight"; and Hart, *Beauty of the Infinite*, 103:

> Nietzsche's post-Christian counternarrative (which is itself perhaps occasionally tainted by resentment rather than honesty) cannot be denied its power and its appeal, but it should be recognized not simply as critique but as always already another *kerygma*. Between Nietzsche's vision of life as an agon and the Christian vision of life as creation—as primordial "gift" and "grace"—there is nothing (not even the palpable evidences of "nature red in tooth and claw") that makes either perspective self-evidently more correct that the other. Each sees and accounts for the violence of experience and the beauty of being, but each according to an irreducible mythos and a particular aesthetics. A battle of tastes is being waged by Nietzsche, and the metaphysical appears therein as a necessary element of his narrative's completeness.

See also Hart, *Beauty of the Infinite*, 124 ff.

61. Nietzsche, *Zarathustra*, 178–79.

62. Nietzsche, *Twilight of the Idols*, 48.

63. Tolkien himself was prone to such "reasoning to God" through the observation of "patterns." See Letter 310, to Camilla Unwin, May 20, 1969, in *Letters*, 399 ff.

64. Nietzsche, "The Convalescent," in *Thus Spoke Zarathustra*, 237–38.

65. Nietzsche, *The Anti-Christ*, sec. 57, 188.

66. Hart, *Beauty of the Infinite*, 95.

67. Nietzsche, *Birth of Tragedy*, sec. 23, 138–39.

68. Ibid., 137.

69. The concluding passage of Cate, *Friedrich Nietzsche*, 576. It is also noteworthy that *Zarathustra*, along with the Gospel of John, was placed in the knapsacks of Nazi soldiers.

70. Boyle, *Sacred and Secular Scriptures*, 255–56.

71. Cf. Boyle, 248–66.

72. Boyle, 262.

73. Ibid.

74. Milbank, *Word Made Strange*, 232n16. As evidence of this Milbank points to *The Hobbit* (Boston: Houghton Mifflin, 1966, 1994), 260: "All the same Mr. Baggins kept his head more clear of the bewitchment of the hoard than the dwarves did. Long before the dwarves were tired of examining the treasures, he became weary of it and sat down on the floor; and he began to wonder nervously what the end of it all would be. 'I would give a good many of these precious goblets,' he thought, 'for a drink of something cheering out of one of Beorn's wooden bowls!'"

75. Hart, *Beauty of the Infinite*, 126.

76. *LOTR* shall designate Tolkien, *Lord of the Rings*.

77. Here I am following Cunningham, *Genealogy of Nihilism*, 174 ff.

78. Here Tolkien anticipates Foucault, but in a much more theologically profound way.

79. Jones, "Preface to *The Anathemata*," in *Epoch and Artist*, 120.

80. Tolkien, "On Fairy-Stories," 156.

81. Ibid.

82. Ibid.

83. Hart, *Beauty of the Infinite*, 124.

84. Ibid., 34.

85. Žižek, *Puppet and the Dwarf*, 48. The reference is to Chesterton, *Orthodoxy*, 164. A more adequate critique of Žižek's provocative suggestion (and his account of "The Doctrine of Unconditional Joy") would require more space than allotted here.

86. Tolkien, "On Fairy-Stories," 155–56.

87. Jones, "Preface to *The Anathemata*," in *Epoch and Artist*, 130.

88. Tolkien, "On Fairy-Stories," 155n2.

89. This is an egregiously oversimple summary of the argument in Cunningham's *Genealogy of Nihilism*.

90. Blondel, *Action*, 403. See Cunningham, *Genealogy of Nihilism*, 179 ff.

91. Tolkien, "On Fairy-Stories," 113.

92. Nietzsche, *Human, All Too Human*, sec. 340, 392.
93. Jones, "Religion and the Muses," in *Epoch and Artist*, 105.
94. De la Taille, *Mystery of Faith*, quoted in Jones, "Art and Sacrament," in *Epoch and Artist*, 179.
95. Cf. 1 Cor. 15:36–58.

BIBLIOGRAPHY

Aquinas, Thomas. *Summa Theologiae*. Translated by the Fathers of the English Dominican Province. Westminster, MD: Christian Classics, 1981.

Augustine. *The City of God against the Pagans*. Edited by R. W. Dyson. Cambridge: Cambridge University Press, 1998.

———. *The Trinity*. Translated by Edmund Hill. Brooklyn: New City, 1991.

Blondel, Maurice. *Action: Essay on a Critique of Life and a Science of Practice (1893)*. Translated by Oliva Blanchette. Notre Dame, IN: University of Notre Dame Press, 1984.

Boyle, Nicholas. *Sacred and Secular Scriptures: A Catholic Approach to Literature*. Notre Dame, IN: University of Notre Dame Press, 2005.

Burrell, David B. "From the Analogy of 'Being' to the Analogy of Being." In *Faith and Freedom: An Interfaith Perspective*, 113–26. Oxford: Basil Blackwell, 2004.

Candler, Peter M., Jr. "Theology at Midnight: Friedrich Nietzsche and the Grammar of Atheism." M. Phil. thesis, Cambridge University, 1997.

Carpenter, Humphrey. *Tolkien: A Biography*. New York: Ballantine, 1977.

Cate, Curtis. *Friedrich Nietzsche*. London: Pimlico, 2003.

Chesterton, G. K. *The Autobiography of G. K. Chesterton*. San Francisco: Ignatius, 1988.

———. *The Ball and the Cross*. New York: Dover, 1995.

———. *Heretics*. San Francisco: Ignatius, 1986.

———. *Orthodoxy*. San Francisco: Ignatius, 1995.

Cunningham, Conor. *Genealogy of Nihilism*. London: Routledge, 2003.

De la Taille, Maurice. *The Mystery of Faith*. London: Sheed & Ward, 1940.

Eco, Umberto. *The Aesthetics of Thomas Aquinas*. Translated by Hugh Bredin. Cambridge, MA: Harvard University Press, 1988.

Eliot, T. S. *Collected Poems, 1909–1962*. London: Faber & Faber, 1963.

Hart, David Bentley. *The Beauty of the Infinite: The Aesthetics of Christian Truth*. Grand Rapids, MI: Eerdmans, 2003.

Huizinga, Johan. *Homo Ludens: A Study of the Play Element in Culture*. Boston: Beacon, 1950.

Jones, David. *Epoch and Artist*. London: Faber & Faber, 1959.

Middleton, Christopher, ed. *Selected Letters of Friedrich Nietzsche*. Indianapolis: Hackett, 1996.

Milbank, John. *The Word Made Strange: Theology, Language, Culture*. Oxford: Basil Blackwell, 1997.

Nietzsche, Friedrich. *The Birth of Tragedy*. In *The Basic Writings of Nietzsche*, translated by Walter Kaufmann. New York: Modern Library, 1992.

———. *Daybreak: Thoughts on the Prejudices of Morality*. Translated by R. J. Hollingdale. Cambridge: Cambridge University Press, 1982.

———. *Ecce Homo*. In *The Basic Writings of Nietzsche*, translated by Walter Kaufmann. New York: Modern Library, 1992.

———. *The Gay Science*. Translated by Walter Kaufmann. New York: Vintage, 1974.

———. *Human, All Too Human: A Book for Free Spirits*. Translated by R. J. Hollingdale. Cambridge: Cambridge University Press, 1986.

———. *Thus Spoke Zarathustra*. Translated by R. J. Hollingdale. London: Penguin, 1969.

———. *Twilight of the Idols*. Translated by R. J. Hollingdale. London: Penguin, 1990.

———. *The Twilight of the Idols/The Anti-Christ*. Translated by R. J. Hollingdale. New York: Penguin, 1990.

———. *Writings from the Late Notebooks*. Edited by Rüdiger Bittner. Translated by Kate Sturge. Cambridge: Cambridge University Press, 2003.

Porter, James I. *Nietzsche and the Philology of the Future*. Stanford, CA: Stanford University Press, 2000.

Rahner, Hugo. *Man at Play*. New York: Herder & Herder, 1972.

Rosen, Stanley. *The Mask of Enlightenment: Nietzsche's "Zarathustra."* Cambridge: Cambridge University Press, 1995.

Shippey, Tom. *The Road to Middle-earth: How J. R. R. Tolkien Created a New Mythology*. New York: Houghton Mifflin, 2003.

Soskice, Janet Martin. *Metaphor and Religious Language*. Oxford: Oxford University Press, 1985.

Thatcher, David S. *Nietzsche in England, 1890–1914*. Toronto: University of Toronto Press, 1970.

Tolkien, J. R. R. "Beowulf: The Monsters and the Critics." In *The Monsters and the Critics and Other Essays*, edited by Christopher Tolkien. Boston: Houghton Mifflin, 1984.

———. *The Letters of J. R. R. Tolkien*. Edited by Humphrey Carpenter with the assistance of Christopher Tolkien. Boston: Houghton Mifflin, 1981.

———. *The Lord of the Rings*. 3 vols. Boston: Houghton Mifflin, 1994.

———. "On Fairy-Stories." In *The Monsters and the Critics and Other Essays*, edited by Christopher Tolkien. London: Allen & Unwin, 1983.

————. *The Silmarillion*. Edited by Christopher Tolkien. New York: Houghton Mifflin, 2001.

Toulmin, Stephen. *Cosmopolis: The Hidden Agenda of Modernity*. Chicago: University of Chicago Press, 1990.

Turner, Denys. *Faith, Reason and the Existence of God*. Cambridge: Cambridge University Press, 2004.

Ward, Elizabeth. *David Jones, Mythmaker*. Manchester: Manchester University Press, 1983.

Žižek, Slavoj. *The Puppet and the Dwarf: The Perverse Core of Christianity*. Cambridge, MA: MIT Press, 2003.

CHAPTER 5

A PORTRAIT OF THE POET
AS AN OLD HOBBIT

Engaging Modernist Aesthetic Ontology
in The Fellowship of the Ring

Phillip J. Donnelly

> Probably at the bottom of the confrontation between *The Lord of the Rings*
> and its critics there lies some total disagreement over the nature of the
> universe, a disagreement surfacing in strong instinctive, mutual antipathy.
> Nothing will cure this. However, it ought to be possible to bring the reasons
> for it out into the light, and by doing so to show that whatever may be said
> of Tolkien's view of reality, it was neither escapist nor thoughtless.
>
> —T. A. Shippey, *The Road to Middle-earth*

Critical treatments of Tolkien's relation to "modernity" and "modernism" are now many and varied; such criticism, however, tends not to consider what Tom Shippey calls "Tolkien's view of reality," or his ontology.[1] Tolkien's fiction arguably engages both the cultural conditions widely referred to as "modernity" and the aesthetic responses to those conditions that characterize literary "modernism."[2] Given the fraught and potentially circular character of any attempt to stipulate specific formal aspects of modernism, the argument here takes its points of departure from one exemplary instance: the writing of

James Joyce. As we shall discover, Tolkien's writing suggests that the root problem of both cultural modernity and aesthetic modernism is in the "view of reality" that they share: the belief that reality consists of strife between violent chaos and coerced order.[3] Against the resulting tendency to imagine "freedom" as subjective randomness and "order" as coerced constraint, Tolkien implies that reality is a gift that is not necessarily violent.[4] An "aesthetic ontology," as I use the phrase here, can refer either to an account of reality (ontology) implied by a given work of art or to an account of reality implied by an aesthetic theory (a theory of human making, *poiesis*). As the fiction of both Tolkien and Joyce reveals, however, these two aspects of aesthetic ontology become inseparable when imaginative writing articulates an aesthetic theory or depicts an artistic process. For this reason, my analysis of Tolkien's writing focuses on his use of inset verse narratives, as they present unique occasions for second-order reflection on the act of poetic composition.[5] The main argument here focuses on three episodes involving such inset narratives in *The Fellowship of the Ring*. When taken together, these episodes portray the artistic development of Bilbo Baggins, from a composer of traveling lyrics and bathing songs to a composer of heroic court poetry on the myth of Eärendil. The argument begins, however, by first describing (rather than defining) some of the characteristically modern assumptions regarding the composition of imaginative literature that Stephen Dedalus illustrates in James Joyce's *Portrait of the Artist as a Young Man*. We shall also note briefly some particular aspects of inset narrative that bear on the present analysis. As we then consider three of the verse narratives embedded in Tolkien's *Fellowship of the Ring*, we can begin to understand how their framing entails a critique not only of aesthetic attitudes that had become dominant in English culture by the early twentieth century but also of the view of reality that they assume.

Because *The Lord of the Rings* has long been recognized for its neo-medieval content and archaic modes of diction, critics have variously attempted to show, by contrast, the implicitly contemporary aspects of Tolkien's work. Thus, Shippey, for example, argues that Tolkien engages characteristically twentieth-century themes and that

Tolkien's corpus is comparable in some major respects to Joyce's.[6] In the latter case, Shippey points out that there are extended comparisons that may be made between Tolkien and Joyce, including not only a common interest in philology but also a similar set of relationships among their respective texts. Both wrote an early short work (*The Hobbit* and *Portrait*) that "shares some characters" with an "obvious main work" (*Lord of the Rings* and *Ulysses*), followed later by "posthumous publication of first drafts" (*History of Middle-earth* and *Stephen Hero* or *James Joyce Archive*).[7] Neither Shippey's claims nor those of the argument here suggest that Tolkien is directly responding to Joyce; the purpose here is simply to consider an illuminating comparison. I propose, however, that Tolkien's most direct thematic riposte to the aesthetic vision exemplified by Joyce's *Portrait* appears in *Fellowship of the Ring* rather than in *The Hobbit*. Nevertheless, *Fellowship of the Ring* presents that thematic engagement significantly through the same character who is the protagonist in *The Hobbit*: Bilbo Baggins. This is why the analysis here focuses on these three specific instances of inset verse narrative from among the various alternative characters and episodes. These particular episodes in *Fellowship of the Ring* provide not only depictions of three moments in the development of Bilbo Baggins as a poet; each episode also provides a point of direct contrast to the aesthetic assumptions embodied by the character of Stephen Dedalus.

Margaret Hiley has argued that Tolkien's use of myth is closer to the "mythical method" of literary modernists, such as Pound, Joyce, and Eliot, than has been appreciated thus far.[8] In the final stage of this argument we shall return to Hiley's claims, but several of her central points are worth noting here at the outset. She initially posits that "myth" in general involves a fundamental misrepresentation of itself: its stories derive authority from presenting themselves as organic realities rather than as the human constructions that they are.[9] Modernist writers often adapted mythic discourse, appropriating its authoritative effects, in order to overcome problems pertaining to subjectivism and the randomness of temporal experience.[10] Tolkien, according to Hiley, makes similar use of myth's authoritative effects but also threatens to encompass the "Primary World" of the reader within the world of his mythic fiction.[11] As we shall find, one of the most important effects of Tolkien's use of inset narrative is to imply a continuity between the world of his mythic *legendarium*[12] and the main narrative world in *Lord of the Rings*, as well as between his entire fictive world and the world of the reader. The argument here ultimately aims to outline the character of these implied continuities. We should notice already, however, that Hiley's structuralist analysis presumes that temporal reality is fundamentally chaotic. In effect, the argument depends on the view that art is necessarily an imposition of order upon a preexistent reality that is the random flux of time. This suggests a further way in which the tacit ontology of modernity (chaos and coercion) continues to inform not only the aesthetic assumptions of literary modernism but also its critics. Ultimately, I contend that the very way in which Tolkien frames inset verse narratives in *Fellowship of the Ring* engages the aesthetic assumptions of Stephen Dedalus in *Portrait*, and the ontology implied by those aesthetic assumptions.

NARRATING MODERN ARTISTRY

Beyond its status as a representative modernist work, Joyce's *Portrait* is especially well suited to this discussion because of its participation in a genre that is continually self-reflective about the writing of imaginative literature. As Maurice Beebe points out, however, "the tradition of artist fiction, which had developed steadily for more than a century, reached a crest in the first two decades of the twentieth century"; by 1921, "both the artist and the adolescent had become hackneyed subjects of fiction."[13] As evidence for this claim, Beebe cites a passage from Aldous Huxley's novel *Crome Yellow*, in which the young poet, Denis, is "chagrined" to hear a new acquaintance preemptively describe the plot of the novel that he has just confessed to writing:

> "Little Percy the hero was never good at games, but he was always clever. He passes through the usual public school and the usual university and comes to London, where he lives among the artists. He is

bowed down with melancholy thought; he carries the whole weight of the universe upon his shoulders. He writes a novel of dazzling brilliance; he dabbles in Amour and disappears at the end of the book into the Luminous Future."

Denis blushed scarlet. Mr. Scogan had described the plan of his novel with an accuracy that was appalling. He made an effort to laugh. "You're entirely wrong," he said. "My novel is not in the least like that." It was a heroic lie. Luckily, he reflected, only two chapters were written. He would tear them up that evening when he unpacked.

Mr. Scogan paid no attention to his denial, but went on: "Why will you young men continue to write about things that are so uninteresting as the mentality of adolescents and artists?"[14]

Huxley is, of course, having some fun at the expense of not only Joyce but also of readers like Mr. Scogan who fail to appreciate "real literature." When Huxley's novel was published in 1921, Tolkien was finishing his first year as a Reader of English Language at Leeds University. Only in 1922, with the publication of *Ulysses*, and still more strikingly with the publication of *Stephen Hero* in 1944, would it become apparent how great was the ironic distance between the protagonist and the author of *Portrait*.[15] We are not concerned here, however, to establish the extent to which Joyce personally endorses, or rejects, for example, the quasi-Thomist aesthetic theory presented in *Portrait*.[16] Instead, I draw attention here to three characteristically modernist assumptions regarding the nature of artistic expression that appear in Stephen's developmental narrative in *Portrait*: an insistence upon the primacy of individual "freedom," in opposition to the community; a detachment of aesthetics from ethics; and a subordination of friendship to the demands of artistic "freedom."

First, Stephen believes that an authentic artist is constituted as such through a specific kind of opposition between the self and the community, whether religious, national, or local, from which the writer comes. In such a view, true art can be produced only in complete freedom—the quest for which ultimately leads Stephen to leave Ireland. By the beginning of *Ulysses*, we discover that Stephen seems to have failed in his attempt to become a master artificer; nevertheless, according to Stephen, as he describes his aims in *Portrait*, a writer should seek "the mode of life or art whereby [his] spirit could express itself in unfettered freedom."[17] Moreover, such aesthetic freedom is also necessarily a freedom to reject any limit (whether moral or metaphysical) upon desire. As Stephen explains to Cranly: "I am not afraid to make a mistake, even a great mistake, a lifelong mistake and perhaps as long as eternity too." This view of freedom is consistent with the characteristically post-Romantic assumption that authentic selfhood entails the obligation to do what one desires. At one level, such discourse assumes that any moral order outside the self is a coercive constraint on the desires of the subject; the ensuing challenge is then to explain how the freedom from all such constraint can be distinguished from randomness. Conversely, human creative action, in such a view, is understood as an attempt to impose, however temporarily, one's own order upon a fundamentally chaotic reality.

We can discern a second crucial modern presupposition in a passage where Stephen explains his view of tragedy. In the final section of *Portrait*, having drawn away from his companions for a conversation with Lynch, Stephen states suddenly:

> —Aristotle has not defined pity and terror. I have. I say—
> Lynch halted and said bluntly:
> —Stop! I won't listen! I am sick. I was out last night on a yellow drunk with Hogan and Goggins.
> Stephen went on:
> —Pity is the feeling which arrests the mind in the presence of whatsoever is grave and constant in human sufferings and unites it with the human sufferer. Terror is the feeling which arrests the mind in the presence of whatsoever is grave and constant in human sufferings and unites it with the secret cause.
>
>   . . .
>
> —Tragic emotion, in fact, is a face looking two ways, towards terror and towards pity, both of which are phases of it. You see I use the word arrest. I mean that tragic emotion is static. Or rather the dramatic emotion is.[18]

Stephen goes on to explain that true beauty must not provoke the "kinetic" emotions of either desire or revulsion but should induce "an esthetic stasis." Lynch's comic interruptions of Stephen's discourse in this passage bear considerably on how the reader should take these pronouncements.[19] But the key point here is that Stephen presumes that tragic effect can be detached from ethical judgment. His definition of tragedy speaks of "suffering" and "pity" without reference to moral judgment. By contrast, in Aristotle's account, the very perception of tragedy as such depends on the arbitrary *in*justice of the protagonist's suffering.[20] Manifestly deserved suffering does not produce tragic effect. The Aristotelian view of tragic pity cannot be separated from a network of ethical presuppositions regarding the meaning of "justice" that makes the distinction between deserved and undeserved suffering intelligible.[21] Stephen, though not necessarily Joyce, seems to presume that such a separation has already occurred. Nor is it mere coincidence that the severing of aesthetics from ethics appears in combination with the privileging of spatialized stasis; the temporality that constitutes the shared field of *phronesis* and *poiesis* has dropped from consideration.[22] As Joseph Buttigieg points out, the larger trajectory of *Portrait* involves an attempt to overcome precisely such spatialization of the temporal process that is characteristic of modernity.[23] Stephen's adopting such a view as his own is thus ultimately ironic with respect to the novel as a whole; nevertheless, the point remains that Stephen shares the characteristically modern assumption that aesthetic action can be detached from ethical understanding.

A third aesthetic assumption embodied by Stephen is a willingness to subordinate friendship to the demands of artistic freedom. As Stephen declares, "I do not fear to be alone or be spurned for another or to leave whatever I have to leave." To which Cranly replies:

—Alone, quite alone. You have no fear of that. And you know what that word means? Not only to be separate from all others but to have not even one friend.
—I will take the risk, said Stephen.[24]

Once again, even if Joyce later undercuts Stephen's pretensions to solitariness, there persists for Stephen the belief that, whatever problems friendship might pose regarding the configurations of the self and the other, a change in literary or artistic technique is sufficient to address those challenges. Furthermore, in such a view, the development of a given artist's abilities do not depend in any crucial way upon the temporal particularities of extended friendships. Each of these three elements—the primacy of individual freedom, the severing of aesthetics from ethics, and the subordination of friendship to the demand for such freedom—are not necessarily endorsed by Joyce and appear variously among post-Romantic aesthetic attitudes, sometimes implicitly criticized, sometimes celebrated. In *Portrait*, however, such assumptions form an especially close combined arrangement in the character of Stephen.[25] As we shall see, Tolkien's *Lord of the Rings* presents a model for artistic development that contrasts with each of the three attitudes embodied by Stephen in *Portrait*. Tolkien presents that alternative model indirectly through the use of inset narrative.

The use of inset narrative, as a fictive mode, is as ancient as Homer and continued to be used in the early twentieth century by a variety of writers, most notably Joseph Conrad.[26] In general, such stories involve a mode of irony that hinges on the difference between the implications that a given story has for characters inside the main framing narrative and the contrasting implications that the same story has for readers outside the main narrative. The most commonly noted historical analogue for Tolkien's use of inset narrative is arguably *Beowulf*. We should, however, distinguish the use of inset narrative in *Beowulf* from two other aspects of the Old English epic that are widely noted in Tolkien criticism: the use of "legendary back-stories" and the use of "interlace" narrative structure. The first element is noted by Tolkien in "Beowulf: The Monsters and the Critics," namely, the narrative persistently refers to comparative historical or legendary events outside the main action. In effect, the *Beowulf* poet, according to Tolkien, draws extensively upon a preexisting series of "connected legends" for his own narrative purposes, with the resulting effect that the poem evokes a "sense of perspective, of antiquity with a greater and yet darker antiquity behind."[27] In *Lord of the Rings*, such fictional "antiquity" glimpsed at various points in the story, whether through passing narrative references or conversational allusions, is given a more full exposition in *The Silmarillion* and the posthumous volumes published as *The History of Middle-earth*. Although such legendary back-stories form part of the argument here, most of such intertextual connections do not come to readers in the form of inset narrative. By contrast, our attention here is upon the *relation* between inset verse narratives and their larger fictional frames in *Lord of the Rings*.

Various critics have also noted the second element of interlace narrative structure in both *Lord of the Rings* and *Beowulf*. But whether we consider John Leyerle's account of interlace structure in *Beowulf* or Richard West's discussion of the similar structural elements in Tolkien's fiction, we can see that both studies focus on the interruptions in and interweaving of the main narrative action.[28] This interlace technique enables a "very subtle kind of cohesion," through the varied tracing of characters' actions as they intersect and diverge.[29] *Lord of the Rings* employs both inset narrative and interlace structuring of the main narrative; my point, however, is that Tolkien does not deploy the former to achieve the latter and that the two narrative strategies should not be conflated or necessarily linked. The use of what are sometimes called the "digressions" in *Beowulf* arguably comes closest to the deployment of inset verse narrative in Tolkien's fiction.[30] In the episodes from Tolkien that we shall focus on here, however, he uniquely foregrounds the very interaction between the inset story and its frame: that interaction, in turn, embodies an alternative to the modernist aesthetic assumptions and their underlying ontology.

THE POET AS HOBBIT

In the first half of *Fellowship of the Ring*, readers encounter poetic verse that ranges widely in form, content, and quality, performed by various characters amid the main action.[31] But if we consider two specific narrative poems composed by Bilbo (and a further one that he translated), we can begin to discern an implicit narrative of artistic apprenticeship. This overall development involves three transitions: first, from a composer of what I call "mundane lyric poetry" to a composer of folk narrative; second, from a composer of folk stories to a translator of heroic legend; and finally from a translator to a composer of original adaptations of heroic legend. Apparently, Bilbo first began writing lyric poetry in response to his adventures described in *The Hobbit*. By the time he hosts his "eleventy-first" birthday party, at the beginning of *Fellowship of the Ring*, he already has a reputation, of sorts. We are told that the guests "rather dreaded the after-dinner speech of their host," which involved the risk that he would be "liable to drag in bits of what he called poetry" (*LOTR*, 28). The topics of Bilbo's lyric poems tend to be unexalted, or mundane, but some of them evidently become part of a local oral hobbit culture, as we encounter them repeated at various points by other characters who know them by heart. Such poems concern topics like bathing, saying farewell, traveling, or returning home.[32]

Some readers may, of course, complain about the quality of the verse generally found in *Lord of the Rings*. Such complaints, however, seem to result from a failure to consider the larger narrative context of the poetry—even less-than-brilliant poetry can reveal something important about the characters who recite or compose it, or the world that they inhabit.[33] Consider Bilbo's "bath song":

> *Sing hey! For the bath at close of the day*
> *that washes the weary mud away!*
> *A loon is he that will not sing:*
> *O! Water Hot is a noble thing! (LOTR, 99)*

If we are inclined not to be deeply impressed by such poetry, we should remember that we share such a reaction with the vast majority of the hobbits. Nearly the whole Shire is invited to Bilbo's eleventy-first birthday party, but there is no indication that even a small number of hobbits do anything but dread the expected "poetry." Nevertheless, Bilbo's bath song is known by heart among some of Frodo's friends, like Pippin. The larger context of the story implies that there is, indeed, no correlation between literary excellence and a poem's circulation in any given oral culture: being doggerel does not disqualify a poem from popular use, as long as it is memorable and suits the occasion.

Among the more somber lyric poems that Bilbo composes is the traveling song, starting "The Road goes ever on and on," a verse of which Bilbo and Frodo each sing upon their respective departures from the Shire. Early in *Fellowship of the Ring*, Bilbo recites one stanza:

> *The Road goes ever on and on*
> *Down from the door where it began.*
> *Now far ahead the Road has gone,*
> *And I must follow, if I can,*
> *Pursuing it with eager feet,*
> *Until it joins some larger way,*
> *Where many paths and errands meet.*
> *And whither then? I cannot say.* (*LOTR*, 35)

Two "previous" stanzas of this song appear near the end of *The Hobbit*, and they are composed by Bilbo upon his return from his "there and back again" adventure.[34] When Frodo repeats the same stanza recited by Bilbo, he makes just one change, replacing the words "eager feet" in line 4 with "weary feet" (*LOTR*, 72). As Shippey points out, this change is part of an important broader shift in emotional register between the two versions of the poem because of their respective contexts: Frodo, unlike Bilbo in either of the above contexts, is leaving for what he expects to be exile. Tellingly, Frodo cannot recall whether the poem is Bilbo's or whether he has just composed it himself.[35] Still later, we meet Frodo's version of the same stanza again in *The Return of the King*, but this time recited by a sleepy Bilbo in Rivendell (*LOTR*, 965). The use of this particular lyric poem is probably the most complex among Bilbo's various compositions on mundane topics, as the fragments are performed in such different contexts.[36] The performance of this poem near the end of *Return of the*

King directs readers' attention at that point also to the end of *The Hobbit* and to the beginning of *Fellowship of the Ring*. At the same time, such repetition indicates the enduring worth in some of what might seem Bilbo's "lowest" poetry. Most notably, Bilbo's writing of lyric poetry also eventually prepares him for composing what I call "folk narrative."

Our first indication that Bilbo has ever written such stories comes just before we encounter one of them, during the stay of the four hobbits at The Prancing Pony in Bree. In an attempt to keep Pippin from accidentally revealing too much regarding their errand or reminding his common-room listeners of the disappearing Bilbo Baggins, Frodo suddenly interrupts Pippin's story regarding Bilbo's birthday disappearance. After getting everyone's attention and saying a few words, however, Frodo simply "hesitated and coughed":

> Everyone in the room was now looking at him. "A song!" shouted one of the hobbits. "A song! A song!" shouted all the others. "Come on now, master, sing us something that we haven't heard before!"
>
> For a moment Frodo stood gaping. Then in desperation he began a ridiculous song that Bilbo had been rather fond of (and indeed rather proud of, for he had made up the words himself). It was about an inn; and that is probably why it came into Frodo's mind just then. Here it is in full. Only a few words of it are now, as a rule, remembered. (*LOTR*, 154)

He then begins the song:

> *There is an inn, a merry old inn*
> *beneath an old grey hill,*
> *And there they brew a beer so brown*
> *That the Man in the Moon himself came down*
> *one night to drink his fill.* (*LOTR*, 155)

The ensuing story involves characters ranging from a fiddle-playing cat and humor-loving dog to a dancing cow and silver spoons. The main action of the story, however, seems to present an etiological myth, which, in effect, cites the overindulgence in fine ale as an explanation for the moon's periodic appearance during the daytime.

Although Frodo has memorized Bilbo's poem and we are never told exactly when it was composed, we can draw some important inferences regarding its composition: first, it is presented as something apparently "original," in response to a demand for novelty; second, in contrast to the various bits of lyric poetry we have met thus far, this narrative poem is connected to a self-conscious sense of accomplishment on Bilbo's part; third, the overall movement of its main action, notwithstanding its outlandish mode, is one of celestial descent and ascent (as the Man in the Moon comes down and eventually returns to the sky, albeit late). The element of comedic circularity provides an important point of comparison with the inset heroic narratives, as we shall see, but it also resembles Frodo's own adventures to some extent. Most importantly, the composition of this "folk narrative" clearly represents a kind of artistic progress for Bilbo, even as he continues to develop the poetic skills that he first honed in composing lyric verse. This is not to imply that all, or even any, of Bilbo's narrative poetry is superior to his lyric poetry, but simply to observe that this shift represents an expansion in Bilbo's range of possible genres and as such requires that he develop new poetic skills. Those who find "The Man in the Moon" poem simply unbearable as poetry might take a closer look to see whether they recognize an ironic depiction of their own poetic tastes. This poem is arguably the closest thing that we ever get to an "original composition," in the sense privileged by modernity; Frodo offers the song in response to a demand for novelty. The story suggests that to make the demand for novelty the defining characteristic of one's aesthetic taste is to risk eliciting compositions far rougher than Bilbo's.

The performance of "The Man in the Moon" also serves to advance the action of the main story—in crucial ways that seem ultimately contrary to the apparent intentions of any particular character. After having a second mug of ale, Frodo is persuaded to repeat his performance of the song, while standing on a table, so that others could learn the words and sing along. In repeating the words in the penultimate stanza, "the cow jumped over the moon," Frodo falls disastrously:

> He leaped in the air. Much too vigorously; for he came down, bang, into a tray full of mugs, and slipped, and rolled off the table with a crash, clatter, and bump! The audience all opened their mouths wide for laughter, and stopped short in gaping silence; for the singer disappeared. He simply vanished, as if he had gone slap through the floor without leaving a hole! (*LOTR*, 157)

The result is disastrous not simply because of the social discomfort that the visiting hobbits must suffer but because three different suspicious people in the common-room immediately leave in order, presumably, to inform the Black Riders that they have seen a disappearing hobbit who is probably named "Baggins." At one level, this revelation precipitates the pursuit of the Black Riders, making their chase and approach even more immediate than it had been before the party reached Bree. Frodo imagines that he had accidentally slipped the Ring onto his finger when he tried to break his fall. But he also wonders "if the Ring itself had not played him a trick; perhaps it had tried to reveal itself in response to some wish or command that was felt in the room" (*LOTR*, 157). Although Frodo's speculation is never confirmed or denied, even if his speculation is accurate, the event also has important favorable consequences, the most important of which is to enable and fortify the decision of the hobbits and Strider to undertake the rest of the journey to Rivendell together. Even if the Ring was responding to some willed self-revelation, the larger story suggests another intention aimed at bringing good out of evil, in the same way that the apparent failure of the Man in the Moon evidently became absorbed into a larger cosmic harmony of heavenly motion. The similar role played by good ale in the respective "falls" of Frodo and the Man in the Moon also suggests a comparison of the two stories. But especially striking here is the combination of necessary details in both stories that forges a causal connection between an apparently gratuitous detail ("the cow jumped over the moon") in the inset narrative and an event (Frodo's jumping) that proves crucial to the unfolding of the main action in the framing narrative.

The implications of this story extend still further when the narrator explains that "only a few words of it are now, as a rule, remembered." At that point, the speaker effectively connects the world of the main narrative to the world of the implied reader. The children's rhyme to which the narrator alludes is, of course, a version of the old rhyme:

Hey diddle diddle,
The cat played the fiddle
The cow jumped over the moon;
The little dog laughed to see such sport,
And the dish ran away with the spoon.[37]

This rhyme has been described as "probably the best known nonsense verse in the language."[38] Tolkien makes analogous connections between the story and reader elsewhere, when he refers generally to the beginning of the "age of men." In "The Man in the Moon," however, we encounter a concrete connection to a detail in the cultural life of most people in mid-twentieth-century English-speaking culture. In effect, the relation between the world of the reader and that of the main narrative is directly analogous to the relationship between the world of the main narrative and that of the legendary back-stories presented in *Silmarillion*. The latter relationship, however, runs in the opposite chronological direction and is not yet apparent in *Fellowship of the Ring*. Only through later developments, like the next two inset narratives that we shall consider, do we begin to sense more directly the historical relation between the "Third Age" and the stories of elder days. The crucial point here is that the "Man in the Moon" story serves to suggest the "future looking" continuity, as it were, between the world of Middle-earth and that of the reader. In effect, Bilbo's folk narrative is a complete version of a story that is only echoed in the nursery rhyme fragment that we now have. That relationship between fragment and larger story is analogous to the relationship between the stories in *Silmarillion* and the fragments of such legend that we overhear throughout *Lord of the Rings*. In having the narrator make such a comment, Tolkien is not simply disparaging nursery rhymes. Rather, the comment opens the potential for wonder: how many such paleolinguistic fragments do we utter daily without any sense of the forgotten worlds, stories, and people by which they came to us? Such wonder could well induce an unsuspecting reader toward affections resembling philology. The story suggests that, for those who have ears to hear, the world of the reader, no less than the Secondary World of the story, offers opportunities to encounter anew the linguistic antiquities among which we live and move. It also implies that even doggerel, if it is memorable, can be redemptive, insofar as its memorability can resist the permanent loss of such remaining fragments from the life of a language and people. As we shall see, such implications arise, however, not from subsuming the Primary World into the text, but from analogies between the inset fictive world's relation to the main narrative and the main story's relation to the world of the reader.

THE HOBBIT AS (ALMOST) HEROIC POET

When Strider and the four hobbits eventually reach Rivendell, we hear Bilbo perform one of his own compositions, but the style of narrative is strikingly different from "The Man in the Moon": he performs for the court of Elrond his own version of the myth of Eärendil. Before considering Bilbo's performance, however, we might well ask how he ever developed the poetic skill to produce poetry susceptible of so much more *gravitas*. An important detail regarding that development appears amid the intervening journey toward Weathertop. The hobbits are listening to Strider's account of the "ancient lore" surrounding the location of Weathertop, when Merry asks, "Who was Gil-galad?":

But Strider did not answer, and seemed to be lost in thought. Suddenly a low voice murmured:

> *Gil-galad was an Elven-king.*
> *Of him the harpers sadly sing:*
> *The last whose realm was fair and free*
> *Between the Mountains and the Sea.*
>
> *His sword was long, his lance was keen,*
> *His shining helm afar was seen;*
> *The countless stars of heaven's field*
> *Were mirrored in his silver shield.*
>
> *But long ago he rode away,*
> *And where he dwelleth none can say;*
> *For into darkness fell his star*
> *In Mordor where the shadows are.*

The others turned in amazement, for the voice was Sam's. "Don't stop!" said Merry.

"That's all I know," stammered Sam, blushing. "I learned it from Mr. Bilbo when I was a lad. He used to tell me tales like that, knowing how I was always one for hearing about Elves. . . . He was mighty book-learned he was dear Mr. Bilbo. And he wrote *poetry*. He wrote what I have just said."

"He did not make it up," said Strider. "It is part of a lay that is called *The Fall of Gil-galad*, which is in an ancient tongue. Bilbo must have translated it. I never knew that." (*LOTR*, 181–82)

There is no denying that the author of "The Man in the Moon" has some limited powers of poetic invention, but Bilbo's later composition clearly draws upon more than the talent evident in such earlier work. He apparently learned to write heroic poetry in the common tongue by translating the ancient legends. His ability to compose his own verse rendition of the Eärendil story thus depends implicitly on a long apprenticeship in that narrative mode through the work of translation.

Strictly speaking, a poetic apprenticeship that progresses from lyric poetry to folk narrative to translation of heroic narrative to composition of heroic narrative does not quite correspond with any particular ancient or medieval developmental model.[39] Nevertheless, we can identify some general characteristics in this particular development. First, the progress in genres tends to be in the direction of increasingly public speech—involving a shift from concerns limited to the self and toward the concerns of a wider community. Second, the development of Bilbo's heroic narrative voice comes about through the practice of translation. The idea that translation work could serve as an effective way not simply to imitate another writer but to develop one's own poetic voice was common through the Renaissance and arguably persisted as late as the twentieth century.[40] Such subjection of the artistic self to the external authority of another's imaginative writing goes against the modern sensibilities noted earlier. Similarly, *Fellowship of the Ring* depicts a corresponding shift in Bilbo's social context as his poetry changes. His relocation from the Shire to the court of Elrond, though not determinative, obviously enables Bilbo to imagine an audience that could appreciate the exalted modes of heroic poetry. Although Sam enjoyed Bilbo's translations in private, the crowd at The Prancing Pony would obviously not appreciate such poetry as much as they did "The Man in the Moon." Tolkien thus depicts a process of interaction between the individual poet and the community, rather than a constitutive opposition between artist and community.

However, we never hear the rest of the Gil-galad story as Bilbo translated it. Even Frodo's later summary of those events is cut short. Instead, Strider tells the story of Beren and Lúthien. Still, the truncated performance of Bilbo's Gil-galad translation provides an important part of the context for his own poem when we encounter it later. When Strider and the hobbits are camped on Weathertop, Merry asks Strider, "Do you know any more of that old lay that you spoke of?":

"I do indeed," answered Strider. "So also does Frodo, for it concerns us closely." Merry and Pippin looked at Frodo who was staring into the fire.

"I know only the little that Gandalf has told me," said Frodo slowly. "Gil-galad was the last of the great Elf-kings of Middle-earth. Gil-galad is *starlight* in their tongue. With Elendil, the Elf-friend, he went the land of——"

"No!" said Strider interrupting, "I do not think that tale should be told now with the servants of the Enemy at hand. If we win through to the house of Elrond, you may hear it there, told in full."

"Then tell us some other tale of the old days," begged Sam . . .

"I will tell you the story of Tinúviel," said Strider, "in brief—for it is a long tale of which the end is not known; and there are none now, except Elrond, that remember it aright as it was told of old. It is a fair tale, though it is sad, as are all the tales of Middle-earth, and yet it may lift up your hearts." (*LOTR*, 186–87)

As far as we are told, when the hobbits do finally "win through to Rivendell," rather than hear the story of Gil-galad, at least initially, they hear Bilbo's Eärendil poem.[41] Yet the substitute story that Strider tells, the story of Beren and Lúthien Tinúviel, is actually more appropriate than the Gil-galad story in providing for the reader, who is outside the main narrative, the necessary background for Bilbo's mythic poem.

Except for the greater attention given to the descriptive details of physical setting, the style of Strider's poem is, especially in its final stanza, reminiscent of the densely allusive and compressed emplotment that we encounter in the *Beowulf* inset verse narratives. After describing how the mortal Beren won the love of Lúthien, daughter of Thingol the Elf-king, the poem ends:

> *O'er stony mountains cold and grey,*
> *Through halls of iron and darkling door,*
> *And woods of nightshade morrowless.*
> *The Sundering Seas between them lay,*
> *And yet at last they met once more,*
> *And long ago they passed away*
> *In the forest singing sorrowless.* (*LOTR*, 189)

The presence of the uncomprehending hobbits allows Strider to give them (and the reader) an extended explanation of the larger context and later events in the story. Much suffering ultimately resulted from Beren and Lúthien's short-term success in taking from Morgoth one of the silmarils that was to be "the bride-price of Lúthien to Thingol" (*LOTR*, 189). Regarding the final lines, Strider explains:

> Yet at the last, Beren was slain by the Wolf that came from the gates of Angband, and he died in the arms of Tinúviel. But she chose mortality, and to die from the world, so that she might follow him; and it is sung that they met again beyond the Sundering Seas, and after a brief time walking alive once more in the green woods, together they passed, long ago, beyond the confines of this world. (*LOTR*, 189)

Strider also identifies Beren and Lúthien as the ancestors of both Elrond and "the Kings of Númenor," which we later find out is Strider's (i.e., Aragorn's) own lineage. This inset story thus implicitly identifies the world of the inset legendary narrative, despite the vast lapse of time, as the self-same world of the framing narrative, inhabited by the descendants of the legendary characters. During the later council at Rivendell, this continuity in worlds becomes still more explicit when Elrond identifies himself as an eye-witness to the fall of Gil-galad (*LOTR*, 237). But Strider's immediate explanation (*LOTR*, 189–90) also implies that when Bilbo later chooses to tell the story of Eärendil, the subject of his poem is the ancestor of both his host, Elrond, and Strider/Aragorn. Eärendil is, in fact, Elrond's father, and Eärendil's other son, the mortal Elros, is the ancestor of Aragorn. Moreover, Eärendil's wife, Elwing, is the granddaughter of Beren and Lúthien.[42] When Strider says, regarding the story of Beren and Lúthien, that "the end is not known," his statement bears two possible meanings. He could mean simply that knowledge of the complete legend has dropped from memory or that he realizes the story is ultimately still unfolding, even as he speaks. The larger narrative context implies both meanings. Thus, in telling the story of Eärendil, Bilbo is, in a sense, providing a sequel in continuity with Strider's story, while the main story implies that the subject of Bilbo's narrative also is part of a still ongoing action.

Upon his recovery after reaching Rivendell, Frodo is reunited with Bilbo, just when Bilbo claims to be nearing the completion of a new poem. He tells Elrond that he needs the help of Aragorn (Strider) to finish the poem. Elrond tells Bilbo to finish the poem so that the elves may hear it later in the evening and offer their judgment (*LOTR*, 224–25). This context then creates an awkward audience-response dynamic for the initial reception of Bilbo's heroic poem, because the immediate question that the elves are trying to answer in listening to the tale is, in effect, "Which parts of the poem were written by Bilbo and which parts did Aragorn add?" Readers first encounter the poem amid what Frodo takes to be a kind of waking dream, as he hears an initially unknown voice begin to chant:

> *Eärendil was a mariner*
> *that tarried in Arvernien;*
> *he built a boat of timber felled*
> *in Nimbrethil to journey in;*
> *her sails he wove of silver fair,*
> *of silver were her lanterns made,*
> *her prow was fashioned like a swan,*
> *and light upon her banners laid.* (*LOTR*, 227)

Like events in Aragorn's earlier poem, many of the events that Bilbo's poem mentions are explained in more detail in *Silmarillion*.[43] The most important details that Bilbo could presume to be part of his elvish listeners' knowledge include the following: that Eärendil came to possess one of the silmarils; that he attempted to sail to Valinor and succeeded only after he was joined by his wife, Elwing, who came to him in the form of a "great white bird," bringing the silmaril to him; and that Eärendil eventually became "an orbed star," "the Flammifer of Westerness" (*LOTR*, 230), bearing the light of the silmaril in the heavens and ultimately being decisive in the final battle against Morgoth.[44] In the same way that the story of Beren and Lúthien culminates in, as it were, an "exit" from the "circles of the world," the Eärendil story ends with a linear departure to the heavens. Both heroic legends, in this respect, seem to contrast with "The Man in the Moon," but like Bilbo's folk narrative, the Eärendil story seems to offer an etiological account, in this case concerning the star known as the "Flammifer of Westerness" (*LOTR*, 230), rather than the cycles of the moon.

The elves never get a direct answer to their somewhat academic question regarding which part of the poem is indebted to Aragorn, but Bilbo later tells Frodo:

> "As a matter of fact it was all mine. Except that Aragorn insisted on my putting in a green stone. He seemed to think it important. I don't know why. Otherwise he obviously thought the whole thing rather above my head, and he said that if I had the cheek to make verses about Eärendil in the house of Elrond, it was my affair. I suppose he was right." (*LOTR*, 231)

Only much later will readers discover that the "green stone," the elf-stone, is the token of Aragorn's own kingship. The presumption on Bilbo's part arises apparently from the fact that Eärendil is Elrond's father. But the most important point to notice here is the anticlimactic reception of the poem on all sides. On the one hand, the elves do not really respond to either the form or content of the poem. Their interests at that moment are, in fact, most similar to the kind expressed regarding *Beowulf* among early twentieth-century historical linguists.[45] On the other hand, Aragorn seems to dismiss the poem as presumptuous. Most striking of all, Bilbo agrees that a genuine understanding of the ostensible subject of his own poem is probably beyond him. What are we to make of this odd reception?

Although Bilbo has become capable of composing verse appropriate to heroic subjects of ancient legend, for him to do so involved reaching beyond his capacities or at least beyond the range of experiences that would be clearly intelligible to him as a hobbit. What then is Bilbo fitted for? He is suited for writing prose narrative like *The Hobbit*; a narrative composed, as it were, from a hobbit's-eye view and one that does not involve pretensions to greater knowledge than that to which a hobbit of his character and experience is capable. Bilbo's poetic abilities and narrative understanding remain closer to the self-understanding offered by Merry, after meeting with Aragorn and Gandalf in Gondor's Houses of Healing. Pippin reflects, "We Tooks and Brandybucks, we can't live long on the heights":

> "No," said Merry. "I can't. Not yet, at any rate. But at least, Pippin, we can now see them, and honour them. It is best to love first what you are fitted to love, I suppose: you must start somewhere and have some roots and the soil of the Shire is deep. Still there are things deeper and higher; and not a gaffer could tend his garden in what he calls peace but for them, whether he knows about them or not. I am glad that I know about them, a little. But I don't know why I am talking like this." (*LOTR*, 852)

Bilbo's development as a composer of stories culminates not in the mixed reception of his Eärendil poem but in the "big book with plain red leather covers," which he passes on to Frodo and which Frodo eventually gives to Sam, who, in turn, bequeaths the book to his descendants (*LOTR*, 1004, 1072). Because of his possession of the Ring, Bilbo lives for an exceptionally long time, even for a hobbit, and is, in fact, 128 years old when he performs his Eärendil poem. Few characters could offer a more striking contrast to the image of the adolescent artist that had become "hackneyed" during the decade before Tolkien wrote *The Hobbit* (between 1930 and 1932).[46] Rather than write "a novel of dazzling brilliance" before disappearing "into the Luminous Future," Bilbo's rather mediocre success in composing heroic poetry after years of apprenticeship suggests that he finds his calling in composing his own original (prose narrative) portion of what comes to be known as "The Red Book of Westmarch" (*LOTR*, 14). We thus get finally a portrait of the poet as an old hobbit who must settle for being a storyteller and who can happily depend on those after him to finish even that work.

FRIENDSHIP GIVING FICTIVE TIME

There are several other instances of inset narrative that we could have considered here, but I contend that these three particular episodes, in addition to presenting an implicit account of Bilbo's development as a poet, engage directly the three modern aesthetic assumptions described at the outset. First, Frodo's performance of Bilbo's "Man in the Moon" poem engages modern assumptions about artistic freedom. Then, in the truncated "Fall of Gil-galad" story and its substitute we encounter the inseparability of poetic art from ethical action. Finally, Bilbo's performance of his own version of the Eärendil myth reveals the gently ironic role of friendship in poetic composition. Ultimately, the dynamic framing of these inset narratives implies a view of time that offers an alternative to the modern assumption that reality consists of a strife between chaos and coercion.

In purporting to be an "original" composition, Bilbo's "Man in the Moon" poem comically depicts the modern privileging of artistic novelty—the work of an artist free from community. The fact that this most outlandish poem is arguably Bilbo's most successful, in terms of immediate audience response (it "tickled their fancy"; *LOTR*, 156), also suggests that such claims to originality often mirror the very tastes of the community from which the artist would purport to be free. If we also consider the topic of artistic freedom more broadly in *Lord of the Rings*, we can appreciate that Bilbo's poetry develops only through interaction with various social contexts, rather than erupting from an originary subjectivity. Nevertheless, there is a striking outward similarity between Stephen Dedalus and Bilbo Baggins. It could be argued that, like Stephen, who needs to leave Ireland, Bilbo becomes a poet only as a result of his leaving the Shire and undergoing the adventures recounted in *The Hobbit*, adventures that result in Bilbo losing his "respectability" in much of hobbit society. By the time we meet him again at the beginning of *Fellowship of the Ring*, Bilbo's exceptionally long life has resulted in a deepening sense of isolation from the wider community. The fact that Bilbo's creative capacities are sparked and fed by his sense of difference from the rest of the Shire seems to parallel directly the modernist insistence upon an opposition between the artist and the community from which the artist arises. But there is a crucial difference—much depends on the character of such opposition. The ambitions of an aspiring modernist like Stephen entail a rejection of the moral universe upon which his community is based—insisting upon the construction of his own alternative moral framework. By contrast, Bilbo's world has been enlarged, in the sense that he knows about and has engaged in conversation with beings (e.g., dragons and elves) whose very existence many in the Shire find doubtful. Clearly, both Bilbo and, to an even greater extent, Frodo, embody a critique of the provincialism that controls most hobbits' lives. Bilbo's constitution as a poet, however, does not require a wholesale rejection of the entire ethos of the Shire. His interaction with elves has given him a stance from which to see more clearly some of the foibles of his own kind, but the elvish perspective is never entirely his own. Most importantly, Bilbo's development as a poet does not depend upon a claim to be free from all moral order external to himself.

The truncated performances of the Gil-galad story, in addition to providing us with a glimpse of Bilbo as translator, also imply a direct connection between poetry and ethics. This point arises in two ways. On the one hand, Aragorn stops the second attempt to tell the Gil-galad story because of the close proximity of the Riders. Aragorn is not superstitious, as though he thought the story, or even the use of the name "Mordor," magically invoked the Enemy's power. If he had believed that, he would not have suggested that the story be told later, when they reach Rivendell. Rather, Aragorn's response reveals an understanding that the occasion of a story's performance is intrinsic to its moral bearing. Similarly, by offering the story of Beren and Lúthien in place of the fall of Gil-galad, Aragorn does so in the hope of lifting the hearts of the hobbits, that is, he hopes to strengthen the courage of the hobbits against the impending assault of the ringwraiths, who depend so much on fear. Against the modernist tendency to deny that poetry has any *telos* beyond itself, the framing of these stories results in two crucial implications, namely, that stories have an ethical trajectory and that such ethical bearing is not separable from the complex conditions involved in any given performance of a story. Tolkien thus implies that there is a direct connection between the good and the beautiful (enjoyment); however, the dynamics of the framing narrative imply that such a connection does not reside simply in a given aesthetic object as such but in the living action of a story's ongoing performance and reception.

Finally, Bilbo's experience in presenting his version of the Eärendil myth offers a direct contrast to the belief that friendship should be subordinated to aesthetic freedom. At one level, Bilbo explicitly acknowledges his need for Aragorn's help in finishing the poem. In a more crucial way, Aragorn's evaluation of the poem also helps Bilbo not to overestimate the worth of his own accomplishment. Aragorn openly warns Bilbo, as only a friend could, that his poem risks presumption. Likewise, the elves who hear the poem, in their lighthearted teasing of Bilbo for delighting possibly too much in his own poetry, offer to him (by means of their friendship) a kind of self-knowledge regarding his poetic abilities. At the same time, the overall trajectory of *Lord of the Rings* also presents friendship as not only the place for virtuous action but as constituting the "loom" and the "fabric," as it were, of poetic activity:

> Frodo went through his papers and writings with Sam, and he handed over his keys. There was a big book with plain red leather covers; its tall pages were now almost filled. At the beginning there were many leaves covered with Bilbo's thin wandering hand; but most of it was Frodo's firm flowing script. It was divided into chapters but Chapter 80 was unfinished and after that were some blank leaves....
>
> "Why, you have nearly finished it, Mr. Frodo!" Sam exclaimed. "Well, you have kept at it, I must say."
>
> "I have quite finished, Sam," said Frodo, "The last pages are for you." (*LOTR*, 1004)

In effect, Bilbo's first portion of the Red Book corresponds to the plot of *The Hobbit*, Frodo's portion corresponds to the events narrated in *Lord of the Rings*, while Sam and his descendants, among others, evidently composed the chronology and other materials that eventually appear in the appendices.[47] Partially because of his wider and deeper experience, Frodo is able to write of things that Bilbo cannot; the story remains, however, one narrated from a hobbit's-eye view, and even Frodo's writing requires more than his own wisdom can provide. He thus finally subtitles the book: "(as seen by the Little People; being the memoirs of Bilbo and Frodo of the Shire, supplemented by the accounts of *their friends and the learning of the Wise*.) Together with extracts from Books of Lore translated by Bilbo in Rivendell" (*LOTR*, 1004; emphasis added). The last sentence, along with comments from the prologue, suggest that Bilbo is the fictive "translator" and "editor" of the elvish lore presented in *Silmarillion*. Although Bilbo does not finish writing the Red Book, he takes the important step of beginning the project, and he is largely responsible for the literary education of both Frodo and Sam. Bilbo's development into a heroic-verse poet of moderate capacity is one of the necessary, but not sufficient, background causes that enable him, but also Frodo and Sam, to participate in composing what eventually becomes the "Red Book of Westmarch." The friendships between first Bilbo and Frodo and then Frodo and Sam are thus not only depicted in the narrative but become part of the metafictional means by which the story purportedly comes to us. Both the imaginary composition and preservation of the story thus arise in multiple ways from intergenerational friendships. At the same time, such shared work and enjoyment is not subordinated to but woven into the same fabric as Bilbo's translations and poetic compositions.

In the same way that the framing of these inset narratives challenges modern aesthetic assumptions, Tolkien's explicit account of the fantasy genre and his inset narrative practice both entail an alternative to the ontology informing that aesthetic. Tolkien defines "fantasy" as a genre that combines two human capacities: the ability to form "mental images of things not actually present," even of things not possibly present, and the capacity for what he calls "sub-creation," "the achievement of the expression which gives (or seems to give) 'the inner consistency of reality.'"[48] Tolkien is certainly a master at evoking such "inner consistency," but his fiction also connects his Secondary World to the Primary World of his implied readers. In this sense, *Lord of the Rings* arguably occupies a middle ground between what Tolkien calls "Chestertonian Fantasy," whose setting enables a humbling defamiliarization of the Primary World and a more strict kind of "fantasy" whose entire Secondary World is distinct from the Primary World but has "the inner consistency of reality."[49] This point is important because, as Tolkien points out, fantasy is "not primarily concerned with possibility, but with desirability."[50] Merely plausible possibility distinguishes fiction generally from the claims to actuality that attend historical narratives. The nature of such possibility underlies, for instance, Aristotle's use of the term "universal" to indicate what makes "poetry" superior to mere "history."[51] As Paul Ricoeur points out, "the universals a plot engenders are not Platonic ideas."[52] The universal claims of theoretical discourse can entail universal necessity or entail universal imperatives; by contrast, "poetic" or fictive universals involve a mere claim to plausible possibility: the claim that in a given situation, a certain kind of character would likely act in such and such a manner.

Nevertheless, to the extent that *Lord of the Rings* presents a self-consistent world that includes things "not actually present," the story does involve a key element of what Tolkien calls "fantasy." The Secondary World–making of fantasy "seeks shared enrichment, partners in making and delight, not slaves"; such making stands in contrast to what Tolkien calls "magic," which aims to effect "an alteration in the Primary World" through the "domination of things and wills."[53] In Tolkien's insistence upon the possibility of genuinely "shared enrichment," we glimpse the alternative account of reality that he assumes. For Tolkien, human art may be, but is not necessarily, a forceful imposition upon a fundamental chaos. He does not, of course, deny the existence of evil (or that art could be rooted in such coercion); he merely denies its ultimate reality; the fairy-tale genre, in his words, "does not deny the existence of *dyscatastrophe*, of sorrow and failure"; rather, "it denies (in the face of much evidence, if you will) universal defeat."[54] The root difference here is between understanding human art as a gift that results from being "made in the image and likeness of a Maker" or as a cunning attempt to wrest stability from the flux of reality.[55] Tolkien insists that art can (potentially) result in "shared enrichment" rather than the mere subjection of other wills and things; this insistence issues from a belief that the world inhabited by the human maker depends on the gratuitous character of reality as convivial harmony (contingent but fitting) rather than as either violent chaos or coerced order.

Whether Tolkien's fiction is consistent, in actual practice, with the explicit aims of such an ontology remains, however, an open question. According to Margaret Hiley, Tolkien's use of myth entails the subjection of the reader's world to the will of the author. She suggests that *Lord of the Rings* is potentially coercive because of the ways in which it configures the relationship first between the inset world of myth and the main narrative world and then between the world of the main narrative and that of the reader. At one level, Tolkien effectively gives myth the status of historical events internal to his fictional world. This is a problem because "myth" functions like ideology, being "the ultimate construct" that nevertheless "seeks to hide this [fact of its construction] by posing as what Barthes calls 'nature.'" Various modernists deployed language that was "stolen" (Barthes's term) from myth in order to make the claims in their own texts implicitly "cosmic" and "timeless," thereby stabilizing the world outside the self and imposing an order on temporal succession that would otherwise be random.[56] In this view, Tolkien's use of myth is more dangerous than customary modernist appropriations of myth because Tolkien's use of such "stolen language" is more covert. Tolkien's myth still might not, in itself, be a problem if his narrative did not also imply that the Secondary World of his story was continuous with the Primary World of the reader, as Hiley states: "This linking of the Secondary with the Primary World is also another mythic attempt to hide the constructed nature of the Secondary World. If it poses as a kind of prehistory of our own world, it is less obviously imaginary; it claims to be nature. And thus it claims validity in our world."[57]

The root of the difficulty in Hiley's own argument becomes apparent when she claims that myth functions to impose order on an otherwise random series of temporal moments. Such an idea of "empty time" presumes the modern capacity to disregard ourselves, to adopt the view from nowhere and to know what time is like when no intelligence is present. In effect, her argument presumes that the violence of imposing order upon such chaos is the founding violence of human culture. Thus, as Hiley admits, Barthes's structuralist theory of myth, "which itself is presented as an absolute method of analysis, is of course open to the same criticism he directs at myth. This is a problem in much of structuralist analysis."[58] Several implications follow from such a statement. First, it presumes that a claim to "universality" in a fictional text (myth) is identical to "universality" in a theoretical discourse ("absolute method"). Second, by deploying a structuralist critique of Tolkien's writing, despite the acknowledged incoherence of the judgments that structuralism purports to enable, the analysis arguably involves as much interpretive violence as that which is imputed to Tolkien. Such violence in this case, however, is not a problem (according to Hiley) but is merely a necessary aspect to any cultural ordering amid the chaos of temporal succession. Thus, to fault Tolkien for creating a Secondary World that purports to "encompass" the Primary World,[59] according to the claims of such an argument, is simply to choose the totalizing claims of structuralism over the supposedly totalizing claims of Tolkien's mythical narrative.

But does Tolkien's story really involve such an imposition upon the Primary World? The failure to distinguish between fictional and theoretical universality underlies the failure to understand that the link between Tolkien's fictive world and the Primary World is one of mere possibility. Hiley seems to acknowledge this distinction, but misses the point, when she cites Tolkien's claim that events in *Lord of the Rings* occur in "a purely imaginary (though not wholly impossible) period of antiquity."[60] To which Hiley responds: "Is the spatial dimension therefore real while the temporal one is not?"[61] The problem here is that a story regarding possible events imagined to occur in the "real world" (spatially) is simply a definition of fiction generally, as distinct from historical narration. In effect, if we seriously grant Hiley's claim that Tolkien subsumes the Primary World in his fictional world, then the "Man in the Moon" episode would implicitly claim to offer a historical account of the origins of that particular nursery rhyme in the Primary World. Such a view, I submit, misconstrues the episode in a profound way. The capacity of that inset story and its frame to provoke genuine readerly reflection regarding the history of nursery rhymes or language generally in the Primary World subsists in the status of the narrative event as a universal fictive possibility, not in a purported claim to be a historical account. Hiley acknowledges that what Tolkien calls "magic," a technique for altering the Primary World through the "domination of things and wills," "would seem to correspond exactly with Barthes's characterization of myth [as that] which distorts the perception of the primary world to gain authority."[62] She similarly admits that in Tolkien's view fantasy, by contrast, "seeks shared enrichment, partners in making and delight, not slaves,"[63] but she dismisses the attempt to make such a distinction:

> This is a pleasant theory, but it proves difficult to work in practice. Tolkien himself stated that in creating a Secondary World, "as you are the master your whim is law."[64] Can this master really have "partners in making"? Indeed, as Tolkien's Secondary World in its mythic character reaches out to encompass the Primary World as well, this perhaps places him closer to the authoritarian magician than he would have been comfortable with.[65]

At one level, such a dismissal merely announces that there is no alternative to the ontology of chaos and coercion. More importantly, the line quoted from *Sauron Defeated*, "your whim is law," concerns specifically the operation of what Tolkien describes as the capacity to form "images of things not actually present." Such imaginative making pertains specifically to the creation of a fictional subcreated world, precisely not to the links between the fictional world and the Primary World. In effect, *Lord of the Rings* presents a possible antiquity, the very imagining of which enriches the Primary World of the present, not by controlling it or by providing definitive etiological myths, but by defamiliarizing the commonplace elements shared within the fictively continuous world of text and reader.

Ultimately, we find the most subtle evidence for Tolkien's rejection of the chaos-coercion ontology in the view of time implied by his framing of inset narratives. At one level, there is the simple fact of

Bilbo's age, the fact that he is an "old hobbit" rather than a "young man." Bilbo undergoes a long apprenticeship before composing his own heroic-verse narrative. In a still larger sense, the intergenerational friendships that fictionally give rise to the main narrative involve prolonged temporal development. In fact, the whole temporal process in *Lord of the Rings* is for Bilbo a gift, including his work of translation. In a literal sense, Bilbo finally bequeaths all of his writing, both compositions and translations, as a gift to Frodo. Bilbo's verse narrative compositions are also "elvish" in the sense that they offer to others the gift of shared enjoyment. Insofar as the main narrative of the Secondary World identifies itself as dependent on the "Red Book of Westmarch," Tolkien's fictions claim no more control over the Primary World than do Bilbo's inset narratives over their respective fictive audiences. By contrast, as Tolkien explains in one of his letters, "the basic motive" for the use of "magic" by characters like Sauron is to annihilate time: to reduce "to a minimum (or vanishing point)" "the gap between the idea or desire and the result or effect."[66] If time is merely chaotic flux, then its elimination is only the necessary triumph of order. What drops from consideration, of course, is the possibility of an order that is not coerced. Tolkien's particular use of inset narrative foregrounds rather than conceals the status of myth as a work of human imagination, but it also foregrounds the gift of temporal order out of which such narrative compositions arise. The emphatically extended temporal character of both Bilbo's poetic development and of the metafictional account of the friendships that shape the Red Book stories imply that, because reality is a gift, time is more than a series of empty homogenous moments. In this way, the very relation between the framing narrative and the inset stories implies that time, as an aspect of reality, is an ordering condition for poetic composition. What is ultimately most remarkable about the achievement of Tolkien's narrative invention is the capacity to locate an entire subcreated fictional world in a realm of imagined ancient possibility. Tolkien's depiction of the poet as an old hobbit implies that the gift of time uniquely enables—as a necessary but not sufficient cause—both the conviviality and the *poiesis*, both the ale and the song, imagined throughout *Fellowship of the Ring*.

NOTES

1. Two notable instances of such criticism would be Chance and Siewers, *Tolkien's Modern Middle Ages*, and Honegger and Weinreich, *Tolkien and Modernity*. The essays in these collections are consistent with the general tendency not to consider that Tolkien's relation to "modernity," however defined, hinges upon differences in ontology.

2. Without presuming to define either of these fraught terms in a comprehensive or prescriptive manner, I take "modernity" to refer to a broad set of cultural habits and material conditions ultimately rooted in the attempt to master fortune by singular reliance upon human calculation. By contrast, I use "modern*ism*" to indicate a slightly more specific cluster of early twentieth-century artistic attempts to address the personal and social consequences of modernity. If one were to insist upon historical points of reference, the term "modern," as I use it here, could be identified with a set of intellectual and broadly cultural developments that became manifest in Europe between the fourteenth and early seventeenth centuries and whose effects continue to the present. This would include everything from the Petrarchan turn to the subject to the Newtonian mechanism to the Enclosures Act to Henry Ford. The terms modern*ist* and modern*ism* indicate a smaller but more contestable range of early twentieth-century artistic and literary trends. These terms enable only the most general historical distinctions and do not imply that either modernity or modernism names a homogenous movement. For a broader discussion of the fissures within so-called literary modernism, in relation to both modern philosophical assumptions and postmodernism, see Thornton, *Antimodernism*.

3. Such a view of reality is, of course, an ancient view that modernity revives. My account of modernity has been influenced by the work of John Milbank and David B. Hart. In *Theology and Social Theory*, Milbank contends that "a hidden thread of continuity between antique reason and modern, secular reason" is "the theme of original violence" (5)—a coercion that establishes cultural and social order against the presumed reality of a threatening chaos (cf. 259–325). In *Beauty of the Infinite*, Hart explains how such an ontological binary continues to inform postmodern accounts of aesthetics and ethics (35–93). In this regard, literary modernism often radicalized certain features of early modern philosophy and similarly informs much of what passes for "postmodern" philosophy. One direct connection between literary modernism and postmodern philosophy appears, for example, in Jacques Derrida's acknowledgment of his debt to Joyce: "Every time I write, and even in the most academic pieces of work, Joyce's ghost is always coming on board" (see "Two Words for Joyce," 149). My argument here, however, does not require (or offer) a position regarding the debate between those critics who "claim Joyce for deconstruction" and those who "see his works as involving discernible values and presenting a critique of the

modernist-postmodernist-deconstructionist mentality" (see Thornton, *Anti-modernism*, 21).

4. An account of Tolkien's positive alternative to modern ontology appears in the final section of this essay.

5. In what follows, I use the word "poetry" (and related terms) in a pre-Romantic sense to indicate "imaginative writing" generally and not lyric poetry, or even verse, exclusively. See, for example, Aristotle, *Poetics*, 1447b.

6. See Shippey, *Road to Middle-earth*, 126–32, and his more recent *J. R. R. Tolkien*, 310, respectively.

7. Shippey, *J. R. R. Tolkien*, 310.

8. Hiley, "Stolen Language," 838. The phrase "mythical method" is from Eliot, *Selected Prose*, 177.

9. Hiley, "Stolen Language," 839–41.

10. Ibid., 841–42.

11. Ibid., 847–53.

12. I use the term *legendarium* to indicate the constellation of connected mythic stories Tolkien composed, including those in *Silmarillion* and those in the posthumously published *History of Middle-earth* series.

13. Beebe, "Artist as Hero," 341. For a more detailed account of *Portrait*'s relation to the existing Bildungsroman tradition and the irony inherent in such apprenticeship fiction, see Thornton, *Antimodernism*, 65–81.

14. Huxley, *Crome Yellow*, 30–31.

15. Booth, *Rhetoric of Fiction*, 333.

16. See, for example, Joyce, *Portrait*, 204–16; cf. Booth, *Rhetoric of Fiction*, 328–36.

17. Joyce, *Portrait*, 246.

18. Ibid., 204–5.

19. Cf. Buttigieg, *"Portrait of the Artist,"* 103.

20. Aristotle, *Poetics*, 1453a.

21. Ricoeur, *Time and Narrative*, 59.

22. Although Tolkien's fiction embodies, I contend, a particular continuity between the temporal fields of human artistry and ethical action, I am indebted to Ricoeur's *Time and Narrative* for developing this point in a general way (e.g., 40–48).

23. Buttigieg, *"Portrait of the Artist,"* 68–108.

24. Joyce, *Portrait*, 247.

25. As I suggest above, one interpretive difficulty here (which does not need to be resolved for the present argument) arises from the fact that Joyce's ironic treatment of Stephen was not widely acknowledged by critics until after the publication of *Ulysses*, or *Stephen Hero*, if even then. Cf. Booth, *Rhetoric of Fiction*, 330–36, and Hugh Kenner, "The *Portrait* in Perspective," in *James*

Joyce: Two Decades of Criticism, augmented ed., ed. Seon Givens (New York: Vanguard, 1963), 132–74.

26. For example, in *Heart of Darkness*, Conrad's main narrator of the framing story describes the teller of the inset story, Marlow, as one for whom "the meaning of an episode was not inside like a kernel but outside, enveloping a tale which brought it out only as a glow brings out a haze, in the likeness of one of these misty halos that sometimes are made visible by the spectral illumination of moonshine" (Conrad, *Heart of Darkness*, 68). In effect, Conrad radicalizes the form of inset narrative by implying a maximal importance for the frame in its relationship to the inset story, even as he minimizes the size of such a framing narrative.

27. Tolkien, "Beowulf," 31.

28. See, respectively, Leyerle, "Interlace Structure of *Beowulf*," and West, "Interlace Structure of *The Lord of the Rings*."

29. West, "Interlace," 79.

30. For an account similar to my ensuing argument here, regarding how Tolkien draws upon the "digressions" in *Beowulf* as a model for intertextuality in his own fiction, see Nagy, "The Great Chain of Reading."

31. Several of the poems throughout *LOTR* appear also in Tolkien, *Adventures of Tom Bombadil*. The relationship between these poems and their narrative contexts in *LOTR* warrants a separate study. *LOTR* shall designate Tolkien, *The Lord of the Rings*.

32. See, respectively, *LOTR*, 99, 104, 72, 76.

33. For a detailed defense of Tolkien's poetry, see Geoffrey Russom, "Tolkien's Versecraft in *The Hobbit* and *The Lord of the Rings*," in *J. R. R. Tolkien and His Literary Resonances: Views of Middle-earth*, eds. George Clark and Daniel Timmons (Westport, CT: Greenwood, 2000), 53–69.

34. Tolkien, *The Hobbit*, 325–26.

35. Shippey, *Road to Middle-earth*, 140–41.

36. For a detailed discussion of some important connections between these various parts and versions of this lyric poem, see Shippey, *Road to Middle-earth*, 139–44.

37. Honegger, in "Man in the Moon," 46, cites the version of the rhyme given in Opie and Opie, *Oxford Book of Nursery Rhymes*, 213. I have altered line 2 in keeping with a version recalled from my own memory.

38. Opie and Opie, *Oxford Book of Nursery Rhymes*, 203. For a detailed historical account of Tolkien's possible sources and the development of variations in the Man in the Moon stories, see Honegger, "Man in the Moon."

39. For example, Virgil's career of poetic development "from the pastoral *Eclogues* and *Georgics* to the epic *Aeneid*" arguably provided a model for multiple Renaissance poets, according to Rosenberg (*Oaten Reeds and Trumpets*, 17).

40. Revealingly, Tolkien reports that, in his own experience as a child, he had been "insensitive to poetry, and skipped it if it came in tales." He developed a capacity to enjoy poetry, however, through the study of Latin and Greek, "and especially through being made to try and translate English verse into classical verse" (see Tolkien, "On Fairy-Stories," 135). This development also seems to suggest a parallel to Bilbo's experience.

41. During the council at Rivendell, Elrond does discuss, speaking as an eye-witness, Gil-galad and the "Last Alliance of Elves and Men"; however, readers are never given a direct account of the battles involved (*LOTR*, 236–39). Still later, readers are told that the hobbits hear many other stories, including the full account of the story of Beren and Lúthien, but this general mention of other stories is the closest that we ever come to an explicit suggestion that the hobbits hear the full story regarding Gil-galad.

42. Cf. Tolkien, *Silmarillion*, 162–87, 306. As Elrond later explains to Frodo during the council at Rivendell: "Eärendil was my sire, who was born in Gondolin before its fall; and my mother was Elwing, daughter of Dior, Son of Lúthien of Doriath" (*LOTR*, 237). A fuller account of the ancestry is given in *Silmarillion*, where the larger correspondence between the marriage of Beren to Lúthien and that of Aragorn to Arwen becomes more apparent; like Lúthien of old, Arwen chooses mortality.

43. Tolkien, *Silmarillion*, 246–55. The fact that the first and only instance of Bilbo's own heroic verse narrative compositions that we encounter fully as readers concerns Eärendil helps to sharpen the sense of parallel between Bilbo's and Tolkien's respective artistic developments. In Tolkien's case, his encounter with two lines from the Old English poem *Crist* regarding "Earendel, brightest of angels" inspired him to compose a short poem titled "The Voyage of Earendel the Evening Star." That short poem eventually became the "Lay of Earendel," which, in turn, contained the seeds for much of the mythology that became Middle-earth. See Carpenter, *J. R. R. Tolkien*, 64–71.

44. Tolkien, *Silmarillion*, 252.

45. See, for example, Tolkien, "Beowulf," 6, where he responds to Archibald Strong, who claims that *Beowulf* is primarily interesting as "an important historical document."

46. Chance, "*Lord of the Rings*," xi.

47. The prologue to *Fellowship of the Ring* presents a fascinating "manuscript history" of the "Red Book of Westmarch," which is alleged to be the main "source" for the history of the War of the Ring. To that original (and now lost) volume of Bilbo's and Frodo's memoirs (known as simply the "Red Book") was "annexed" and bound in "a single red case" Bilbo's "three large volumes" of translated elvish lore that he had given to Frodo. To these was later added a fifth volume "containing commentary, genealogies, and various other matter concerning hobbit members of the Fellowship" (*LOTR*, 14). These five volumes to-

gether comprised the "Red Book of Westmarch," a complete and most important transcript of which survived only as a result of a scribe in Gondor being commissioned by Pippin's great-grandson to make an exact copy of the text that Pippin had taken with him "when he retired to Gondor" (*LOTR*, 14).

48. Tolkien, "On Fairy-Stories," 138–39.

49. Ibid., 138–47.

50. Ibid., 134.

51. Aristotle, *Poetics*, 1451b.

52. Ricoeur, *Time and Narrative*, 41.

53. Tolkien, "On Fairy-Stories," 143. As Tolkien explains in the same passage, "at the heart of many man-made stories of the elves lies, open or concealed, pure or alloyed, the desire for a living, realised sub-creative art, which (however much it may outwardly resemble it) is inwardly wholly different from the greed for self-centered power which is the mark of the mere Magician."

54. Tolkien, "On Fairy-Stories," 153.

55. Ibid., 145.

56. Hiley, "Stolen Language," 841–43.

57. Ibid., 854; cf. 845–51.

58. Ibid., 858.

59. Ibid., 857

60. Tolkien, quoted in Carpenter, *Inklings*, 98.

61. Hiley, "Stolen Language," 853.

62. Ibid., 857.

63. Tolkien, "On Fairy-Stories," 143.

64. Tolkien, *Sauron Defeated*, Vol. 2 of *The History of Middle-earth* (Boston: Houghton Mifflin, 1992), 240.

65. Hiley, "Stolen Language," 857.

66. Tolkien, *Letters*, 200.

BIBLIOGRAPHY

Aristotle. *Poetics*. Translated by James Hutton. New York: Norton, 1982.

Barthes, Roland. *Mythologies*. Translated by Jonathan Cape. London: Vintage, 1993.

Beebe, Maurice. "The Artist as Hero." Reprinted in *A Portrait of the Artist as a Young Man*, edited by Chester G. Anderson, 340–57. New York: Penguin, 1968.

Booth, Wayne. *The Rhetoric of Fiction*. Chicago: University of Chicago Press, 1961.

Buttigieg, Joseph A. "*A Portrait of the Artist*" *in Different Perspective*. Athens: Ohio University Press, 1987.

Carpenter, Humphrey. *The Inklings: C.S. Lewis, J.R.R. Tolkien, Charles Williams, and Their Friends.* Boston: Houghton Mifflin, 1979.

———. *J.R.R. Tolkien: A Biography* (1977). London: Allen & Unwin, 1988.

Chance, Jane. *"The Lord of the Rings": The Mythology of Power.* New York: Twayne, 1992.

Chance, Jane, and Alfred K. Siewers, eds. *Tolkien's Modern Middle Ages.* New York: Palgrave, 2005.

Conrad, Joseph. *Heart of Darkness/The Secret Sharer.* New York: Signet, 1910.

Derrida, Jacques. "Two Words for Joyce." Translated by Geoff Bennington. In *Post-Structuralist Joyce: Essays from the French*, edited by Derek Attridge and Daniel Ferrer, 145–60. Cambridge: Cambridge University Press, 1984.

Eliot, T.S. *Selected Prose of T.S. Eliot.* Edited by Frank Kermode. London: Faber and Faber, 1963.

Emig, Rainer. *Modernism in Poetry.* London: Longman, 1995.

Hart, David B. *The Beauty of the Infinite: The Aesthetics of Christian Truth.* Grand Rapids, MI: Eerdmans, 2003.

Hiley, Margaret. "Stolen Language, Cosmic Models: Myth and Mythology in Tolkien." *Modern Fiction Studies* 50, no. 4 (2004): 838–60.

Honegger, Thomas. "The Man in the Moon: Structural Depth in Tolkien." In *Root and Branch: Approaches towards Understanding Tolkien*, edited by Thomas Honegger, 9–76. Zurich: Walking Tree, 1999.

Honegger, Thomas, and Weinreich, Frank, eds. *Tolkien and Modernity.* 2 vols. Zurich: Walking Tree, 2006.

Huxley, Aldous. *Crome Yellow.* New York: Harper, 1922.

Joyce, James. *A Portrait of the Artist as Young Man* (1916). Edited by Chester G. Anderson. New York: Penguin, 1968.

Leyerle, John. "The Interlace Structure of *Beowulf*." *University of Toronto Quarterly* 37 (1967): 1–17.

Milbank, John. *Theology and Social Theory: Beyond Secular Reason.* Oxford: Blackwell, 1993.

Nagy, Gergely. "The Great Chain of Reading: (Inter)textual Relations and the Technique of Mythopoiesis in the Túrin Story." In *Tolkien the Medievalist*, edited by Jane Chance, 239–58. London: Routledge, 2003.

Opie, Iona, and Peter Opie, eds. *The Oxford Book of Nursery Rhymes.* 2nd ed. Oxford: Clarendon, 1952.

Ricoeur, Paul. *Time and Narrative.* Vol. 1. Translated by Kathleen McLaughlin and David Pellauer. Chicago: University of Chicago Press, 1984–1988.

Rosenberg, D.M. *Oaten Reeds and Trumpets: Pastoral Epic in Virgil, Spenser, and Milton.* Lewisburg, PA: Bucknell University Press, 1981.

Shippey, T.A. *J.R.R. Tolkien: Author of the Century.* Boston: Houghton Mifflin, 2000.

———. *The Road to Middle-earth.* Boston: Houghton Mifflin, 1983.

Thornton, Weldon. *The Antimodernism of Joyce's "Portrait of the Artist as a Young Man."* Syracuse, NY: Syracuse University Press, 1994.

Tolkien, J. R. R. *The Adventures of Tom Bombadil* (1961). London: Allen & Unwin, 1975.

———. "Beowulf: The Monsters and the Critics." In *The Monsters and the Critics and other Essays*, edited by Christopher Tolkien, 5–48. London: Allen & Unwin, 1983.

———. *The Hobbit, or There and Back Again* (1966). Boston: Houghton Mifflin, 1996.

———. *The Letters of J. R. R. Tolkien*. Edited by Humphrey Carpenter with the assistance of Christopher Tolkien. Boston: Houghton Mifflin, 1981.

———. *The Lord of the Rings* (1966). Boston: Houghton Mifflin, 1994.

———. "On Fairy-Stories." In *The Monsters and the Critics and Other Essays*, edited by Christopher Tolkien, 109–61. London: Allen & Unwin, 1983.

———. *The Silmarillion*. 2nd ed. Edited by Christopher Tolkien. Boston: Houghton Mifflin, 1999.

West, Richard C. "The Interlace Structure of *The Lord of the Rings*." In *A Tolkien Compass*, edited by Jared Lobdell, 77–94. La Salle, IL: Open Court, 1975.

CHAPTER 6

POURING NEW WINE
INTO OLD BOTTLES

Tolkien, Joyce, and the Modern Epic

Dominic Manganiello

The Lord of the Rings and *Ulysses* are perhaps the two most influential novels of the twentieth century, and yet they have never received any extended comparative analysis. The very idea of placing the name of Tolkien beside that of Joyce struck some literary critics for decades as an incongruous, even "blasphemous" proposition.[1] Detractors still tend to look down on the Oxford writer as a mere dabbler who has been completely overshadowed by the towering Irish canonical modernist. But as Tolkien's stature continues to grow, such negative judgments seem increasingly wide of the mark, and they are beginning to recede into the background. With the renewal of academic interest in this prominent member of the Inklings, the time is now ripe to examine together the major works of these two epochal writers. When *Lord of the Rings* first appeared in 1954–1955, it generated, "on a modest scale," as R. J. Reilly put it, the kind of critical controversy that accompanied the publication of *Ulysses* in 1922.[2] Since the "trilogy" did not fit any preconceived categories, Tolkien was generally credited with almost single-handedly inventing the fantasy genre. Like *Ulysses*, moreover, *Lord of the Rings* compelled readers to reconsider, among other subjects, the relationship between epic and novel. Although both modern writers were similarly engaged in updating the oldest of literary forms, they took up their task from opposing angles. In *Ulysses*, Joyce famously presented the artist as a "counter-creator"[3] who constructs "the epic of a world abandoned by God,"[4] but in *Lord of the Rings*, Tolkien revived the familiar trope of the world as a book written by human scribes or "sub-creators" and glossed by the hand of providence. The decentered universe of *Ulysses* bears the imprint of an ironic spirit that calls everything into doubt, whereas the cosmic order of *Lord of the Rings* retains discernible traces of a divine signature inscribed upon it. In his fiction, Tolkien responded to the challenges modernity posed in the first part of the twentieth century as a result of political and social upheaval, but he did so without subscribing to the aesthetic ideology of modernism or adopting the stance of ironist in the way Joyce had done. Tolkien's paradigm of collaborative authorship thus serves to deflect the antitheological bias of Joyce's exclusively human comedy. From these antithetical approaches to *mythopoeia* other key differences in outlook between the two writers emerge. In what follows, I will focus, in particular, on a distinctive feature of these landmark novels: the depiction of the hero.

THE BOOK AND THE WORLD

In *A Portrait of the Artist as a Young Man*, Joyce introduced the well-known figure of the godlike artist who remains not only "within" *but also* "above his handiwork."[5] Both immanent and transcendent, this indifferent deity reappears in *Ulysses*, now cast in a decidedly negative light. During his discourse in the library, Stephen Dedalus pictures God, for example, as a flawed Shakespearean playwright who wrote the folio of this world quite badly.[6] Unable to decipher God's poor calligraphy, Stephen claims that he can nevertheless detect the "criminal thumbprint on the haddock" of the "hangman god" who demands cruel sacrifices from his creatures.[7] Ironically, this malevolent demiurge gradually withdraws from his defective creation, leaving behind a "god-shaped hole" to fill.[8] The literary genius therefore "reoccupies" the position vacated by God, to use Hans Blumenberg's phrase,[9] acting as the new "standard of all experience, material and moral."[10] By setting himself up as a rival maker, Stephen adopts the rebellious stance of Joyce, as Marilyn French observes:

> Joyce, the arrogant seer, ate the apple of the knowledge of good and evil, read God's book, the world, and became himself a god. Then Joyce, the arrogant creator, made his world, careful to reproduce symbolically what he had "found in the world without as actual."[11]

The epiphany of the *atheos absconditus*, a hidden, nonexistent God, *prompted* the author of *Ulysses*, in other words, to construct his fictional universe upon the incertitude of the Void.[12]

The world as book remains the principal image in *Ulysses*, but Joyce inflects it so as to undermine the conventional trope. The metaphor of the rhizome rather than the tree, Deleuze and Guattari maintain, best describes Joyce's revision of the biblical model. The modern "radicle-text," which adopts the synthetic logic of the "and," subverts the totalizing impulse of the classical "root-book," which follows the binary logic of the "either-or."[13] As a "rhizomatic" novel with "multiple roots" in ancient myth, *Ulysses* parodies the cultural coherence of the Middle Ages by replacing it with the "chaos" of modernity.[14] All myths are relative in Joyce's novel, as in James Frazer's *The Golden Bough*; Christianity holds no claim to uniqueness or truth. Umberto Eco puts the matter succinctly: "If you take away the transcendent God from the symbolic world of the Middle Ages, you have the world of Joyce."[15] Instead of Dante's paradigmatic concentric circles that revolve around a divine center, Joyce presents "an inconstant series of concentric circles of varying gradations of light and shadow" in order to disclose a decentered universe.[16] The Joycean signatory of this fragmented book competes with the primal divine *fiat*, having remade the world in the author's own image and likeness by way of the aesthetics of "chaosmos."

In sharp contrast, Tolkien returned to an arborescent model of literature, envisaging a Tree of Tales on whose manifold branches countless leaves burgeon. Writing about the *rooted* works that appeared in the "encyclopaedic" fourteenth century, he marveled at the skill of medieval authors in giving "new life to old tales." They succeeded—despite some spillage—in pouring the "new wine" of Christian theology into the "old bottles" of folk traditions.[17] Although similarly inspired to "make it new," Tolkien as a modern fantasy writer believed that he should resist the "anxiety to be original" that obsessed his modernist contemporaries. The fantasist returns to what is already given in order to "make something new"; he never creates anything *de novo.* His subcreation is therefore founded upon the observance of "fact," on the "hard recognition that things are so in the world as it appears under the sun." Storymaking is a natural human activity because, as Tolkien himself delcared, we make in a "derivative mode"; that is, "we are made: and not only made, but made in the image and likeness of a Maker."[18] In this way, Tolkien restores the biblical connectedness between *homo faber* and his creator, the link that Joyce had severed.[19]

Tolkien also retains the traditional image of the world as a great book in which human characters cooperate freely with the plot devised by the "supreme Artist and Author of Reality."[20] *Lord of the Rings* dramatizes the distinction Northrop Frye draws between competing scriptures: "secular scripture tells us that we are creators; [sacred scripture] tell[s] us that we are actors in a drama of divine creation and redemption."[21] Sam Gamgee, for example, registers the crucial point that the heroes of old did not seek adventures in order to relieve the boredom of their prosaic lives: "Folk seem to have been just landed in them, usually—their paths were laid that way" (*LOTR,* 696).[22] They were content to play a small part in a larger story not of their own making. That is why, as Frodo Baggins adds, the great tales never end (*LOTR,* 697).

The paradoxical idea of coming to terms with a conclusive end in an ongoing saga helps to explain why many readers continue to find *Lord of the Rings* an "exciting story."[23] The theology at work behind Tolkien's metaphysical vision can perhaps best be elucidated by Chesterton's remarks on narrative:

> To a Christian existence is a *story*, which may end up in any way. In a thrilling novel (that purely Christian product) the hero is not

eaten by cannibals; but it is essential to the existence of the thrill that he *might* be eaten by cannibals. The hero must (so to speak) be an eatable hero.[24]

The drama of personal choice makes a story exciting because it contains the potent element "of what theology calls free will."[25] Just as Frodo freely accepts the onus of the Ring at the Council of Elrond, so too he freely (albeit not without enormous pressure from Sauron and the Ring itself) rejects it on Mount Doom: "I do not choose to do what I came to do. I will not do this deed" (*LOTR*, 924). This apparently negative climax reflects another salient aspect of the Christian understanding of time and history: "Life (according to the faith) is very like a serial story in a magazine: life ends with the promise (or menace) 'to be continued in our next.'"[26]

Tolkien provides an apt image of this open-ended ending in the final pages of *Lord of the Rings*, where a big book with plain red covers is prominently on display. Having begun to write in it, Bilbo and Frodo leave one chapter unfinished for Sam to fill in (*LOTR*, 1003–4). Though immersed in the writing of their little pilgrim stories, the principal hobbits are free agents who feel, at the same time, that another hand, that of providence itself, both "writes" and is "written of," however tacitly, in the telling. Their individual chapters are continually glossed by the author and finisher of an open-ended story, which is ever ancient and ever new. Even when minor characters falter, the episode turns out well; for the divine chronicler writes straight with crooked lines. Thus does the narrative of *Lord of the Rings* describe an epic of a world still cared for by the storyteller.

HEROES BIG AND SMALL

The myriad tellers of the eighteen chapters that constitute *Ulysses* are often unreliable, as are the oscillating perspectives they provide on the main character, Leopold Bloom. The instability of narration prompted Marilyn French, among other critics, to suggest that Joyce grounded his entire novel on an "uncertainty principle": "There is no fixed style, no fixed narrational point of view, and even the structure moves inconstantly. The inconstancy of the characters is a micro-cosmic analogy to that of the world which is the novel. *Ulysses* is an epic of relativity."[27] The relativization of styles in *Ulysses* reflects an underlying moral relativism that accounts for the new kind of hero that Joyce plans to introduce.

To achieve this aim, Joyce transports Homer's Odysseus to twentieth-century Ireland, having him walk the streets of Dublin in the person of Bloom. Even though the "dreary sameness" of every-day life seems far removed from the exciting world of epic romance with its clanking mail and halo-like gallantry, Joyce claimed that the modern age exudes a unique aura of its own.[28] Thus does Bloom's mental odyssey take but a single day, as his most commonplace actions contribute to the "great human comedy in which each has share" down the ages.[29] The parallel *Ulysses* sets up between con-temporaneity and antiquity through the so-called mythical method[30] forms part of a larger redemptive vision, according to David Lodge:

> The representation of a demythologized world, a world "fallen into the quotidian" (Heidegger's phrase) is thus ingeniously redeemed by allusion to the lost mythical world—aesthetically redeemed by our perception of the structure, and spiritually redeemed by our perception of human continuity between the two worlds.[31]

Although Joyce foregrounds the qualities that Bloom holds in com-mon with the rest of humanity, Lodge seems not to notice that he does so by transvaluing the values associated with traditional epic heroism.

As a young man, Joyce once asked, quoting Wagner's *Parsifal*, "Who is good?"[32] but later insisted that his modern Ulysses should be construed as a "good man." He conceived of Bloom as a "com-plete all-around character," but not in the sense of being ideal.[33] "Life we must accept as we see it before our eyes, men and women as we meet them in the real world, not as we apprehend them in the world of faery," Joyce affirmed.[34] A true-to-life portrait allows the observer to see the subject from all sides and in *chiaroscuro*. One of the periph-eral characters in *Ulysses*, Lenehan, unwittingly underlines this point with his remark, "He's a cultured allroundman . . . there's a touch of the artist about old Bloom."[35] The implicit irony lies in the fact that at the time this compliment is paid to Bloom, he is out of earshot browsing through some racy reading material in a bookstall. The scene is emblematic of the novel's approach to the hero's ambiguous sexual conduct. Bloom never strives for moral perfection, as the ancient Greeks or later Christians would understand the concept. Instead of imitating Odysseus's gentlemanly behavior towards Nausicaa in Homer, for example, Bloom becomes sexually aroused by Gerty MacDowell (the Irish counterpart to the young Greek princess) and "literally worship[s] at the shrine" of her sexuality.[36] Through this act of idolatrous transgression, Bloom remains, paradoxically, a "decent" man since, by the end of the episode, he once again shows kindness to his fellow human beings.[37]

Yet Bloom's alleged honesty must be set in the context of the Western moral tradition that he seeks at once to recapitulate and overcome. Like Diogenes in the ancient world before him, Blaise Pascal in the seventeenth century, for example, had expressed a desire to find "an all-round good man."[38] The French philosopher understood the concept of honesty to imply an adherence both to a code of honor and to moral uprightness. His *honnête homme* was cognizant of the fact that "no one is good but God only" (Luke 18:19). This meant, as St. Augustine explained, that "we were created good by the Good; for 'God made man upright' [Eccles. 7:9], but by our own free will, we became evil."[39] Drawing on this biblical exegesis, John Newton in the late eighteenth century glossed Alexander Pope's admired line in his *Essay on Man*, "an honest man's the noblest work of God," as follows:

A Christian is the noblest work of God in this visible world, and bears a much brighter impression of his glory and goodness than the sun in the firmament. And none but a Christian can be strictly and properly honest: all others are too much under the power of self to do universally to others as they would others should do unto them, and nothing but a uniform conduct upon this principle deserves the name of honesty.[40]

Ulysses departs from this Christian tradition by calling into question the radical distinction between good and evil. Rather than holding to the ideal of *honnêteté* derived from scripture and Augustine, as it was also embraced by both Pascal and Newton, Joyce dramatizes Rousseau's principle of uninhibited self-disclosure. His presentation of Bloom's inner dreams and desires thus stand under no sort of transcendent judgment. "Am I the only honest person that has come out of Ireland in our time?" Joyce once asked pointedly.[41]

Given Joyce's critique of moral absolutism, it seems exceedingly odd to identify *caritas* as Bloom's dominant virtue. Yet certain critics argue that Bloom shows his goodness not only in private life with reference to sexual toleration but also in the public sphere when he takes a stand against violence. Two key episodes in *Ulysses* support this view. The first occurs in Barney Kiernan's pub during an altercation with the chauvinistic Citizen. Bloom registers there his resistance to the idea of physical force advanced by the Irish "Cyclops" with a simple definition of love as the opposite of hatred. The unnamed narrator of the chapter scoffs at Bloom's feeble attempt to articulate his conviction: "Love loves to love love. Nurse loves the new chemist. Constable 14A loves Mary Kelly . . . and this person loves that other person because everybody loves somebody but God loves everybody."[42] Despite the ironic tone of this passage, love remains Bloom's genuine testament, since he is supposedly more Christian than the nominal Christians surrounding him in the scene. Bloom also performs a charitable deed later in the novel by rescuing Stephen in his scuffle with two British soldiers and picking him up in "orthodox Samaritan fashion."[43] The phrasing is here too deliberately absurd, but this unassuming act of kindness proves to be a central moment in *Ulysses*. Arguably, it saves the Joycean universe from the incertitude and amoralism of solitary human existence amidst the Void.

His gesture is highly commendable, but Bloom follows Christ's new commandment only partially. *Caritas* is stripped of its full Christian meaning in these episodes because it is converted to humanitarian good will. Marilyn French cites St. Augustine's famous definition of charity in *The City of God* as "the motion of the soul toward the enjoyment of God for His own sake, and the enjoyment of one's self and of one's neighbour for the sake of God" without noting Bloom's only partial fulfillment of the precept.[44] The second commandment—love of neighbor—is invoked without reference to the first—love of God above all creatures. *Caritas* is made to operate as the central principle of Joyce's moral vision, on this view, even though *Ulysses* "posits a world without God."[45]

French argues in a similar vein when she claims that Joyce's hero offers Molly Bloom "the greatest degree of *caritas*."[46] Bloom's acceptance of his wife's adultery on the rationalistic grounds that fidelity and infidelity coincide may be charitable on the surface, but its real purpose is to offer a barb against purity. Life consists of a series of sexual sensations so that no one could ever expect his spouse to have preserved her virtue before marriage or to safeguard her chastity afterwards, Bloom suggests.[47] In any case, committing adultery is "less reprehensible than theft, highway robbery, cruelty to children and animals, obtaining money under false pretences," and so forth.[48] Bloom, in short, minimizes the gravity of the moral transgression that the sixth commandment prohibits. His relativized ethics differ radically from the mercy of Christ, who also forgave an adulteress, but exhorted her at the same time "from now on sin no more" (John 8:11). Joyce's hero takes his cue, instead, from Freud in believing that "all affection is sexual at root."[49] Bloom's consideration for his wife is not based therefore on the law of love, nor does his compassion for others, including Mrs. Purefoy in childbirth and Mrs. Dignam in mourning, spring from anything other than his own individual philanthropy, that is, not from any communally sustained Christian ethos.[50]

Ulysses enacts the principle that man can be good without God, and the individual can be heroic without performing grand gestures. The pervasive use of irony in the novel (such as in the passage on "love" cited above) represents, in Georg Lukacs's view, a kind of "negative mysticism" that fills the void created by God's absence.[51] Marilyn French elaborates on Joyce's use of this favorite literary device:

The image closest to a divine one is the narrator who is omniscient, but who shows the other face of God. Whether the narrator is contemptuous, impersonal, or indifferent, he is always malevolent toward the tiny, foolish, and disgusting creature, man: he is at worst a *dio boia* or hangman god, at best a *deus absconditus.*[52]

Lukacs agrees that irony represents a "demonic" force in the modern novel,[53] but he criticizes Joyce for treating only the superficial aspects of life through an experimental technique that levels all moral and social distinctions: "If Joyce had set Napoleon on the toilet of the petit bourgeois Bloom," the Marxist critic hypothesizes, "he would merely have emphasized what was common to both Napoleon and Bloom."[54] This is probably correct. Joyce was all for deflating grandiosity, as when in the "Cyclops" episode the English are described as "a race of mighty heroes, rulers of the waves, who sit on thrones of alabaster silent as the deathless gods."[55] Napoleon would not have escaped this satiric treatment either. In this respect, Joyce is the heir not only of Jonathan Swift but also of Montaigne, who conveyed his skepticism about the individual's capacity to rise above himself and humanity through a graphic image at the conclusion of the *Essays*: "on the loftiest throne in the world we are still sitting only on our own rump."[56] Even "supermen"—*pace* Nietzsche—are finally subject to the same needs and desires as ordinary people. Joyce mocks all actions of epic proportions by rendering them human-all-too-human. Art is the great leveler, making all men equal.

Tolkien also operates as a literary "democrat" in *Lord of the Rings*, but with a striking difference. His characters are "all equal before the Great Author, *qui deposuit potentes de sede et exaltavit humiles*" ("who has put down the mighty from their thrones and exalted the humble").[57] His "hobbitocentric" tale features "little people, smaller than Dwarves" (*LOTR*, 1) who are humble in the etymological sense of the word. [58] The Latin *humiles*, Erich Auerbach explains, is related to *humus*, "soil"; it literally means "low," "low-lying," "of small stature." Tolkien also alludes to the figurative meanings of this key virtue that undergirds a Christian motif deriving chiefly from the life of Christ—from the low birth and the humiliation of the Passion, to the glory of the Resurrection and the Ascension: "The humility of the Incarnation derives its full force from the contrast with Christ's divine nature: man and God, lowly and sublime, *humiles et sublimes*: both the height and depth are immeasurable and inconceivable: *peraltissima humilitas*."[59]

It is not by happenstance then that the Fellowship departs on December 25 and that Sauron falls on March 25 (the date of the feast of the Annunciation), both dates intimately connected with the Incarnation. Tolkien's treatment of heroism accordingly strikes a balance between the high and low, the very thing Nietzsche detested: "Books for all the world are foul smelling books: the smell of small people clings to them."[60] Unlike the Lilliputians Gulliver meets on his travels, the hobbits are not disdained or satirized. "They are made small," Tolkien points out, "partly to exhibit the pettiness of man, plain unimaginative parochial man—though not either with the smallness or savageness of Swift, and mostly to show up, in creatures of very small physical power, the amazing and unexpected heroism of ordinary men 'at a pinch.'"[61] For most of the tale, it follows, the hobbits remain inconspicuous, though there is more to them than meets the eye. Only the Great Author sees the hidden mettle they display along the *via dolorosa* of complete renunciation, weaving their subtle acts of sacrifice into the grand carpet of providential and eschatological history.

That Tolkien subtly alters the epic ideal of heroism by underlining the importance of humility is made evident from the outset. When Gandalf instructs Frodo on the nature of his mission, for example, the hobbit considers himself the least likely candidate to save Middle-earth. *Nolo heroizari* ("I do not want to be a hero") best describes his initial attitude, since he feels wholly inadequate for the task.[62] Echoing Dante's famous declaration of personal inadequacy, "I'm not Aeneas, and I am not Paul,"[63] Frodo admits, "I am not made for perilous quests" (*LOTR*, 60). In this respect, Frodo resembles Pascal's *honnête homme*.[64] He even wonders why he was ever chosen in the first place. His wise mentor replies that no one can answer such questions. "You may be sure," he counsels the already humbled hobbit, "that it was not for any merit that others do not possess: not for power or wisdom at any rate" (*LOTR*, 60). Like his illustrious predecessors, Frodo must learn that "only a small part is played in great deeds by any hero" (*LOTR*, 263). Elrond confirms the wizard's point of view, but with a significant corollary: "This quest may be attempted by the weak with as much hope as the strong. Yet such is oft the course of deeds that move the wheels of the world: small hands do them because they must, while the eyes of the great are elsewhere" (*LOTR*, 262).

Tolkien transvalues Nietzsche's attempted deconstruction of Christian humility as a disguised form of the will to power, and thus his equation of moral evil with moral weakness by alluding to St. Paul's aphorism: "God chooses weak things to confound the strong" (1 Cor. 1:27).[65] Nietzsche's ideal of hard self-reliance proves utterly insufficient in Tolkien's work. The power of the powerless lies in their willingness to let their lives correspond to the grace given to accomplish the appointed task.[66] Frodo discovers the paradox that only when he is weak can he claim to be strong. Unlikely heroes take center stage in *Lord of the Rings*, whereas epic characters undergo a certain ironic displacement. Significantly, it is Aragorn, the returning king, who confirms the new heroic order: "with him [Frodo] lies the true quest. Ours is but a small matter in the great deeds of this time" (*LOTR*, 416).

Tolkien presents heroism as a noble ideal, but one that takes into account personal shortcomings. Frodo's turnabout on Mount Doom provides a case in point. It can be said that the Ringbearer fails, strictly speaking, to carry out his prime directive at the very end, but his failure does not tarnish what he has accomplished up to this point. From the beginning he is pitted against a foe beyond his strength and must confront insuperable obstacles to reach his destination. Once there, Frodo, weakened by many months of torment, starvation, and exhaustion, plus the exposure to the Ring's spell, is understandably unable to withstand the intolerable pressure it exerts on the wearer at its place of origin there at the volcanic Cracks of Mount Doom. That he gets as far as he does against such formidable odds is an amazing feat by any standard. His fortitude, his perseverance, his capacity for self-sacrifice, his fidelity to the cause are all unparalleled. Few, if any, of the other members of the Fellowship could rise to the occasion in such exemplary fashion.[67] In the light of this broader perspective, Frodo's moral lapse can be seen as "a more significant and real event than a mere 'fairy-story' ending in which the hero is indomitable."[68] The hobbit with feet of clay remains a sterling hero in the eyes of his fellows.

The "ennoblement (or sanctification) of the humble"[69] in *Lord of the Rings* occurs against a backdrop of moral realism that acknowledges the existence of One who can bring good out of evil.[68] The wonderfully diverse creatures of Middle-earth recognize an objective moral order, as Aragorn affirms: "Good and ill have not changed since yesteryear; nor are they one thing among Elves and Dwarves and another among Men" (*LOTR*, 428). It seems fitting, then, that Frodo, who expends every fiber of his being as "an instrument of Providence," should receive aid from that source to make up for what he lacks.[70] Frodo's compassion for Gollum throughout the journey to Mordor also comes into play at this critical juncture. For Nietzsche, pity was a synecdoche for Christianity, a negative virtue that stifled the life-giving power of will.[71] In stark contrast, Gandalf declares that "the pity of Bilbo [in showing mercy to Gollum] will rule the fate of many"—Frodo not least of all (*LOTR*, 58). When the misshapen hobbit betrays his oath of service by biting off his master's Ring-laden finger, Frodo does not delay in forgiving Gollum: "But for him, Sam, I could not have destroyed the Ring . . . so let us forgive him!" (*LOTR*, 926). Frodo's act of mercy, the fruit of *caritas*, gains him mercy. His magnanimity produces a situation that allows him to avert personal and universal disaster. The Writer of the Story intervenes to amend Frodo's dread failure to destroy the Ring, enabling the quest to succeed.[72]

Both Frodo and Sam, unlike ancient heroes, learn that fame is not an end in itself. In Cirith Ungol, for instance, Sam momentarily thinks of himself as having the stuff that legends are made of: "he saw Samwise the Strong, Hero of the Age, striding with a flaming sword across the darkened land, and armies flocking to his call as he marched to the overthrow of Barad-dûr" (*LOTR*, 880). Love of the master to whom he has pledged his service combined with "plain hobbit-sense" help him to snap out of his daydream. Frodo faces a similar temptation. His reluctance to return to the Shire—formerly his deepest longing—generates, as Tolkien commented, "a last flicker of pride: [a] desire to have returned as a 'hero,' not content with being a mere instrument of good."[73] Usually unassuming, the hobbits momentarily put on airs. Despite their frailty, they come to realize that each age requires what Aragorn calls "valour without renown" (*LOTR*, 767). The glory belongs to another Name, even if in the novel it remains nameless.

If in the new kingdom established with the return of Aragorn "the presence of the greatest does not depress the small," then the opposite also holds true.[74] During the coronation ceremony that takes place on the Field of Cormallen, a remarkable scene unfolds: "to Sam's surprise and utter confusion [Aragorn] bowed his knee before [the hobbits]; and taking them by the hand, Frodo upon his right and Sam upon his left, he led them to the throne, and set . . . them upon it" (*LOTR*, 933). Tolkien dramatizes in this instance what Chesterton calls "the great paradox of Christianity": "Carlyle was quite wrong; we have not got to crown the exceptional man who knows he can rule. Rather we must crown the much more exceptional man who knows he can't."[75]

Aragorn's surprising gesture validates what Saruman says begrudgingly of Frodo: "You have grown, Halfling. . . . Yes, you have grown very much. You are wise" (*LOTR*, 996).[76] The truth of this statement applies equally to Sam. The hobbits have grown in moral, not chiefly in physical, stature—though the ent-drafts have enabled Merry and Pippin to increase in stature. Thus are the previously unsung heroes generously praised in song by the minstrel of Gondor. Implicitly, this celebration takes the two hobbits back to a conversation in which they expressed genuine surprise at their own exploits:

"I wonder if we shall ever be put into songs or tales. We're in one, of course, but I mean: put into words you know, told by the fireside, or read out of a great big book with red and black letters, years and years afterwards. And people will say: 'Let's hear about Frodo and the Ring!' and they'll say: 'Yes, that's one of my favourite sto-

ries. Frodo was very brave, wasn't he, dad?' 'Yes, my boy, the fa-
mousest of the hobbits, and that's saying a lot.'"

"It's saying a lot too much," said Frodo, and he laughed. . . .
"Why, Sam," he said, "to hear you makes me merry as if the story
was already written. But you've left out one of the chief characters:
Samwise the stouthearted. 'I want to hear more about Sam, dad.
Why didn't they put in more of his talk, dad? That's what I like, it
makes me laugh. And Frodo wouldn't have got far without Sam,
would he, dad?'" (*LOTR*, 697).

From being virtually unknown to becoming renowned among
their kind, the hobbits develop in a manner that is signaled by a
modulation of styles, both high and low, including colloquial and
elevated prose.[77] The narrative situation of the novel as a whole calls
for the use of a "common speech" when members of different races
gather together. This "cross-referencing of styles" remains a significant feature of Tolkien's incarnational poetics.[78] *Lord of the Rings*
draws on the venerable tradition of the *sermo humilis*, which, like
the Gospels themselves, put the doings of exalted figures and ordinary fishermen on the same stylistic footing. A providential anti-
irony brings the least pretentious of heroes to "regions where . . .
tears are the very wine of blessedness" (*LOTR*, 933). In this fellowship, rulers and their subjects do not enter into a master-slave relationship (Hegel), but serve one another in love (St. Augustine).

The ideal of rendering service to others for the common good distinguishes Tolkien's Augustinian vision from Joyce's humanistic project. Both writers invoke the famous Pauline metaphor of a community composed, like the human body, of diverse yet complementary
members that are unified through Christ their head (1 Cor. 12:12ff.).
Joyce, however, secularizes the biblical idea of *corpus Christi*, as
Donald F. Theall points out, "through the association of Bloom with
Christ and Bloom's body with the corporate body" of Dublin, the
civitas terrena.[79] Even though his messianic ambitions, destined to
be fulfilled in "the golden city which is to be, the new Bloomusa-
lem," are gently mocked in the "Circe" episode, Joyce's hero retains
his faith in natural human solidarity as the highest good.[80]

The chief protagonists of *Ulysses* uphold this central principle during their brief encounter, but they fall short of embracing a fully realized communal ideal. Although the fledgling artist and ordinary citizen merge momentarily into "Blephen Stoom," they fail to achieve a true communion of persons.[81] Each acknowledges the other "in his selfhood," as Marilyn French says, but "each may end up finally with only himself on his own doorstep."[82] They go their separate ways, remaining strangers to each other and to the world around them. This failed attempt at forming a genuine and lasting fellowship reflects the "cosmic irony" at work in *Ulysses*.[83] "Ultimate reality" in Joyce's novel does not derive from a benevolent divine source but resides instead "in the humanity of the characters, the sands and stones of Dublin, and the void which contains them all."[84] Bloom and Stephen accordingly end their modern odyssey on the bleak note of skepticism sounded by Nietzsche in *The Genealogy of Morals*: "man would sooner have the void for his purpose than be void of purpose."[85]

If *Ulysses* affords a consistently ironic perspective on the "hopeless bind that is human life" in the earthly city,[86] then *Lord of the Rings* offers a countervision based on a providential hope that exists beyond the void and the walls of the world.[87] In spite of their eventual separation, Bloom and Stephen are united in their "heterodox resistance" to traditional Christian teachings, especially concerning the practice of the new commandment.[88] Joyce, in fact, considered the "whole structure of heroism" that required self-sacrifice instead of "individual passion" as the motivating impulse for human conduct to be "a damned lie."[89] The hero of his novel is consequently a common man who shows solicitude for others, but one who abides by an individualistic ethic. Tolkien's hobbits, on the other hand, strive to maintain the bonds of a fellowship that is at once human and mystical. The success of their venture depends on mutual support, not personal effort, and on "the general sanctity (and humility and mercy) of the sacrificial person" who trusts in a power greater than his own.[90] Frodo and Sam become "ordinary" heroes in what Chesterton describes as "the correct sense of the term; which means the acceptance of an order; a Creator and the Creation."[91] Whereas Joyce celebrates "the eternal affirmation of the spirit of man in literature," Tolkien pays homage to the "supreme Artist and the Author of Reality."[92] By freely binding themselves in love to each member of the Company and to the gentle rule of a returning king who serves his subjects in turn, the hobbits glimpse the towers of the true city, the *civitas Dei*, a transcendent society grounded in *caritas*.

NOTES

1. Cf. Shippey, *J. R. R. Tolkien*, 310.

2. Reilly, "Tolkien and the Fairy Story," 128.

3. Steiner, *Grammars of Creation*, 109.

4. Lukacs, *Theory of the Novel*, 88.

5. Joyce, *Portrait of the Artist*, 233.

6. Joyce, *Ulysses*, 273.

7. Ibid., 668.

8. Rushdie, "Is Nothing Sacred?" 107.

9. Blumenberg, *Legitimacy of the Modern Age*, xvi–xvii.

10. Joyce, *Ulysses*, 250.

11. French, *Book as World*, 267.

12. For discussion of the *atheos absconditus*, see Lukacs, *Realism in our Time*, 44.

13. Deleuze and Guattari, *Thousand Plateaus*, 25.

14. Ibid., 6–7.

15. Eco, *Aesthetics of Chaosmos*, 7.

16. Joyce, *Ulysses*, 870.

17. Tolkien, "Sir Gawain and the Green Knight," 90.

18. Tolkien, "On Fairy-Stories," 144–46.

19. I have treated the Dantesque aspects of Tolkien's theory of subcreation in Manganiello, "*Leaf by Niggle*," 121–37.

20. Tolkien, *Letters*, 101.

21. Frye, *Secular Scripture*, 157.

22. *LOTR* shall henceforth designate Tolkien, *Lord of the Rings*.

23. Tolkien, *Letters*, 212. I have explored the topic of endings in relation to the image of the book in Manganiello, "Neverending Story," 5–14. For an interesting treatment of Tolkien's idea of the book with reference to the great medieval manuscript tradition, see Flieger, "Tolkien and the Idea of the Book," 283–99.

24. Chesterton, *Orthodoxy*, 136.

25. Ibid., 126.

26. Ibid., 136. Tolkien's treatment of personal identity also grows out of a fundamentally narrative apprehension of life. Galen Strawson has recently challenged the concept of selfhood understood with reference to what he calls the "ethical Narrativity thesis" that enjoins an individual to gather together his experiences in the form of a coherent story that will serve as the basis for the aim of a good life. Human self-experience can be "diachronic," Strawson maintains, in the sense of "something that has relatively long-term . . . continuity, something that persists over a long stretch of time, perhaps for life." In stark contrast, the enactments of an individual life can also appear as a series of unconnected episodes. The "episodic" person does not "figure oneself, considered as a self, as something that was there in the (further) past and will be there in the (further) future, although one is perfectly well aware that one has long-term continuity considered as a whole human being" ("Against Narrativity," 430). Diachronic and episodic accounts of human experience overlap in both *Ulysses* and *Lord of the Rings*. Joyce presents his protagonist living his daily routine in eighteen episodes that seem at times loosely linked, but in fact show Bloom playing the role of a modern-day Odysseus in accordance with the author's revised script of Homer's epic. For his part, Tolkien employs the medieval interlace technique to mirror the flux of events happening at once in his narrative, but he weaves these dangling threads together to place each character's adventure in the context of a universal story. By representing the episodes of an individual life as part of a greater narrative whole, Tolkien's ethical vision resembles more closely the work of contemporary narrative theorists, such as Alasdair MacIntyre, Paul Ricoeur, and Charles Taylor.

27. French, *Book as World*, 17.

28. Joyce, *Critical Writings*, 45.

29. Ibid., 45.

30. Eliot, "*Ulysses*, Order, and Myth,"177.

31. Lodge, *Modes of Modern Writing*, 139.

32. Joyce, *Critical Writings*, 76.

33. Budgen, *Joyce and the Making of "Ulysses,"* 17–18.

34. Joyce, *Critical Writings*, 45.

35. Joyce, *Ulysses*, 301–2.

36. Ibid., 471.

37. Marilyn French claims Bloom's "decency and honesty provide a norm, a standard, in a chapter on sexuality that points to the hypocrisy, craven deceit, and artificiality in society's approach to, or rather retreat from, the subject" (*Book as World*, 166).

38. Pascal, *Pensées*, 204.

39. Augustine, "Sermon XI," 295.

40. Newton, *Letters*, 427.

41. Joyce, *Letters*, 187. Also see article by Manganiello, "Reading the Book of Himself," 149–62.

42. Joyce, *Ulysses*, 433.

43. Ibid., 704.

44. French, *Book as World*, 42.

45. Ibid., 38.

46. Ibid., 47.

47. Joyce, *Ulysses*, 863.

48. Ibid., 865.

49. French, *Book as World*, 218.

50. For an opposing view, see Sicari, *Joyce's Modernist Allegory*, who argues that Joyce presents Bloom as a Christian hero.

51. Lukacs, *Theory of the Novel*, 90.

52. French, *Book as World*, 6.

53. Lukacs, *Theory of the Novel*, 92.

54. Lukacs, *Writer and Critic*, 180.

55. Joyce, *Ulysses*, 422.

56. Montaigne, *Essays*, 46.

57. Tolkien, *Letters*, 215.

58. Ibid., 237.

59. Auerbach, *Literary Language*, 39–41.

60. Nietzsche, *Beyond Good and Evil*, 43.

61. Tolkien, *Letters*, 158n.

62. Tolkien states, "*nolo heroizari* is of course as good a start for a hero, as *nolo episcopari* for a bishop" (*Letters*, 215). Cf. Chesterton's remark: "Carlyle's hero may say, 'I will be king'; but the Christian saint must say, '*nolo episcopari*'" (Chesterton, *Orthodoxy*, 119).

63. Dante, *Hell*, 2:32.

64. Mesnard comments that Pascal's concept of *honnêteté* is related to the Christian virtue of humility. Cf. Mesnard, *Les Pensées*, 106.

65. Nietzsche redefines the moral concepts of good and evil in the following passage from his *Anti-Christ*: "What is good? All that heightens the feeling of power, the will to power, power itself in man. What is bad? All that proceeds from weakness" (115).

66. Tolkien, *Letters*, 326n.

67. Ibid., 326, 253.

68. Ibid., 252.

69. Ibid., 237.

70. Ibid., 326. For the role providence plays in *Lord of the Rings*, see, for example, the article by Dubs, "Providence, Fate, and Chance," 133–42.

71. Cf. Nietzsche, *Birth of Tragedy/Genealogy of Morals*, 256, 273. Also, at the end of section 2 of *Anti-Christ*, Nietzsche concludes, "The weak and ill-constituted shall perish; first principle of *our* philanthropy. . . . What is more harmful than any vice?—Active sympathy for the ill-constituted and

weak—Christianity" (116). Frodo's compassion for Gollum flows from his Christian charity rather than from a Nietzschean philanthropy. As Tolkien insisted, "that strange element in the World that we call Pity or Mercy . . . is . . . an absolute requirement in moral judgment (since it is present in the Divine nature)" (Tolkien, *Letters*, 326).

72. Cf. Tolkien, *Letters*, 250.

73. Ibid., 328.

74. Tolkien, "On Fairy-stories," 156.

75. Chesterton, *Orthodoxy*, 119.

76. Tolkien explained that "Frodo" was a name he took from the Germanic tradition: "Its obvious connexion is with the old word *frod* meaning etymologically 'wise by experience'" (Tolkien, *Letters*, 224).

77. Cf. Tolkien, *Letters*, 159–60.

78. Kirk, "'I Would Rather Have Written in Elvish,'" 300.

79. Theall, *Joyce's Techno-Poetics*, 104–5.

80. Joyce, *Ulysses*, 606.

81. Ibid., 798.

82. French, *Book as World*, 263–64.

83. Ibid., 19.

84. Ibid., 22.

85. Nietzsche, *Genealogy of Morals*, 299.

86. French, *Book as World*, 22.

87. On the subject of Tolkien's "anti-irony," see Shippey, *J. R. R. Tolkien*, 110–11, and Rosebury, *Tolkien*, 154–57. For an insightful treatment of Tolkien's vision of hope, see Wood, *Gospel according to Tolkien*, 136–48.

88. Joyce, *Ulysses*, 777. Bloom and Stephen adopt a Nietzschean attitude of "absolute skepticism toward all inherited concepts." Cf. Nietzsche, *Will to Power*, par. 409.

89. Joyce, *Letters*, 81.

90. Tolkien, *Letters*, 252.

91. Chesterton, *The Thing*, 51.

92. Joyce, *Ulysses*, 777; Tolkien, *Letters*, 101.

BIBLIOGRAPHY

Alighieri, Dante. *The Comedy I: Hell (L'Inferno)*. Translated by Dorothy L. Sayers. London: Penguin, 1949.

Auerbach, Erich. *Literary Language and Its Public in Late Latin Antiquity and in the Middle Ages*. Translated by Ralph Manheim. New York: Pantheon, 1965.

Augustine. "Sermon XI." In *A Select Library of the Nicene and Post-Nicene Fathers of the Christian Church*, First Series, Vol. 2, edited by Philip Schaff, 294–98. Grand Rapids, MI: Eerdmans, 1996.

Blumenberg, Hans. *The Legitimacy of the Modern Age*. Translated by Robert M. Wallace. Cambridge, MA: MIT Press, 1985.

Budgen, Frank. *James Joyce and the Making of "Ulysses" and Other Writings*. London: Oxford University Press, 1972.

Chesterton, Gilbert K. *Orthodoxy*. Garden City, NY: Image, 1959.

———. *The Thing*. London: Sheed & Ward, 1957.

Deleuze, Gilles, and Felix Guattari. *A Thousand Plateaus: Capitalism and Schizophrenia*. Translated by Brian Massumi. Minneapolis: University of Minnesota Press, 1987.

Dubs, Kathleen E. "Providence, Fate, and Chance: Boethian Philosophy in *The Lord of the Rings*." In *Tolkien and the Invention of Myth: A Reader*, edited by Jane Chance, 133–42. Lexington: University Press of Kentucky, 2004.

Eco, Umberto. *The Aesthetics of Chaosmos: The Middle Ages of James Joyce*. Translated by Ellen Esrock. Tulsa, OK: University of Tulsa Press, 1982.

Eliot, T. S. "*Ulysses*, Order, and Myth." In *Selected Prose of T. S. Eliot*, edited by Frank Kermode, 172–78. San Diego: Harcourt, Brace, 1975.

Flieger, Verlyn. "Tolkien and the Idea of the Book." In *"The Lord of the Rings," 1954–2004: Scholarship in Honor of Richard E. Blackwelder*, edited by Wayne G. Hammond and Christina Scull, 283–99. Milwaukee, WI: Marquette University Press, 2006.

French, Marilyn. *The Book as World: James Joyce's "Ulysses."* Cambridge, MA: Harvard University Press, 1976.

Frye, Northrop. *The Secular Scripture*. Cambridge, MA: Harvard University Press, 1976.

Joyce, James. *The Critical Writings of James Joyce*. Edited by Ellsworth Mason and Richard Ellmann. New York: Viking, 1959.

———. *The Letters of James Joyce*. Vol. 2. Edited by Stuart Gilbert and Richard Ellmann. London: Faber and Faber, 1966.

———. *A Portrait of the Artist as a Young Man*. Edited by Seamus Deane. London: Penguin, 1992.

———. *Ulysses*. London: Penguin, 1992.

Kirk, Elizabeth D. "'I Would Rather Have Written in Elvish': Language, Fiction, and *The Lord of the Rings*." In *Towards a Poetics of Fiction*, edited by Mark Spilka, 289–302. Bloomington: Indiana University Press, 1972.

Lodge, David. *The Modes of Modern Writing: Metaphor, Metonymy, and the Typology of Modern Literature*. Ithaca, NY: Cornell University Press, 1977.

Lukacs, Georg. *Realism in Our Time*. Translated by John and Necke Mander. New York: Harper and Row, 1971.

———. *The Theory of the Novel*. Translated by Anna Bostock. Cambridge, MA: MIT Press, 1971.

———. *Writer and Critic and Other Essays*. Edited and translated by Arthur D. Kahn. New York: Grosset and Dunlap, 1971.

MacIntyre, Alasdair. *After Virtue: A Study in Moral Theory*. 2nd ed. Notre Dame, IN: University of Notre Dame Press, 1984.

Manganiello, Dominic. "*Leaf by Niggle*: The Worth of the Work." *English Studies in Canada* 24 (1998): 121–37.

———. "The Neverending Story: Textual Happiness in *The Lord of the Rings*." *Mythlore* 59 (1992): 5–14.

———. "Reading the Book of Himself: The Confessional Imagination of St. Augustine and Joyce." In *Biography and Autobiography*, edited by James Noonan, 149–62. Ottawa: Carleton University Press, 1993.

Mesnard, Jean. *Les Pensées de Pascal*. Paris: Société d'édition d'enseignement supérieur, 1976.

Montaigne, Michel de. *Montaigne's Essays and Selected Writings*. Translated and edited by Donald M. Frame. New York: St. Martin's, 1963.

Newton, John. *Letters*. In *A Burning and Shining Light: English Spirituality in the Age of Wesley*, edited by David Lyle Jeffrey, 423–33. Grand Rapids, MI: Eerdmans, 1987.

Nietzsche, Friedrich. *Beyond Good and Evil*. Translated by Walter Kaufmann. New York: Random House, 1966.

———. *The Birth of Tragedy/The Genealogy of Morals*. Translated by Francis Golffing. Garden City, NY: Doubleday Anchor, 1956.

———. *The Twilight of the Idols/The Anti-Christ*. Translated by R. J. Hollingdale. London: Penguin, 1965.

———. *The Will to Power*. Translated by Walter Kaufmann and R. J. Hollingdale. London: Weidenfeld and Nicolson, 1968.

Pascal, Blaise. *Pensées*. Translated by A. J. Krailsheimer. London: Penguin, 1995.

Reilly, R. J. "Tolkien and the Fairy Story." In *Tolkien and the Critics*, edited by Neil D. Isaacs and Rose A. Zimbardo, 128–50. Notre Dame, IN: University of Notre Dame Press, 1968.

Ricoeur, Paul. *Oneself as Another*. Translated by Kathleen Blamey. Chicago: University of Chicago Press, 1992.

Rosebury, Brian. *Tolkien: A Cultural Phenomenon*. Houndmills: Palgrave Macmillan, 2003.

Rushdie, Salman. "Is Nothing Sacred?" *Granta* 31 (1990): 97–111.

Shippey, T. A. *J. R. R. Tolkien: Author of the Century*. London: HarperCollins, 2000.

Sicari, Stephen. *Joyce's Modernist Allegory: "Ulysses" and the History of the Novel.* Columbia: University of South Carolina Press, 2001.

Steiner, George. *Grammars of Creation.* New Haven, CT: Yale University Press, 2001.

Strawson, Galen. "Against Narrativity." *Ratio (new series)* 17, no. 4 (2004): 428–52.

Taylor, Charles. *Sources of the Self: The Making of Modern Identity.* Cambridge, MA: Harvard University Press, 1989.

Theall, Donald F. *James Joyce's Techno-Poetics.* Toronto: University of Toronto Press, 1997.

Tolkien, J. R. R. *The Letters of J. R. R. Tolkien.* Edited by Humphrey Carpenter with the assistance of Christopher Tolkien. Boston: Houghton Mifflin, 1981.

———. *The Lord of the Rings.* London: HarperCollins, 1995.

———. "On Fairy-Stories." In *The Monsters and the Critics and Other Essays,* ed. Christopher Tolkien, 109–61. London: HarperCollins, 1997.

———. "Sir Gawain and the Green Knight." In *The Monsters and the Critics and Other Essays,* edited by Christopher Tolkien, 70–108. London: HarperCollins, 1997.

Wood, Ralph C. *The Gospel according to Tolkien: Visions of the Kingdom in Middle-earth.* Louisville, KY: Westminster John Knox, 2003.

CHAPTER 7

THE CONSOLATIONS OF FANTASY

J. R. R. Tolkien and Iris Murdoch

Scott H. Moore

One of the twentieth century's foremost critics of fantasy was Anglo-Irish philosopher and novelist Iris Murdoch (1919–1999). She believed that fantasy was an attempt to manufacture unwarranted consolation by escaping the reality of the human condition. What is less well known is that Murdoch had a deep and abiding affection for the fiction of J. R. R. Tolkien. She read and reread *The Lord of the Rings*. She refers to Tolkien's achievement in her philosophical works and alludes to his characters and his fiction in her own novels. How is one to make sense of this surprising affinity, and does anything of significance follow from it?

Perhaps there is simply an equivocation over the term "fantasy," so that the kind of fantasy that Murdoch opposed is not at all the kind of fantasy that Tolkien created. It could be that there is no equivocation but that Murdoch was simply incoherent with respect to her literary theory and her aesthetic taste. If either of these conjectures were the case, surely nothing of significance would follow for the interpretation of Tolkien. However, it seems to me that neither of these initial objections is valid, but rather that we have good antecedent grounds for rejecting the "incoherence" accusation out of hand. Harold Bloom and others have asserted that Murdoch was often inconsistent with her novels,[1] but it seems unlikely that Murdoch, who took great care with her philosophy, would be guilty of such silly *philosophical* incoherence as this.

Given the appropriateness of juxtaposing Tolkien's literary achievement with Murdoch's philosophical reflection, an investigation is warranted into the nature of fantasy and its concomitant effect on the reader. I argue that Iris Murdoch believed that Tolkien's work belonged among those few compelling works of art that not only legitimately console their readers but also embody the moral vision that Murdoch thought was indicative of authentic virtue and that she sought to embody in her own fiction. Murdoch's engagement with Tolkien will illuminate both Tolkien's own achievement, in particular, and the nature of consolation and fantasy, in general.

To make this argument, I will first establish Murdoch's personal and professional relation to Tolkien, showing that she had an affection for his work and that it substantively influenced her scholarship and her own art. Second, I will examine the concepts of fantasy and imagination as they pertain to Tolkien. Third, I will present a brief overview of Murdoch's objection to fantasy and its relationship to consolation, explaining why any sort of philosophical or literal solace is so deeply problematic for her. Fourth, I will conclude with an explication of what Murdoch called *austere* consolation and its relation to both literary imagination and moral vision. I will thus conclude that, for Murdoch, Tolkien exemplifies precisely the sort of austere consolation that she believed to be exhibited in the highest forms of art.

MURDOCH'S ATTRACTION TO TOLKIEN

Murdoch's and Tolkien's careers at Oxford briefly overlapped, but she was much younger. In many ways, they could not have been more different. Religiously, Tolkien was a strict Roman Catholic; Murdoch a mystical Platonist who denied the existence of any personal God. Professionally, he was a linguist and philologist who reveled in the minute intricacies of grammar and etymology; she was a philosopher given to grand visions of the Good and the True. Politically,

Tolkien was conservative; Murdoch (at least during Tolkien's lifetime) flirted with Leftist parties, including the Communists. Concerning their personal lives, he was the retiring and devoted father and family man; she was the "catch of Oxford" whose multitudinous love affairs contributed to her mystique and notoriety.

For both, however, their commitments to the writing of fiction had the effect of marginalizing them from their professional academic disciplines. Many of Tolkien's colleagues could not fathom his unending work on the fictional Middle-earth, just as Murdoch's unique brand of existentialist fiction won her such inexorable opposition from the analytic philosophical establishment at Oxford that she gave up her formal post at St. Anne's College in 1963.[2] Finally, there is a synchronicity in the appearance of their major works of fiction: Murdoch's first novel, *Under the Net*, was published in the same year (1954) as *The Fellowship of the Ring*. Murdoch and Tolkien were also friends, though she knew his son, Christopher, far better than the philologist himself. Christopher Tolkien and Murdoch's husband, John Bayley, were colleagues at New College, and they worked closely together for many years. In the midst of Murdoch's decline with Alzheimer's disease and again after her death in 1999, Christopher Tolkien wrote warm, affectionate letters of condolence to Bayley.

In the 1970s, Murdoch purchased Tolkien's "roll top" desk, at which she spent many hours writing and answering correspondence.[3] "*The Lord of the Rings*," notes A. N. Wilson, "she read and reread, enjoying detailed conversations about it with its author, or with Christopher Tolkien, the author's son."[4] According to Wilson, Murdoch loved talking with the elder Tolkien about "the more abstruse points of elvish lore" and would defend *Lord of the Rings* against cynical criticisms made against it by Bayley.[5] There is much that is dubious in Wilson's scandalous memoir *Iris Murdoch: As I Knew Her*, but these claims seem entirely plausible, especially the reference to a close family friend and colleague such as Christopher Tolkien (who was also one of Wilson's tutors at New College).

Any extended conversations Murdoch might have had with Tolkien *père* would have come late in his life. In a letter to Michael

Tolkien dated September 9–10, 1965, the father notes, "But I suppose my greatest surprise was 4 days ago to get a warm fan-letter from Iris Murdoch. And if that name is just an 'Ava Gardner' to you, it can't be helped."[6] That Tolkien was "surprised" to receive such a letter implies that, prior to 1965, he was not aware of her interest in and affection for his work. Indeed, the "Ava Gardner" comment makes it clear that Murdoch was not a close family friend who would be known to Michael. (In 1964, Tolkien had been introduced to the movie star at an Oxford gathering, and apparently neither one knew why the other was famous.) Tolkien retired from Oxford to Poole near Bournemouth in 1968, and he returned to Oxford only in 1972, the year before his death. In all likelihood, any "detailed conversations" between Tolkien and Murdoch would have occurred between 1965 and 1968. In addition to her multiple readings of *Lord of the Rings*, Murdoch had copies of *The Silmarillion* and *Unfinished Tales* in her working library in Oxford.[7] She also owned a copy of *Oxford Poetry 1915*. This slim volume contains the first appearance in book form of a work by Tolkien, his poem "Goblin Feet." The book was a gift from "A" in October 1955, and it remained quite valuable to her.[8]

Explicit references to Tolkien and *Lord of the Rings* arise at several moments in her fiction and in her philosophy. For instance, in the 1971 novel *An Accidental Man*, the silent and misunderstood Dorina quietly broods while reading *Lord of the Rings*. Dorina's quest for goodness and freedom is, on the surface, quite different from that cultivated by the Fellowship of the Ring. She lives a quiet, hellish life away from her abusive husband, Austin. And yet there are interesting parallels between Dorina's quest and the book that so consumes her. She is on a journey for truth, peace, and security. She is surrounded by her own fellowship, one that is similarly broken by selfishness and pride. Dorina does not finish *Lord of the Rings*, alas, before her tragic drowning.

In her 1985 novel, *The Good Apprentice*, Murdoch even inserts a reference to one of Tolkien's characters. At the conclusion of the novel, Edward takes his father's, Jesse's, ring and the chain given to him by his half-sister, Ilona, and puts them on: "It was like a religious ceremony. He tested his feelings. No warmth, no vision, quiet relics. It occurred to him that he might put the ring on to the chain and wear it round his neck, like Frodo. The idea amused him. He put the relics away, let them rest; and he wondered whether in the future, in some emergency, he might not, with greater expectation and with more remarkable results, put on Jesse's ring."[9]

Murdoch's penultimate novel (published in 1993) was *The Green Knight*. This reformulation and retelling of the medieval story of *Sir Gawain and the Green Knight* also integrates its companion poem *Pearl* along with the story of Cain and Abel, the Holy Grail, and more. Carla Arnell has demonstrated persuasively the ways in which Murdoch presents, re-presents, and breaks the *Gawain* legend.[10] Tolkien's 1925 edition (with E. V. Gordon) of *Sir Gawain and the Green Knight* was a mainstay of British literary education during two-thirds of the century. (His translations of *Sir Gawain*, *Pearl*, and *Sir Orfeo* were published posthumously in 1975.) According to Arnell, *Green Knight* demonstrates Murdoch's "penchant for raiding the riches of old myths," firmly establishing her as "one of the most pro-lific mythopoetic writers of the twentieth century," one who wrote in the "great tradition of Lewis, Tolkien and Williams."[11]

Perhaps the most intriguing connection between Tolkien and Murdoch is her tendency to employ *eucatastrophe*, the literary de-vice that Tolkien famously coined. For Tolkien, eucatastrophe is the "good catastrophe, the sudden joyous 'turn'" that produces the happy ending of fairy tales. According to Tolkien, "it is a sudden and miraculous grace: never to be counted on to recur."[12] In a letter to Christopher in November 1944, the elder Tolkien describes eu-catastrophe as "the sudden happy turn in a story which pierces you with a joy that brings tears." It produces this effect in the reader be-cause "it is a sudden glimpse of Truth, . . . a sudden relief as if a major limb out of joint had suddenly snapped back."[13] Eucatastrophe, for Tolkien, has distinct theological connotations that Murdoch would have rejected—namely, the conviction that the divinely created cos-mos will be divinely consummated. Even so, I believe there is substan-tial evidence to show that eucatastrophe is a useful concept for making sense of the notoriously implausible "happy endings" of Murdoch's novels. Moreover, its intimate connection both to metaphors of

vision and to austere consolation reinforce its relevance for understanding Murdoch.

Implicit Tolkien-like themes of the personal quest and the conflict between good and evil also abound in Murdoch's fiction, even
as they appear in the form of philosophical comedies of manners
usually set in twentieth-century London and its environs. *The Black
Prince* is the tale of a failed writer seeking redemption and love in
the most unlikely of places. *The Unicorn* presents a mythopoetic
narrative of loss, captivity, and the tragedy of failed knowledge
and misunderstanding. *The Nice and the Good* shows a protagonist
forced to make multiple journeys into the "underworld" in an attempt to understand how things are and how they came to be. *A
Word Child* is the story of a man fleeing from his past, seeking salvation in words and struggling not to succumb to the same temptation,
which has already ruined his life. *A Fairly Honourable Defeat* presents the classic battle between good and evil as a quest for genuine
love and truth. *The Bell* features a unique company of characters
brought together by fate and laudable intentions, as they struggle to
achieve a good that they can only partially name. *The Book and the
Brotherhood*, *The Time of Angels*, and *Flight from the Enchanter*
each present a questing fellowship as it grapples with evil both within
and without.

FANTASY AND FAIRY STORIES

According to Colin Manlove, Tolkien and Murdoch are both representatives of "English fantasy," albeit of two distinct types. Tolkien
wrote what Manlove calls "secondary world" fantasy of the kind pi-
oneered by George Macdonald, H. G. Wells, and others. In this type
of fantasy, "the writer invents an alternative world with its own
rules." Murdoch, on the other hand, falls into Manlove's category of
"metaphysical" fantasy together with G. K. Chesterton, Charles
Williams, and Muriel Spark. In metaphysical fantasy, we are "asked
to take the supernatural presented as in some sense potentially real."
According to Manlove, "This fantasy often constitutes a fictional ef-

fort to preserve the metaphysical view of life in a world where belief in it is fading."[14] Yet Manlove's own definition of fantasy as "fiction involving the supernatural or the impossible"[15] fails to get at the psychological dimension of fantasy, and he thus fails to engage Murdoch's objection to the term.

In his 1961 book, *An Experiment in Criticism*, C. S. Lewis discusses the differences between literary and psychological uses of "fantasy." As a psychological term, fantasy entails two kinds of delusive "castle-building," whereby imaginative constructions of the mind are mistaken for reality. Castle-building, for Lewis, can be either "morbid" or "normal." Morbid castle-building consists of a "pleasing imaginative construction entertained incessantly, and to his injury, by the patient, but without the delusion that it is a reality. A waking dream . . . of military or erotic triumphs, of power or grandeur . . . is either monotonously reiterated or elaborated year by year. *It becomes the prime consolation, and almost the only pleasure, of the dreamer's life.*"[16] Normal castle-building is a more moderate and temporary recreation in which such inventions are subordinated to one's everyday activities. Normal castle-building can be further divided into "egoistic" and "disinterested" types. In the egoistic, the dreamer is always the hero who makes witty remarks, successfully courts beautiful women, and saves the day. In the disinterested, the dreamer may or may not be present in the dream at all. He makes imaginary journeys to Switzerland, for example, to survey castles and mountains and to observe adventures occurring there. When disinterested castle-building reaches this point, according to Lewis, "more than mere reverie has come into action: construction, invention, in a word *fiction*, is proceeding." Lewis concludes, "There is thus, if the daydreamer has any talent, an easy transition from disinterested castle-building to literary invention. There is even a transition from Egoistic to Disinterested and thence to genuine fiction."[17]

Tolkien takes the matter much further, providing a crucial connection between the psychological and the literary. In his celebrated essay of 1964, "On Fairy-Stories," he connects fairy stories, fantasy, and consolation. For Tolkien, the fairy story does not depend upon elves or fairies themselves, but "upon the nature of *Faërie*:

the Perilous Realm itself and the air that blows in that country."[18] Tolkien notes that fairy stories also offer fantasy, recovery, escape, and consolation, "all things of which children have, as a rule, less need than older people. Most of them are nowadays very commonly considered to be bad for anybody."[19]

For Tolkien, fantasy is not to be confused with dreaming—with that reverie "in which there is no Art." Likewise, fantasy is not to be confused with imagination, which Tolkien denotes as "the mental power of image-making" (and which leads to a romantic confusion of creation and subcreation). Tolkien consistently describes the writing of fiction as an act of "sub-creation" in order to distinguish it from the primary creation that belongs to God alone. God alone creates *ex nihilo*, "out of nothing," but all human making merely re-shapes already-existing things. Art thus provides the link between imagination and subcreation. [20] Fantasy is a "natural human activity" that, in its uncorrupted state, "does not seek delusion nor be-witchment and domination; it seeks shared enrichment, partners in making and delight, not slaves." Furthermore, fantasy does not "de-stroy or insult Reason. . . . On the contrary. The keener and clearer is the reason, the better fantasy will it make." Absent such ability to perceive truth, fantasy perishes or else becomes "Morbid Delusion." Hence Tolkien's conclusion: "Creative Fantasy is founded upon the hard recognition that things are so in the world as it appears under the sun; on a recognition of fact, but not a slavery to it."[21] Creative fantasy is thus designed to make something new out of the old, and thereby to see the world as we were meant to see it. Viewing such fantastic subcreations enables us to "be startled anew (but not blinded)" by what we thought we knew. This, for Tolkien, is the heart of recovery—"regaining a clear view."[22]

Tolkien's use of the metaphors of vision offers a crucial connec-tion to Murdoch. As any reader of Murdoch's philosophy knows, she believed that the moral life is a quest for adequate vision. *Pace* the reigning moral philosophers of her day (e.g., Stuart Hampshire, R. M. Hare et alii) she insisted that the moral life could not be re-duced merely to action or inaction. Drawing on the work of Simone Weil, Murdoch turned to vision and attention as constituting the habits of a virtuous life. For Murdoch, "true vision occasions right conduct,"[23] for "I can only choose within the world I can *see*, in the moral sense of 'see' which implies that clear vision is a result of moral imagination and moral effort."[24] Like Tolkien, she believed that proper seeing disabuses one of the tendency toward *possession*, and artistic masterpieces—including literary masterpieces—are crucial for this task. According to Murdoch, "It is important too that great art teaches us how real things can be looked at and loved without being seized and used, without being appropriated into the greedy organism of the self."[25]

IMAGINATION OR FANTASY?

Yet Murdoch will allow no room for "fantasy" as it is traditionally understood. Fantasy, for her, is too intimately connected with self-aggrandizement and self-deception to be liberating. Against Tolkien's protestations to the contrary, Murdoch describes Tolkien's work as an instance of "imagination," not fantasy. (Tolkien's essay "On Fairy-Stories" was originally published in the volume *Tree and Leaf* in 1964. If Murdoch knew this essay, she refers neither to it nor to Tolkien's distinction between imagination and fantasy.) But though she insists on retrieving the imagination from the clutches of fantasy, Murdoch defines imagination in terms that are remarkably similar to Tolkien's description of fantasy. In her 1978 essay "Art Is the Imitation of Nature," for instance, she asserts, "Imagination, as opposed to fantasy, is the ability to see the other thing, what one might call, to use those old-fashioned words, nature, reality, the world. . . . Imagination is a kind of freedom, a renewed ability to perceive and express the truth."[26] This quotation sounds remarkably similar to Tolkien's claims that "recovery [is] regaining a clear view," and that "creative Fantasy is founded upon the hard recognition that things are so in the world as it appears under the sun." It is the ability to be astounded anew by such "old-fashioned words" as "nature," "reality," and "the world." For Tolkien and Murdoch, this task entails a rejection of both romanticism about the self and scientism about the world.

Tolkien could have vigorously affirmed Murdoch's insight that "we need to return from the self-centered concept of sincerity to the other-centered concept of truth."[27] Like him, Murdoch repeatedly affirms the power and authority of art to reveal the true character and nature of the world. In her famous 1967 essay "The Sovereignty of Good Over Other Concepts," she notes:

> Art shows us the only sense in which the permanent and incorruptible is compatible with the transient; and whether representational or not it reveals to us aspects of our world which our ordinary dull dream-consciousness is unable to see. Art pierces the veil and gives sense to the notion of a reality which lies beyond appearance; it exhibits virtue in its true guise in the context of death and chance.[28]

Two observations follow from the analysis thus far. On the one hand, it seems quite possible that there is a fundamental equivocation in the use of the terms "fantasy" and "imagination" in both Tolkien and Murdoch. Even if there is such an equivocation, on the other hand, it is one that Murdoch forthrightly overcomes through her own stipulative understanding of imagination. Murdoch even appeals to *Lord of the Rings* to distinguish fantasy from imagination. In the same essay in which she describes *Lord of the Rings* as authentic art, she also asserts that "the practice of any art ... involves a struggle against fantasy, against self-indulgence."[29] Murdoch's insistence that artistic production "pierces the veil and gives sense to the notion of reality which lies beyond appearance" is a claim that is deeply compatible with Tolkien's vision, however much he might have objected to her use of terms.

FANTASY AND CONSOLATION

Tolkien's and Murdoch's similar regard for metaphors of vision, and their mutual conviction that imagination/fantasy truly disclose(s) reality seem, however, to clash radically when applied to the subject of fantasy and consolation. Tolkien believed that escape and consolation were legitimate consequences of good fantasy. In fact, Tolkien goes so far as to suggest that all authentic fairy stories *must* have "the Consolation of the Happy Ending."[30] Eucatastrophe "does not deny the existence of *dyscatastrophe*, of sorrow and failure: the possibility of these is necessary to the joy of deliverance; it denies (in the face of much evidence, if you will) universal final defeat and in so far as *evangelium*, giving a fleeting glimpse of Joy, Joy beyond the walls of the world, poignant as grief."[31] Murdoch would seem to be totally opposed, for she vigorously asserts that good art "resists the easy patterns of fantasy"[32] and thus rejects the consolation that flows from it: "The chief enemy of excellence in morality (and also in art) is personal fantasy: the tissue of self-aggrandizing and *consoling* wishes and dreams which prevents one from seeing what is there outside of one."[33] Such antagonism to the consolations of fantasy is an equally recurrent theme in her philosophical writings. She defines fantasy (both in literary art and psychic life) as "the proliferation of blinding self-centered aims and images."[34] Given her repeated recourse of metaphors of vision, it is not insignificant that Murdoch would describe the effect of fantasy as "blinding." She demands, instead, that we keep our attention fixed upon the real situation so as "to prevent it from returning surreptitiously to the self with consolations of self-pity, resentment, fantasy, and despair."[35]

Even the most casual reader of Murdoch's fiction will recognize the repeated criticisms and ridicule to which she subjects fantasy and consolation. In her 1976 novel, *The Sea, The Sea*, Charles Arrowby rediscovers his childhood love and constructs the most absurd fantasy about her. He "rescues" her from her husband and imprisons her in his home, hoping that she will realize her true love for him instead. He even attempts to adopt her own adopted son in order to create the family he never had. There are similar instances of destructive and deceptive fantasizing in other Murdoch novels: Bradley Pearson's fairy-tale romance with young Julian Baffin (*The Black Prince*), Hilary Burde's obsession with Kitty Gunnar (*The Word Child*), Michael Meade's belief that sequestering himself in a lay monastic community will absolve him of his sins and temptations (*The Bell*).

Such romantic fantasizing is also apparent in Tolkien. In *The Return of the King*, Éowyn falls so delusively in love with Aragorn that she attempts to follow him through the Paths of the Dead. She does not really know Aragorn; indeed, she loves not the man himself but the idea of chivalry, adventure, and exotic travel that she imposes on him. In the Houses of Healing, Aragorn observes to Éomer, "I say to you that she loves you more truly than me; for you she loves and knows; but in me she loves only a shadow and a thought: a hope of glory and great deeds, and lands far from the fields of Rohan."[36]

Murdoch agrees that such fantasy blinds one from seeing reality by turning one's focus inward upon oneself. In her 1969 novel, *The Nice and the Good*, for example, it is the Dachau survivor Willy Kost who defines what would constitute true happiness—distinguishing it not merely from delusion but also from perdition—for the conflicted, puritanical John Ducane: it is "a matter of one's most ordinary everyday mode of consciousness being busy and lively and unconcerned with self. To be damned is for one's ordinary everyday mode of consciousness to be unremitting agonizing preoccupation with self."[37] Fantasy, for Murdoch, is thus a self-imposed damnation. "We are not isolated free choosers . . . but benighted creatures sunk in a reality whose nature we are constantly and overwhelmingly tempted to deform by fantasy. Our current picture of freedom encourages a dream-like facility; whereas what we require is a renewed sense of the difficulty and complexity of the moral life and the opacity of persons."[38] The difficulty and the complexity of the moral life consist in this necessary discernment of the evil and suffering that both encompass and inhabit us.

OBEDIENCE, CHOICE, AND FREEDOM

I am convinced that Murdoch discerned the trouble and strain of the moral life also enfleshed in Tolkien's fiction, and that it is one of the many features of his work that attracted her to it. Tolkien's best characters recognize that they are not "free" simply to walk away from the task that is before them. They must follow their appointed path—even in the absence of the knowledge requisite for traveling it. Frodo says, for example, "I will take the Ring, though I do not know the way." This is Murdoch's similar description of the place and nature of choice:

> The place of choice is certainly a different one if we think in terms of a world which is *compulsively* present to the will, and the discernment and exploration of which is a slow business. Moral change and moral achievement are slow; we are not free in the sense of being able suddenly to alter ourselves since we cannot suddenly alter what we can see and ergo what we desire and are compelled by. In a way, explicit choice seems now less important: less decisive (since much of the "decision" lies elsewhere) and less obviously something to be "cultivated." If I attend properly I will have no choices and this is the ultimate condition to be aimed at. . . . The ideal situation is rather to be represented as a kind of "necessity." This is something of which saints speak and which any artist will readily understand.[39]

According to Murdoch, such freedom is not so much a matter of autonomous choice or individual decision but "something very much more like 'obedience.'"[40]

The long and arduous journey of the Fellowship to Mordor entails many decisions, but in most cases they present themselves as calls to obedience that the Nine Walkers must embrace. They must choose the difficult Good over the convenient, the comfortable, or (in Murdoch's deadly term) the "Nice." Frodo's decision to abandon the Fellowship and travel to Mordor alone is an excellent example of such a choice. It has all of the marks of moral virtue as described by Murdoch. After Boromir attempts to seize the Ruling Ring by force, Frodo places it on his finger in order to escape his maddened companion. Suddenly, the invisible Frodo *sees* the reality of a world devastated by Sauron's destruction:

> At first he could see little. He seemed to be in a world of mist in which there were only shadows: the Ring was upon him. Then here

and there the mist gave way and he saw many visions: small and clear as if they were under his eyes upon a table, and yet remote. There was no sound, only bright living images.[41]

The vision turns horrible as Frodo views Sauron's assault on Middle-earth, and as he suddenly "feels" the gaze of the Eye bearing down on him. Tolkien uses the passive voice to describe Frodo's response to the "two powers" struggling within him—the Voice of Gandalf and the Eye of Sauron: "he heard himself crying out." Frodo's decision, first to take off the Ring and then to journey on alone, are both examples of free choices, but they are not instances of radical, autonomous agency. Frodo knows what he *must* do, what he is compelled to do if he is to remain free. The world is, in Murdoch's words, "compulsively present" to his will:

> Frodo rose to his feet. A great weariness was on him, but his will was firm and his heart lighter. He spoke aloud to himself. "I will do now what I must," he said. "This at least is plain: the evil of the Ring is already at work even in the Company, and the Ring must leave them before it does more harm. I will go alone. Some I cannot trust, and those I can trust are too dear to me: poor old Sam, and Merry and Pippin. . . . I will go alone. At once."[42]

Frodo knows he must continue his journey to Mordor—just as he must accept Sam as his often bumbling companion, later as he must trust the treacherous Gollum, and later still as he must show mercy to this same merciless Gollum—all because he has clearly *seen how things are* and because he has morally matured over the course of the Quest. Like Willy Kost in *Nice and the Good*, Frodo is not concerned for himself ("those I can trust are too dear to me"). Gone is the flippant hobbit who wondered why Bilbo did not kill the murderous Gollum when he had the chance. The same freedom also comes to birth even in Sam Gamgee, as he makes a similarly obedient choice to take off the Ring in Shelob's lair. Each acts *freely* because he acts from a deep sense of obligation—Murdoch's "obedience," as it were. Such obedience is the product of attention that

Murdoch describes as "really looking" and thus as the only true basis for moral choice:

> If we ignore the prior work of attention and notice only the emptiness of the moment of choice we are likely to identify freedom with the outward movement since there is nothing else to identify it with. But if we consider what the work of attention is like, how continuously it goes on, and how imperceptibly it builds up structures of value around us, we shall not be surprised that at crucial moments of choice most of the business of choosing is already over. This does not imply that we are not free, certainly not. But it implies that the exercise of our freedom is a small piecemeal business which goes on all the time and not a grandiose leaping about unimpeded at important moments.[43]

This "small piecemeal business which goes on all the time" is the key to the development of moral virtue and the most substantial bulwark against fantasy. The principal fantasy for Murdoch is the temptation to believe that the "Nice" is the "Good." By the "Nice," she means the cozy, tidy, pleasant existence that avoids moral difficulty in order to maintain a comfortable and convenient status quo. For Murdoch, the Nice is "life without muddle." The "Good," by contrast, is often hard and difficult (even to discern), but because it remains "real" it brings significance to one's action and being. The Good is "the magnetic center toward which love naturally moves. False love moves to false good."[44]

Because the Nice always entails a false good, this confusion of the Nice with the Good is demonstrated over and over again in Murdoch's fiction. For instance, Gracie, in *An Accidental Man*, wants to lead a pleasant, tranquil life in Oxford, so as not to confront Ludwig's moral dilemma between his patriotic duty and his dodging of the U.S. military draft by escaping to England. Morgan, in *A Fairly Honourable Defeat*, wants a marriage built on free, simple "happy love" without muddle, and thus flees from her genuinely good but exceedingly difficult husband, Tallis. Uncle Theo, in *Nice and the Good*, is one of the few who has a glimpse of "the distance which

separates the nice from the good, and the vision of this gap had ter-
rified his soul."[45] In each case, and many more besides, Murdoch's
characters give themselves over to fantasy that the nice, cozy life
without muddle is actually the good life. They damn themselves by
refusing the challenge of the difficult and the good.

In Tolkien, we see much the same temptation played out in both
The Hobbit and *Lord of the Rings*. In the opening pages of *The
Hobbit*, Tolkien introduces hobbits to his readers by explaining that
the Bagginses were respected because they were rich and because
they never risked any adventures nor did anything unexpected. Yet
Bilbo's "nice" existence is shattered by the "unexpected party" of
dwarves at his door, just as Frodo's "nice" existence is similarly shattered by the summons to leave the comfort and pleasure of the Shire
in order to undertake the most threatening of all tasks, the destruction of the Ruling Ring. Each decision can be understood as obedience to the Good rather than preference for the Nice.

Murdoch was drawn to *Lord of the Rings* (as opposed, for instance, to *The Chronicles of Narnia* by C. S. Lewis) because it contains no explicit appeal to God. Murdoch was an exceedingly religious atheist, and she was enamored of theology and religious belief,
but the idea of a personally existing God was problematic for her. In
the conclusion to her famous essay "The Fire and the Sun: Why
Plato Banished the Poets," she notes, "To present the idea of God at
all, even as myth, is a consolation, since it is impossible to defend
this image against the prettifying attentions of art."[46] For Murdoch,
"Any story which we tell about ourselves consoles us since it imposes pattern upon something which might otherwise seem intoler-
ably chancy and incomplete. It is the role of tragedy, and also of
comedy, and of painting to show us suffering without a thrill and
death without a consolation."[47]

"Suffering without a thrill and death without a consolation"
seem an utter contradiction of Tolkien's necessary "Consolation of a
Happy Ending." It might appear, therefore, that despite Murdoch's
manifold affection for Tolkien's work, we must end our inquiry
where it began—in divergence, incoherence, and equivocation. And
yet such a negative conclusion is not necessary. It seems to me that

Murdoch placed Tolkien's fiction among those few compelling masterworks of art because it not only legitimately consoles but also convincingly attends to the sort of moral vision that Murdoch depicts in her own fiction.

EUCATASTROPHE, AUSTERE CONSOLATION, AND LOVE

My seemingly outrageous and concluding claim is that Murdoch's fiction can be read as employing Tolkien's category of eucatastrophe, albeit in atheist dress. As I have noted, many of Murdoch's novels have notoriously implausible "happy endings." The numerous weddings, love affairs, and reunions of improbable couples and friends give her fiction a comic edge that is positively Shakespearean. In *The Bell*, shy and frightful Dora Greenfield overcomes death and destruction while ultimately teaching herself to swim (the quintessentially Murdoch image of moral prowess). In *Good Apprentice*, Edward Baltram accepts the definitively unacceptable. In *Green Knight*, there are numerous unexpected unions, including the delicious but highly improbable elopement of the beautiful Aleph with the vicious and awful Lucas, thus joining "the Beauty and the Beast."[48] In *Nice and the Good* we confront seven implausible couplings, including the dog and the cat sleeping together in the same basket!

Is this Tolkien's "sudden and miraculous grace: never to be counted on to recur,"[49] or is it merely farce for Earl's Court? Much more than mere farce, it is the decidedly atheological eucatastrophe that Murdoch only rarely chose to avoid. Eucatastrophe for Tolkien, as we have seen, is a means of affirming not only the existence of God but also the ultimate triumph of God's goodness through the diverse and unexpected contingencies of the world. Does the term "atheological eucatastrophe" therefore even make sense? It does for Murdoch. Atheological eucatastrophe becomes another way of demonstrating the sovereignty of the Good and of her preference for the Good over God. In "Art Is the Imitation of Nature," she makes it clear that she had a high and lasting regard for *Lord of the Rings* because it returns the conflict between good and evil to the forefront where it belongs. It is no less clear that she was drawn to Tolkien (as not to Lewis) because he embeds his theological convictions deeply, even anonymously, within the tale. This "atheological" tactic is something that Murdoch could appreciate and even imitate.

Murdoch laments that most contemporary writers are reluctant to admit that literature, if it recognizes and opposes the challenge of self-indulgence, must be concerned with "the struggle between good and evil." The artistic avoidance of this struggle is an instance of what she called the "crystalline or journalistic" tendency of the twentieth-century novel:

> The nineteenth century novel (I use these terms boldly and roughly: of course there were exceptions) was not concerned with "the human condition," it was concerned with real various individuals struggling in society. The twentieth century novel is usually either crystalline or journalistic; that is, it is either a small quasi-allegorical object portraying the human condition and not containing "characters" in the nineteenth century sense, or else it is a large shapeless quasi-documentary object . . . telling, with pale conventional characters, some straightforward story enlivened with empirical facts. Neither of these kinds of literature engages with the problem [of genuine moral conflict].[50]

Hence her praise for Tolkien's work as "very clearly about the struggle between good and evil" and thus as a contrary example to what she called the crystalline or journalistic novel.[51]

In lamenting "what we have lost," Murdoch notes, "We no longer use a spread-out substantial picture of the manifold virtues of man and society. We no longer see man against a background of values, of realities, which transcend him. We picture man as a brave naked will surrounded by an easily comprehended empirical world. For the hard idea of truth we have substituted the facile idea of sincerity."[52] I believe that this is the principal reason for Murdoch's abiding admiration of Tolkien. He had an extraordinary sense of the substantial background, the values and the realities, which transcend both the characters and the readers. For Tolkien, this "substantial picture" included the languages and prehistories of competing races in Middle-earth. It included "three ages" composed of thousands of years of history. In published and unpublished manuscripts and stories alike, Tolkien creates an entire imaginative world through which to understand the deep struggle between good and evil.

Tolkien's world is not the "easily comprehended empirical world" that Murdoch regarded as the perennial human temptation. Whether it is Merry and Pippin escaping into Fangorn Forest, only to discover not only a magical wood but also a race of ents, whose history and memory predates almost all that is, or Aragorn's journey through the Paths of the Dead to reclaim an unpaid debt of honor, the real world in Tolkien is not the world that appears superficially. It is certainly not the flat, deceptive empirical world that Murdoch believed art must transform and reconfigure in order to make us see the world truly. And this means that she must leave the door open to the possibility of authentic consolation.

Authentic consolation for Murdoch is austere because it is grounded in beauty and love rather than any sort of delusion: "if there is any consolation it is the *austere consolation* of a beauty which teaches that nothing in life is of any value except the attempt to be virtuous."[53] Love, too, is a legitimate consolation. In *Metaphysics as a Guide to Morals*, she affirms, "In spite of all of the warnings mentioned above, love, love of lovers, of family, of friends, is an ultimate consolation and an ultimate savior."[54] Elsewhere she elaborates this central claim:

> It is in the capacity to love, that is to *see*, that the liberation of the soul from fantasy consists. The freedom which is a proper human goal is the freedom from fantasy, that is the realism of compassion. What I have called fantasy, the proliferation of blinding self-centered aims and images, is itself a powerful system of energy, and most of what is often called "will" or "willing" belongs to this system. What counteracts the system is attention to reality inspired by, consisting of, love. In the case of art and nature such attention is immediately rewarded by the enjoyment of beauty. In the case of morality,

although there are sometimes rewards, the idea of a reward is out of place. Freedom is not strictly the exercise of the will, but rather the experience of accurate vision which, when this becomes appropriate, occasions action.[55]

Many readers of Tolkien would embrace this construal of the role played by love and the obedient exercise of the will, for they have seen it fully dramatized in the Fellowship's many acts of loyal friendship and enduring sacrifice. Most of these readers, however, would object to Murdoch's suggestion that such austere beauty teaches that there is nothing of value except the attempt to be virtuous. Surely there are, in Tolkien's world, innumerable matters that have value apart from the attempt to be virtuous: the wonder of the natural world, the value of tradition and poetry, the camaraderie of good friends, the enjoyment of good food, drink, and tobacco, but especially the Company's noble sacrifices on behalf of the truth and beauty and goodness that "lie beyond the walls of the world" because they characterize the triune God.

Yet these objections do not stand as defeaters to Murdoch's construal. It is precisely the unconsoling character of the conclusion of *Lord of the Rings* that I believe appealed to her so convincingly. It is a consolation that does not deny Frodo's final sadness, the ending of the glorious age of the elves, nor the darkness inherent in the coming age of men. It is a consolation that, for her, is devoid of explicit religion.[56] On this last point, she clearly misread Tolkien's intentions with respect to the novel, and yet the text surely stands sufficient unto itself, without any necessarily religious reading of it, as Tolkien himself admitted.

Murdoch was not loath to use such religious terms as "mystical" and "mysticism." For her, the mystical is "an ever-present moral ideal, that of extending ordinary decent morals indefinitely in the direction of perfect goodness. The 'ordinary' good man, aware of the magnetism of good as well as the role of duty, is thus connected to a mystical ideal whether or not he is, in the traditional sense, religious."[57] This sense of the mystical is what Murdoch found abundantly evident in *Lord of the Rings*. The good hobbits of the Shire represent precisely what Murdoch called the "ordinary good man" who is drawn by the magnetism of the good but without recourse to traditional religion. Whether we readers of Tolkien (and Murdoch) find this account persuasive is quite beside the point. What matters is something more important: Iris Murdoch did indeed believe that Tolkien's fiction belonged among those few compelling works of art which legitimately console us because they persuasively embody true moral vision. It is a moral vision built on acts of attention and obedience that make for the authentic virtue she clearly sought to embody in her own fiction. The "miraculous grace never to be counted on to recur" has no eschatological presence in Murdoch's work, but it is nonetheless present as an unexpected *performative* eucatastrophe in both her philosophy and fiction. The "surprising joyous turn" is that, whether in the work of Tolkien or Murdoch, there are consolations of fantasy after all.

NOTES

1. In his review of *The Good Apprentice*, Harold Bloom notes, "Consistency of stance is one of Miss Murdoch's problems. She is both fantasist and realist, each on principle, but her abrupt modulations between the two visions sometimes seem less than fully controlled. Her novels rush by us, each a successful entertainment but none perhaps fully distinct from the others in our memories" ("A Comedy of Worldly Salvation," *New York Times*, January 12, 1986).

2. Murdoch's resignation of her fellowship at St. Anne's is a complicated affair. She resigned in part because of her unwillingness to practice philosophy in the analytic mode, in part because of her desire to devote herself more fully to her fiction, and in part because of an unfortunate relationship with a colleague. See Conradi, *Iris Murdoch*, 456–58.

3. Conradi, *Iris Murdoch*, 569.

4. Wilson, *Iris Murdoch*, 224.

5. A. N. Wilson, "Tolkien Was Not a Writer," *Daily Telegraph*, November 24, 2001. http://www.telegraph.co.uk/culture/4726760/Tolkien-was-not-a-writer.html.

6. Tolkien, *Letters*, 353.

7. These texts, along with J. E. A. Tyler's *The Tolkien Companion*, are now held in the Iris Murdoch Collection at Kingston University, Kingston-upon-Thames, Surrey. Murdoch's copy of *Lord of the Rings* is not contained in this collection.

8. G. D. H. C. [Gerald Crowe] and T. W. E. [T. W. Earp], eds., *Oxford Poetry 1915* (Oxford: B. H. Blackwell, 1915). Inscribed: *"I—What have we done sweet friend? A. Oxford Station (preparing an Oxford Book of Stations) Oct. 1955"* (Iris Murdoch Collection, Kingston-upon-Thames, IML 1308).

9. Murdoch, *Good Apprentice*, 515.

10. Arnell, "So Familiar, Yet So Strange."

11. Ibid., 72.

12. Tolkien, "On Fairy-Stories," 85–86.

13. Tolkien, *Letters*, 100.

14. Manlove, *Fantasy Literature of England*, 4.

15. Ibid., 3.

16. Lewis, *Experiment in Criticism*, 50; emphasis added.

17. Ibid., 53.

18. Tolkien, "On Fairy-Stories," 38–39.

19. Ibid., 67–68.

20. Ibid., 69.

21. Ibid., 74–75.

22. Tolkien claims that he does not want to involve himself with the philosophers by suggesting that the task is to "see things as they are." But, he notes, "I might venture to say 'seeing things as we are (or were) meant to see them'—as apart from ourselves. We need, in any case, to clean our windows; so that the things seen clearly may be freed from the drab blur of triteness or familiarity—from possessiveness" ("On Fairy-Stories," 77–78).

23. Murdoch, "On 'God' and 'Good,'" in *Sovereignty of Good*, 64.

24. Murdoch, "The Idea of Perfection," in *Sovereignty of Good*, 37.

25. Murdoch, "On 'God' and 'Good,'" in *Sovereignty of Good*, 64.

26. Murdoch, "Art Is the Imitation of Nature," in *Existentialists and Mystics*, 255.

27. Murdoch, "Against Dryness," in *Existentialists and Mystics*, 293.

28. Murdoch, "The Sovereignty of Good over Other Concepts," in *Sovereignty of the Good*, 86.

29. Murdoch, "Art Is the Imitation of Nature," in *Existentialists and Mystics*, 255.

30. Tolkien, "On Fairy-Stories," 85.

31. Ibid., 86.

32. Murdoch, "Sovereignty of Good," in *Sovereignty of Good*, 84.

33. Murdoch, "On 'God' and 'Good,'" in *Sovereignty of Good*, 57; emphasis added.

34. Ibid., 65.

35. Murdoch, "Sovereignty of Good," in *Sovereignty of Good*, 89.

36. Tolkien, *Return of the King*, 849.

37. Murdoch, *Nice and the Good*, 179.

38. Murdoch, "Against Dryness," in *Existentialists and Mystics*, 293–94.

39. Murdoch "The Idea of Perfection," in *Sovereignty of Good*, 38–39.

40. Ibid.

41. Tolkien, *Lord of the Rings*, 391.

42. Ibid., 392.

43. Murdoch "Idea of Perfection," in *Sovereignty of Good*, 36.

44. Murdoch, "Sovereignty of Good," in *Sovereignty of Good*, 100.

45. Murdoch, *Nice and the Good*, 348.

46. Murdoch, "The Fire and the Sun: Why Plato Banished the Artists," in *Existentialists and Mystics*, 463.

47. Murdoch, "The Sovereignty of Good over Other Concepts," in *Sovereignty of Good*, 85.

48. Murdoch, *Green Knight*, 421.

49. Tolkien, "On Fairy-Stories," 85–86.

50. Murdoch "Against Dryness," in *Existentialists and Mystics*, 291.

51. Murdoch, "Art Is the Imitation of Nature," in *Existentialists and Mystics*, 255.

52. Murdoch, "Against Dryness," in *Existentialists and Mystics*, 290.

53. Murdoch, "Sovereignty of Good," in *Sovereignty of Good*, 87.

54. Murdoch, *Metaphysics as a Guide to Morals*, 346.

55. Murdoch, "On 'God' and 'Good,'" in *Sovereignty of Good*, 65.

56. Though she owned a copy of the far more overtly religious work, *Silmarillion*, I know of no explicit engagement of this text by Murdoch.

57. Murdoch, *Metaphysics as a Guide to Morals*, 355.

BIBLIOGRAPHY

Arnell, Carla. "So Familiar, Yet So Strange: Mythic Fragments of *Sir Gawain and the Green Knight* in Iris Murdoch's *The Green Knight*." *Mythlore* 24, no. 2 (2004): 72–86.

Bloom, Harold. *Novelists and Novels*. New York: Checkmark, 2007.

Conradi, Peter. *Iris Murdoch: A Life*. London: HarperCollins, 2001.

Lewis, C. S. *An Experiment in Criticism*. Cambridge: Cambridge University Press, 1961.

Manlove, Colin. *The Fantasy Literature of England*. New York: Palgrave, 1999.

Murdoch, Iris. *Existentialists and Mystics: Writings on Philosophy and Literature*. New York: Penguin, 1999.

———. *The Good Apprentice*. New York: Penguin, 1987.

———. *The Green Knight*. New York: Penguin, 1993.

———. *Metaphysics as a Guide to Morals*. New York: Penguin, 1992.

———. *The Nice and the Good*. London: Vintage Books, 2000.

————. *The Sovereignty of Good.* London: Routledge, 1970.

Tolkien, J. R. R. *The Letters of J. R. R. Tolkien.* Edited by Humphrey Carter with the assistance of Christopher Tolkien. New York: Houghton Mifflin, 2000.

————. *The Lord of the Rings.* Boston: Houghton Mifflin, 2004.

————. "On Fairy-Stories." In *The Tolkien Reader.* New York: Del Rey, 1986.

————. *The Return of the King.* New York: Houghton Mifflin, 1983.

————. *The Tolkien Reader.* New York: Ballantine, 1966.

Wilson, A. N. *Iris Murdoch: As I Knew Her.* London: Arrow, 2004.

CHAPTER 8

"THAT THE WORLD NOT BE USURPED"

Emmanuel Levinas and J. R. R. Tolkien on
Serving the Other as Release from Bondage

Joseph Tadie

In memory of Arthur J. Spring:
volo ut sis

The aim of this essay is to foreground Tolkien's appreciation of the role played by those who are assessed as weak and ignorant by the seemingly powerful and wise, but without whom there would be no truly ethical discourse and hence no release from the bondage of self-interest that ensnares all creatures (strong and weak alike) of Middle-earth. Bondage and the release from bondage available to those who become reflectively aware of their own limitation and who then attend scandalously to strange others as servants—this will be my central concern here. I contend that we who write on Tolkien from perspectives that derive from traditions that are Christian need to attend to voices, perspectives, and interpretive frameworks that are not of our persuasion. If Tolkien is to be a topic of serious academic consideration in the contemporary university, then we must attend more closely to his connection to such important non-Christian thinkers as Emmanuel Levinas. This is precisely my aim.[1]

ON BONDAGE

To better appreciate the notion of epistemological bondage, consider Pascal's crucial claim: "'That is my place in the sun.' That is how the usurpation of the whole world began."[2] Here Pascal describes self-interest as a specific form of bondage that besets creatures endowed with reason. It is my contention that Tolkien's interpretation of the trope of bondage and release resonates not only with Pascal but also with another Francophone thinker, Emmanuel Levinas. Although these thinkers have significant and enduring differences that should not be overlooked or erased in an optimism or syncretism so characteristic of modernity, I nonetheless contend that they share a basic estimate of all reasoning creatures (be they dwarf, elf, ent, hobbit, human, or Istari). All creatures endowed with reason are bound by an essentially concupiscent—by a spontaneously emergent—desire to secure justification for their own particular (and wholly conventional) interpretation of the world. If one's particular way of life can be anchored in the unchanging realm of abstract reason—figuratively speaking: in the sun and its power, in fame and reputation—then one can ostensibly safeguard oneself against the charge of being as arbitrary as are those accounts that do not similarly anchor themselves.

For Pascal, the spontaneous movement toward an adequately anchored and wholly self-satisfied solipsism is inevitable for sinful creatures endowed with reason; even so, it still constitutes a culpable usurpation of the world because such a seeker has all the means necessary for noticing that a search so enacted constitutes an abstract, deluded, and utterly unreflective act of usurpation of the world through a self-satisfied concupiscence. Levinas was a close follower of Pascal on this point. Levinas describes such unreflective and bonded usurpation as an attempt to remain *chez soi,* "at home."[3] Or, alternatively expressed, "to begin at my sanctuary."[4] For Levinas, both of these expressions capture the modern proclivity to absorb the radical alterity of the Other into the Same. Levinas contended that modern epistemology and politics were equally incapable of calling into question their respective unreflective reductive tendencies because both relieved themselves of the urgency that comes from attending to prophetic utterance by naming all such attention as "sectarian" and "fanatical." The modern State and modern philosophical Method were allegedly designed to free us from such bias in our reckoning. Like most postmoderns, Levinas is suspicious of this claim.

In what follows, I contend that Tolkien would agree with both Pascal and Levinas in their judgment that creatures endowed with reason are *bound* to participate in a fundamentally violent interpretation of reality and that they thus are prone to instrumentalize reason as a self-justifying force in what many moderns would describe as an otherwise arbitrary tournament of forces called life. For Levinas and for Tolkien alike, reasoning creatures stand in need of conversion away from an unreflective life lived according to the law of attraction and aversion, which is but the concupiscent reduction of the other to the same. Levinas summons us away from a way of life marked by power.that by its essence is "murderous of the other."[5]

Neither Pascal nor Levinas would optimistically imagine that reason and the mind—as they were construed by so many moderns (i.e., operating coolly according to the purest laws of logic, acting as the surest means either for securing victory in the combat for power and persuasion, or aiding and abetting our attempts at securing mastery and possession of nature)—would readily lay hold of transcendent deliverance for those thus entrapped. They are not optimists about the emancipation that Tolkien called "Release from Bondage."[6] Still Levinas and Tolkien agree that release from bondage is possible (even if only provisional and always exceedingly fragile), and their descriptions of the terms of such release are revealed in strikingly similar linguistic gestures.

ON RELEASE FROM BONDAGE

Both thinkers describe this release, this transcendence,[7] in full awareness that their appeal can never impress the *soi-disant* wise and powerful in the way that other modern voices have: "Hear my words, you wisest ones! Check seriously whether I crept into the very heart of life and into the roots of its heart! Wherever I found the living, there I found the will to power; and even in the will of serving I found the will to be master."[8] Like Pascal before them, Levinas and Tolkien are agreed that if Nietzsche had plumbed the deepest reaches of the heart, then not only would he have *seen* the breakup of pure and solitary *reason* and its compelling mystique of certainty, universality, and necessity as they are achieved by a strict adherence to a method governed by logic and its *regulae*, but he would have also *heard* and been humbled to attentive speech shared with others. In his critique of service (which he interpreted as yet one more vehicle of the will to power), Nietzsche failed to listen attentively to what Pascal called the "reasons"[9] of the heart. Such reasons will always fall short of the kind of knowability desired by the rationally reductive and calculating mind, even as they will never of themselves be able to make a display of power sufficient for one who would idolize eagles in the way that Nietzsche seems to have.[10]

Even as Levinas accepts Nietzsche's clamant concern for ethics and his impressive description of will to power (perhaps *in toto*), he diverges decisively from Nietzsche in this special regard—namely, in our most authentic response to becoming reflectively aware of our individual and collective attempts at making our way in the world. It can be argued that, for Nietzsche, aesthetic acts of creation determined only according to personal taste constitute the most authentic way to dwell in a morally indeterminate world. Levinas does not share this aestheticism. Levinas knows that there may be good *reason* to follow Nietzsche, but, in so doing, we effectively stop our ears to the deepest song of the heart, its *reasons*, and its alarming ability to make us vulnerable to an unsettling command. Levinas prefers to describe the proper human response in ethical, not aesthetic, terms:

> "To turn to the truth with one's whole soul"—the Platonic recommendation is not limited to a pedagogy of good sense, preaching effort and sincerity. Does it not aim at the ultimate reticence, the most sly of all, that of a soul which, before the Good, persists in reflecting on itself, and thus arresting the movement unto the other? Is not the force of this "resistance of the unreflected to reflection" the will itself, prior to and posterior to . . . every representation? And is not

the will thus at bottom a humility rather than a will to power? Humility is not to be confused with an equivocal negation of oneself, already proud of its virtue, which, in reflection, it immediately recognizes in itself. This humility is that of him who does not "have time" to make a return upon himself and undertakes nothing to "negate" oneself, save the very abnegation of the rectilinear movement of a work which goes infinitely to the other.[11]

In spite of this cramped, mathematical, and seemingly un-Tolkienian description of the infinite dimension of the ethical relation, Levinas offers an estimable adumbration of Tolkien's appreciation of the release available to the creatures of Middle-earth who find themselves possessed of self-seeking reason.[12] These creatures are eminently equipped to achieve release from their present bondage to the circles of the world with the help of reflective (and therefore reasonable, if not strictly rational) awareness. This release is neither the product nor a project of reason in a calculative or instrumental mode; it is perhaps better described (if we follow Levinas) as an infinite linguistic relation shared between humbled (and often bewildered and even bewuthered)[13] reasoners who attend and serve one another through the marvel of language expressed in a prophetic commandment.

For Levinas, humility is that rare and shining virtue that enables one to attend to the alterity that "commands the ego by way of another's face,"[14] another's speech.[15] Suffice it to say for our purposes that the speech of the other arrives as a command and that "obedience is the proper mode of attending to the commandment. Attending to a commandment is thus not the recall of some prior generous disposition toward the Other."[16] Reflectively grasped and honestly confessed weakness is needed in order to respond obediently to the call of the other, even though it inevitably comes "against all good sense." In his preference for terms such as "commandment," "obedience," and "humility" as the prominent features of creatures endowed with reason, Levinas most decisively reveals his post-Nietzschean position.

Levinas may accept that usurpation and will to power are ultimate impulses for all creatures possessed of reason, but even if this is so, the modern proclivity to tame this will and end such usurpation through the logical control on meaning is at bottom really just another arbitrary preference.[17] Why not obey an other-than-strictly-logical control on meaning?

> To affirm such an orientation and such a sense, to posit a consciousness without reflection beneath and above all the reflections, in short to surprise at the bottom of the ego . . . [by noting the] servant's humility which no transcendental method could corrupt or absorb . . . this is the marvel of language.[18]

The ethical relation is not yet another work of *pure reason*, constrained by method, because reason (if honest) will always recognize that even its supposedly *transcendental* method is yet another of its own productions. Levinas is clear that the kind of transcendence of which he speaks is neither absurd nor irrational nor romantic, even if he openly sings his arguments in prophetic language.[19] "The God 'remaining with the contrite and the humble' (Isaiah LVII, 15), on the margin, a 'persecuted truth,' is not only a religious 'consolation,' but the original form of transcendence."[20] This does not describe a merely humanly made thing. Just because we have a hand in the doing of the work of grace, we do not thereby degrade the alterity of either the prophetic command or the diffusive character of the Good, as shown at the very end of *The Hobbit*:

> "Then the prophecies of the old songs have proved to be true, after a fashion!" said Bilbo.
> "Of course!" said Gandalf. "And why should they not prove true? Surely you don't disbelieve the prophecies because you had a hand in bringing them about yourself? You don't suppose do you that all your adventures and escapes were managed by mere luck, just for your sole benefit? You are a very fine person, Mr. Baggins, and I am very fond of you; but you are only quite a little fellow in a wide world after all!"
> "Thank goodness!" said Bilbo laughing, and handed him the tobacco jar.

In graced moments such as these, Levinas and Tolkien show themselves to be outside the dialectic characteristic of so many moderns who vacillated between either exaltation in or belittlement of the ego.[21] These moments share an other-than-modern—that is, non-ego-centered—sense of anthropology rooted in stories of creation and accounts of time gleaned from their respectively Jewish and Catholic communities. These would rather say that subjectivity (if there is such a thing) starts in the face-to-face encounter with one who is radically other than I. In this way, our very subjectivity itself can be said to arrive in the infinite relation to others, which arrives as a commanding call and elicits an attentive response in speech in the present moment. Both Levinas and Tolkien have heard the prophetic song of the suffering servant and allowed that song to become manifest in their descriptions of the ethical relation, which secures a precariously fragile release from bondage.[22] There is no other word for it: grace.

Tolkien would be sympathetic to Levinas's claim that the best description of transcendence can be made by reference to an infinite ethical relation that is enacted through language between souls who are humble and weak, who are fissured, traumatized, and even held hostage by the other. If such dialogue among the weak constitutes release, it does so in terms that can only strike the modern sensibilities as openly scandalous, suggesting that we are hostage to the Other and that we should attend fearsome enemies by revealing our true names and offering them our heartfelt service. Half-wits will they appear, those who would argue that creatures endowed with reason are meant to serve even those who would sorely abuse them.[23] Yet in this service the usurpation of the world is prevented; indeed, the usurpers are released from bondage to those who would claim their proper role as a humble servant.

ETHICAL DIMENSIONS IN THE LANGUAGE OF *THE HOBBIT*

Levinas's suspicion about sunny concupiscence finds surprising resonance in Tolkien's *Hobbit*. Consider Bilbo, whose very name conjures associations with bondage, connoting fetters or leg chains as it does. Let's imagine him in those "quiet days before the Unexpected Party"[24] and before Gandalf "flustered"[25] him by involving him in an ethical adventure composed of conversions that were catalyzed by attention to odd others, increased reflective awareness, and surprising linguistic growth.

It is a bright morning in the Shire, Bilbo is reclining just outside the shiny green door of his mathom-filled hobbit-hole, his fat stomach filled to the corners (as they say in those parts) not with just one but with a so-called second breakfast too. So sated, he is also vested in brightly colored green and yellow garments, brass buttons glinting and his curly hair bouncing in the bright morning sun. He appears the complete image of blithe insouciance, especially when we take note of his long pipe (which stretches all the way down to his neatly brushed feet) and the "wisps of smoke" issuing from his "jaws and nostrils."[26] This is an image of the usurpation of the whole world. Is this a hobbit or a dragon? Either way, both are usurpers and thieves and both are precariously close to worms.[27]

The first thing we learn about hobbits is that they live in holes in the ground, like worms and dragons. The narrator alerts us that their holes are easily distinguished from "nasty, dirty"[28] oozy-smelly holes of worms: hobbit holes signify "comfort."[29] Even if his hole is not laden with "countless piles of precious things, gold wrought and unwrought, gems and jewels, and silver . . . coats of mail, helms and axes, swords and spears,"[30] there are still strong similarities between the holes of dragons and the holes of hobbits, especially Bilbo's hole. We learn that Bilbo lived in the "most luxurious hobbit-hole . . . to be found either under The Hill or across The Water" and that in that exceedingly comfortable hole he had "settled down immovably."[31] Would Bilbo look different to Gandalf than Smaug looked to Bilbo on catching his first glimpse of that great usurping, unmoving worm?: "There he lay, a vast red-golden dragon, fast asleep; a thrumming came from his jaws and nostrils, and wisps of smoke."[32]

But how is such thrumming usurpation brought to an end? Levinas has given us an important clue. It ends when the voice of an-Other reaches the Self. The voice of a guardian such as Gandalf manifests a message that decisively impinges on the otherwise concupiscent subject. By attending to the other with the humble heart of the servant and by voicing an obedient "Here I am," concupiscent composure is brought up short. The ethically interrupted creature will cease, as long as it remains humble, to "have time" to make a return upon itself. We recall that for Levinas, virtuous humility is vividly manifest in "him who does not 'have time' to make a return upon himself."[33] Tolkien seems to share Levinas's appreciation for this kind of uncomposed humility. Consider Bilbo again:

> To the end of his days Bilbo could never remember how he found himself outside, without a hat, a walking stick or any money, or anything that he usually took when he went out; leaving his second breakfast half-finished and quite unwashed-up, pushing his keys into Gandalf's hands, and running as fast as his furry feet could carry him down the lane, past the great Mill, across The Water, and then on for a mile or more.[34]

What exactly brought Bilbo to such a predicament, so counter to his own individual habits, so entirely out of character for a hobbit? We can say confidently that Bilbo was moved from his bondage neither by persuasion alone nor by good solid logic. We are told that Bilbo had "got something a bit queer in his make-up from the Took side."[35] But he was also very much a Baggins too. Genetically he is disposed to great reputation that is independent of wealth from the Took side, but from the Baggins side he is prone to avoid adventure, a lesser reputation but a more comfortable, if less abundant, wealth. Thus, his genetic predisposition cannot be the whole story. There is no question that Bilbo's move from his homey hole was motivated, at least in part, by the song of the dwarves: "As they sang the hobbit felt the love of beautiful things made by hands and by cunning and by magic moving through him, a fierce and jealous love, the desire of the hearts of dwarves."[36] We can affirm that greed and "something Tookish"[37] were motive forces, but still we wonder if there was not at least one other motive force acting there and then. Can we say that Bilbo had become flummoxed through an obedient attention to an order received from a face?

In order to develop an answer, let's first consider Levinas's distinction between the two ways in which a transforming *order* or a converting command can be received. The first way depends on reason alone. Accordingly, we resist imagining that Bilbo received "an order by first perceiving it and then subjecting [himself] to it in a decision taken after having deliberated about it."[38] That Bilbo did perceive Gandalf with his eyes cannot be doubted: "All that the unsuspecting Bilbo saw that morning was an old man with a staff. He had a tall pointed blue hat, an old grey cloak, a silver scarf over which his long white beard hung down below his waist, and immense black boots."[39] After seeing him and deliberating about his perceptions of him, Bilbo "decided that [the old man] was not quite his sort, and wanted him to go away."[40] Left to themselves, the rational procedures associated with perception, reflection, deliberation, and decision will never humble a reasonable creature to a command so urgent that it would lead one as "solid and comfortable"[41] as Bilbo to go running off down the lane on an adventure in such an unprepared and ill-conceived way.

Bilbo's first release from hobbit common sense and from his own concupiscent *conatus essendi*[42] came from an order that registers in another and not strictly rational manner. In this second way, an order "attests to or measures an infinite authority" and is best described as "obligation," "command," "imperative," or "irrecusable responsibility."[43] Gandalf's face commanded Bilbo, who, still sunk in stupid hobbit concupiscence, proceeded to see, deliberate, and judge Gandalf, as would any other hobbit—reductively, as "a nuisance and a disturber of the peace."[44] Bilbo wished the old man would go away: "But the old man did not move."[45] So far from moving off without incident, Gandalf stood "leaning on his stick and *gazing* at the hobbit without saying anything, till Bilbo got quite uncomfortable and even a little cross."[46] Gandalf nicely embodies Levinas's second type of order, the imperative of an-Other:

[The other can] present me his face—oppose himself to me beyond all measure, with the total uncoveredness and nakedness of his defenseless eyes, the straightforwardness, the absolute frankness of his gaze. The solipsist disquietude of consciousness, seeing itself, in all of its adventures, a captive of itself, comes to an end here: true exteriority is in this gaze which forbids my conquest. Not that conquest is beyond my too weak powers, but I am no longer able to have power: the structure of my freedom is . . . completely reversed. Here is established a relationship not with a very great resistance, but with the absolutely other, with the resistance that has no resistance, with ethical resistance. It opens the very dimension of infinity, of what puts a stop to the imperialism of the same and the I. We call a face the epiphany of what can thus present itself directly, and therefore also exteriorly, to an I. . . . The epiphany of a face is wholly language.[47]

In a surprising way, the beginning of the end of Bilbo Baggins's unreflective usurpation originates in a reversal marked by a marvelously complicated linguistic interchange. Bilbo opens the exchange full of a staunch, sunny, and somatic certainty: " 'Good Morning!' said Bilbo, and he *meant* it. The sun was shining, and the grass was very green."[48] Gandalf, by contrast, emerges as a speaker with an impressive, if less than sunny, interrogative uncertainty: " 'What do you *mean*?' he said. 'Do you wish me a good morning, or mean that it is a good morning whether I want it or not; or that you feel good this morning; or that it is a morning to be good on?' "[49] Levinas could not have imagined a more ethically evocative interrogation. Bilbo could not feel less comfortable and he could hardly have imagined that, in less than two days' time, he would be running off after the very same dwarves who would insult him in his own home, not only by presuming on his habitual hospitality and threatening to break all his fine things, but also by rudely impugning his formidable reputation in calling him both a "little fellow bobbing on the mat" and a "Burglar."

Bilbo attempts to dissemble, to dismiss Gandalf's pointed question, and thus to avoid the "nasty," "disturbing," and "uncomfortable" imperative he has received by diverting their exchange away from dialogue and into the promise of somatic satisfaction, disguised under the smoky mantle of hobbit hospitality and generosity:

"'All of them at once,' said Bilbo. 'And a very fine morning for a pipe of tobacco out of doors, into the bargain. If you have a pipe about you, sit down and have a fill of mine! There's no hurry, we have all day before us!' Then Bilbo sat down on a seat by his door, crossed his legs, and blew out a beautiful grey ring of smoke."[50]

Levinas and Tolkien (every bit as much as Gandalf) share a reflective suspicion of this kind of indolent comfort and its easy generosity. Remember Levinas's caution, "Attending to a commandment is . . . not the recall of some prior generous disposition toward the Other."[51] Tolkien describes hobbits and their "native" and unthinkingly inherited dispositions. Hobbits were not only "inclined to be fat," "shy," "merry," and "dressed in bright colors," but "they were hospitable and delighted in parties, and in presents, which they gave away freely and eagerly accepted."[52] "In other matters they were, as a rule, generous and not greedy, but contented and moderate."[53] The natural hobbit tendencies toward hospitality, contentment, and generosity are not the stuff of which either ethical discourse or virtue is made, though it may well offer the silent background against which these occur.[54] Ethical discourse will make steep demands that run contrary to the "natural" or "inherited" hobbit approach to relations with others: "All hobbits were, in any case, clannish and reckoned up their relationships with great care."[55]

Tolkien and Levinas both claim that a reflective reasoning will always call this kind of careful clannish reckoning into question through an appeal to what Tolkien would call an "extravagant generosity."[56] It is "extravagant" because it must be lived even toward others who appear to uncritical common sense only as objectionable and trouble-making creatures. The litany of the objectionable others is both long and varied: Gandalf himself, but also those as fearsome as Lazy Lob and Attercop are for Bilbo; one as slow and booming as Treebeard is for Merry and Pippin; one as spiteful and stalking as Gollum is for Sam. Gandalf sees Bilbo's attempt to misuse and abuse language in an attempt to remain *chez soi* by relying on the virtues of his clan (giving hospitality, providing creature comfort, and showing generosity) for what it is, but he is not put off by it. Gandalf has made a habitual practice of extravagant generosity by learning the language and ways of creatures such as Bilbo Baggins, in spite of Bilbo's lazy linguistic habits and his hardened hobbit heart.

Gandalf responds to Bilbo's retreat with an upsetting urgency: "Very pretty! . . . But I have no time to blow smoke rings this morning. I am looking for someone to share an adventure that I am arranging, and it's very difficult to find anyone."[57] As one who is ethically alert, Gandalf has no time to return upon himself, that is, he is not unreflectively dominated by self-interest, gustatory pleasure, or conventional hospitality. Neither is he concerned for reputation as it governed the Bagginses nor for money as it dominated the Tooks.[58] Even Bilbo, unreflectively sunk as he is in hobbit common sense, has at least *some* reflective awareness, and, thanks to it, he can name *exactly* why Gandalf is having a hard time finding anyone in the Shire who might be open to the adventure of transcendence, and thus to ending the adventures of the ego-controlled self.

> "I should think so—in these parts! We are plain quiet folk and have no use for adventures. Nasty disturbing uncomfortable things! Make you late for dinner! I can't see what anybody sees in them," said our Mr. Baggins, and stuck one thumb behind his braces, and blew out another even bigger smoke-ring.[59]

It is shortly after this exchange that Bilbo greets Gandalf with a thoughtless "good morning." What began as an automatic act full of indolence and concupiscent self-indulgence ends as an intent and pointed insult. "'Good morning!' [Bilbo] said at last. 'We don't want any adventures here, thank you! You might try over The Hill or Across the Water.' By this he meant the conversation was at an end."[60] Gandalf hears Bilbo's meaning, and he could hardly have been surprised at the rapidity of Bilbo's shift in meaning, obviously bound by unreflective instinct and unexamined hobbit common sense as he is. Gandalf comments pointedly, "Now you mean you want to get rid of me, and that it won't be good till I move off."[61]

In his Baggins-like concern for reputation, Bilbo feels the sting of Gandalf's judgment and so attempts a thinly veiled act of damage control: "Not at all, not at all, my dear sir! Let me see, I don't think

I know your name?"[62] Obdurate Bilbo thus remains, sunk in that most common epistemic assumption of an indissoluble link between seeing and knowing.[63] Unreflective reliance on sight and knowledge will always bind the creature endowed with reason from turning to what can only be heard and reflectively grasped as a command arriving from the radical other as a "proper name."[64]

After the revelation of Gandalf's name, Bilbo is decisively interrupted, at a loss, and altogether unhinged, as is signaled in his exasperated exclamations, "Good gracious me! . . . Dear me! . . . Bless me."[65] Levinas might say that Bilbo has been thrust, in Gandalf's act of self-naming, into the infinity of the ethical dimension. The real signal that such a command has been issued and attentively heard is revealed in words that are quite ordinary and whose significance can be easily missed (indeed their full significance is clearly missed by Bilbo himself): "I beg your pardon."[66] These words are uttered with little reflective awareness and even less of the typical hobbit care. Still, for Levinas, these words would be clear evidence of a beginning to the end of Bilbo's unreflective usurpation, indicating as they do an incipient awareness of "guilt with regard to the other."[67]

So flustered is he that Bilbo eventually asks Gandalf's pardon for a second time. Gandalf responds, "I give it you." We still have yet to learn exactly what charges are going to be leveled against Bilbo, but Gandalf has heard the voice of the other begging pardon, asking forgiveness. Some responsibility for the other has also dawned on Bilbo, but not in a wholly rational and certainly in a less than fully collected manner. Levinas would not be tempted to dismiss the import of this shift because of the rag-tag, partial, and less-than-perfectly reflective character of this particular opening toward transcendence:

> Responsibility for the Other does not come down to a thought going back to an *a priori* idea, previously given to and rediscovered by the "I think." The natural *conatus essendi* of a sovereign ego is put into question by . . . the Other, in the ethical vigilance through which the sovereignty of the "ego" can recognize itself as "hateful," and its "place in the sun" as the "image and beginning of the usurpation of the whole world."[68]

Bilbo is not yet capable of seeing his ego as hateful and usurping (much less understanding exactly how and why Gandalf and the dwarves name him "thief"), but still he seems to have begun, in however halting, stuttering, and unreflective a manner, to put "the other before the same."[69]

BILBO'S ADMISSION OF GUILT AS AN ETHICAL OPENING IN *THE LORD OF THE RINGS*

Gandalf could both see and hear this dragon for what he was. It would take Bilbo quite some time to understand the charges he heard there in those meetings with Gandalf and the dwarves. But it is quite clear that he eventually did become more aware; that is, he did achieve at least some release from his bondage to his self-satisfied place in the sun. In order to gather evidence for our claim, we will turn to *The Fellowship of the Ring* and consider a revealing moment from the Council of Elrond. In that moment, we hear heartfelt admissions and apologies from a more transformed Bilbo than we saw at the first encounter with Gandalf in *The Hobbit*. He is still very much the hobbit Bilbo of old, replete with his characteristic concupiscence, which is expressed now not only as a gastronomic obsession so much as something else. Boromir has asked Elrond:

> "How do the Wise know that this ring [is the Ring]? And how has it passed down the years, until it is brought hither by so strange a messenger?"
>
> "That shall be told," said Elrond.
>
> "But not yet, I beg, Master!" said Bilbo. "Already the Sun is climbing to noon, and I feel the need of something to strengthen me."
>
> "I had not named you," said Elrond smiling. "But I do so now. Come! Tell us your tale. And if you have not cast your story into verse, you may tell it in plain words. The briefer, the sooner you shall be refreshed."
>
> "Very well," said Bilbo. "I will do as you bid. But I will now tell the true story, and if some here have heard me tell it otherwise"—he

looked sidelong at Glóin—"I ask them to forget it and forgive me. I only wished to claim the treasure as my very own in those days, and to be rid of the name of thief that was put on me. But perhaps I understand things a little better now. Anyway, this is what happened."[70]

Bilbo has admitted his abuse of language through his lying, just as he also openly embraces his voracious greed and his concern for reputation over truth: he is, after all, still very much a Took and a Baggins. Even if he has become reflectively aware of his own limitations and frailty in these ways—his lying and cheating and egotism—there is still something else, a new wraith-like tendency at work in him, a form of dragon sickness that must be rare for hobbits, intellectual pride:

> To some there Bilbo's tale was wholly new, and they listened with amazement while the old hobbit, actually not at all displeased, recounted his adventure with Gollum, at full length. He did not omit a single riddle. He would have given also an account of his party and disappearance from the Shire if he had been allowed; but Elrond raised his hand.
> "Well told, my friend," he said, "but that is enough at this time."[71]

One might argue that the transformed Bilbo needs to reflect more closely on the example given to him by Elrond and Gandalf. As in Boromir's description of the Periannath in general, Bilbo remains one of those who "had been held of small account by Elves and by Men, and neither Sauron nor any of the Wise save [Gandalf] had in all their counsels given thought to them."[72] Boromir thought them "strange." Like Gandalf, so too Elrond had allowed his reasonable reckoning to suffer intussusception by the speech of these strange, small, and seemingly insignificant others. In the terms deployed here, we would say that such wise and powerful creatures were not unduly attached to their intellectual superiority and their worldly influence; instead, they remained humble—attentive to those who would normally be considered beyond the pale of concern among the enlightened and cultured.[73] This humility is hard-won and, as we saw above, it poses a deep difficulty for this transformed hobbit and for even such well-disposed and cultured humans as Boromir.

There is another instructive moment at the Council of Elrond that perfectly illustrates how difficult it is for the well-educated and the well-disposed to imagine that a creature as lowly and strange as a hobbit might be integral to the realization of a task as exalted as the Quest. In this case, the wise and powerful figure is not Boromir, but instead Erestor the elf:

> "Thus we return once more to the destroying of the Ring," said Erestor, "and yet we come no nearer. What strength have we for the finding of the Fire in which it was made? That is the path of despair. Of folly I would say, if the long wisdom of Elrond did not forbid me."
>
> "Despair or folly?" said Gandalf. "It is not despair, for despair is only for those who see the end beyond all doubt. We do not. It is wisdom to recognize necessity, when all other courses have been weighed, though as folly it may appear to those who cling to false hope. Well, let folly be our cloak, a veil before the eyes of the Enemy! For he is very wise, and weighs all things to a nicety [note the modern preference for quantitatively based metrics as the exclusive means for worthwhile or useful assessment] in the scales of his malice. But the only measure he knows is desire, desire for power; and so he judges all hearts. Into his heart the thought will not enter that any would refuse it, that having the Ring we may seek to destroy it. If we seek this, we shall put him out of reckoning."
>
> "At least for a while," said Elrond. "The road must be trod, but it will be very hard. And neither strength nor wisdom will carry us far upon it. This quest may be attempted by the weak with as much hope as the strong. Yet such is oft the course of deeds that move the wheels of the world: small hands do them because they must, while the eyes of the great are elsewhere."[74]

Gandalf's counsel and Elrond's claim must sound preposterous when measured by conventional reason and common sense, that is, from the point of view of those who live by power and its privileges or from the point of view that prefers quantitative analysis to qualitative transformation. And we must admit, it does sound absurd to put forward the notion that one of the surest means for securing military victories and establishing political kingdoms involves both a dialogical engagement with strange creatures who seem no more significant than worms and a willingness to remain open to qualitative transformation of one's immediately given, one's traditionally held and deeply beloved way of construing the world. It is difficult to be dislodged from the *chez soi*.

Yet such is the stuff of which the strange song of the heart that serves as the *cantus firmus* of Tolkien's work is composed: those who wish to secure release from bondage to self-aggrandizing power, self-important wisdom, or constraining custom must recognize, accept, and embrace their own weakness and limitation[75] by implicating themselves in a linguistically grounded adventure with odd-seeming others. In the case of Gandalf, Elrond, and Erestor, this means more than just tolerating the little people, the unlikely inhabitants of holes hidden in hillsides and meadows. It means risking relationship with them.[76] In the case of Bilbo and Frodo, this means engaging elves, dwarves, Istari, dragons, such as Smaug, and the contemptible Wormtongue and Gollum, not to mention many others.

Such is the difficult principle that emanates from the heart[77] and that will always humble the laborious lucubrations of the wise, the sensible stratagems of the powerful, and the colloquial and calculating concerns of weak ones, such as the hobbits themselves. In the life of humility, a release from epistemological bondage appears as a gift emanating from the other in speech that is rooted in an authentically reflective consciousness. It is speech that, on hearing the name of the other, can properly respond to the command of the other in a subjectivity that is not sly and strong but rather available and weak—totally attentive in the present moment. Such is the disposition of the suffering servant in Tolkien. It is owing to precisely that so-called weak spot in his plan that Bilbo would eventually taste the closest thing he probably ever knew of release from bondage. Bilbo finally becomes openly, honestly, and manifestly what the dwarves once said he was: a thief. His burgling identity shines most clearly when, in their "escape" from the elves, the barrels in which they have been stowed away strike a "stony pier":

> Poor dwarves! Bilbo was not badly off now. He slipped from his barrel and waded ashore, and then sneaked along to some huts that he could see near the water's edge. He no longer thought twice about picking up a supper uninvited if he got the chance, he had been obliged to do it for so long, and he knew now only too well what it was to be really hungry, not merely politely interested in the dainties of a well-filled larder. Also he thought he had caught a glimpse of a fire through the trees, and that appealed to him with his dripping and ragged clothes clinging to him cold and clammy.[78]

Levinas would recognize that sun-warmth-seeking tendency anywhere! Many other features of Tolkien's imagined world are in harmony with the basic contour of this position. He and Gandalf know that the ethical adventure with peculiar others will lead the wise and powerful away from the usual haunts of power, wisdom, and even habits as reputedly wholesome as generosity. These have had to learn that "they have not come to *do* things as [much as] to learn to be, and that they must not come like a mechanic with tools of knowledge and theory to repair what is broken."[79] Instrumentalized reason will never afford us the ability to undertake the risk of the ethical adventure, nor will it afford us so counter a command as to attend as a humble servant on even our enemies. It is not easy to imagine that I am somehow guilty for the guilt of all.

RELEASE FROM BONDAGE DEPENDS ON SERVICE ON ODD OTHERS

Tolkien has a lesser-known account of release from bondage called the "Quest of Erebor." In it, we witness Gimli asking Gandalf a crucial question, "Was [the whole of Bilbo and Frodo's adventure] your design?" Gimli the dwarf loves things cunningly designed and made by hands. I think Gandalf's response is so full of humility, so counter to modern interpretations of instrumentalized reason and its reckoning, and resonates so completely with the main themes we have been rehearsing here via Levinas, that it should function as our conclusion.

It is worth noting that Gandalf's face is bathed in the light of a *setting* sun as he makes his response to this uncharacteristically inquisitive dwarf. He is, after all, the first to break an age-old bias to which his whole tribe had, since they were first awakened, been decisively bound: "Dwarves thought all Elves were all stupid, which was a very stupid thing to think." Gimli, by forging the bonds of friendship with Legolas, follows the wisdom of his heart rather than the knowledge learned from his prior relationships with his people, thus achieving an important release from bondage. A dwarf having become friend to an elf! It is certainly true that Gandalf (like Elrond) has become aware of, and has been in constant combat with, his own sun-seeking tendency—his own truck with bias, violence, and the proclivity for possession and control. Proof positive is found in his willingness to meet with dwarves such as Gimli and hobbits like Bilbo and Frodo. Yet, for all his apparent and mindfully actualized altruism, even Gandalf is still vulnerable to the distorting influence of the sunny usurpation of the world. Even if it is now setting for him, it is still shining on him, influencing him and his reckoning. There is no final, complete, and total release from bondage as long as a creature moves in the circles of the world. Even if the killing of the dragon and the return of the king were achieved for the most part by "the counsel and vigilance"[80] of Gandalf, the wizard still remains reticent to imagine that his efforts were the only efficacious ingredients in the Quest. He responds to the dwarf's question thus:

> "I do not know the answer. For I have changed since those days, and I am no longer trammeled by the burden of Middle-earth as I was then. In those days I should have answered you with words like those I used with Frodo . . . in that distant time I said to a small and frightened hobbit: Bilbo was *meant* to find the Ring, and *not* by its maker, and you therefore were *meant* to bear it. And I might have added: And I was *meant* to guide you both [Frodo and Bilbo]."[81]

Again, the fragility of Gandalf's attentive and humble service is apparent in these details. Gandalf uses language that is fit for the moment. The things that he said to the "small and frightened" Frodo then may not have been *true* in any rigorous sense (and he might not say them now), but neither were they false. Gandalf answers Gimli's question whether the whole adventure had been his design by saying that he himself does not know. This is an authentic confession of finitude and dependence. Gandalf is appropriately humble because he has been attentive to the call emanating from the face of a seemingly strange other: "In those days I should have answered you with words like I used with Frodo, only last year in the spring."[82] I contend that in Gandalf's ultimate answer, one can pick up, yet again, a deep resonance with Levinas. Tolkien has led the wizard away from modern interpretations of heady instrumentalized *reason* to hearty *reasons* shared linguistically with odd others in the posture of a good servant: "I used in my waking mind only such means as were allowed to me, doing what lay to my hand according to such reasons as I had. But what I knew in my heart . . . that is another matter."[83]

NOTES

1. Tolkien scholar Jane Chance is an exemplary figure for engaging Tolkien to the postmodern context and its concerns. Chance boldly put Tolkien into dialogue with influential postmodern thinkers like Michel Foucault, Julia Kristeva, & Luce Irigiray. See Jane Chance, *The Lord of the Rings: The Mythology of Power* (University Press of Kentucky, 2001). While there are some infelicities and lacunae in this or that detail, still her approach remains exemplary and has informed the work of other significant scholars, see *Tolkien's Modern Middle Ages*, eds. Jane Chance and Alfred K. Siewers (Palgrave Macmillan, 2005), for proof.

2. Levinas, *Otherwise Than Being or Beyond Essence*, epigraph.

3. Levinas, *Totality and Infinity*, 33.

4. Levinas, *Otherwise Than Being or Beyond Essence*, vii.

5. Levinas, *Totality and Infinity*, 47.

6. Tolkien, *Silmarillion*, 162.

7. This wooly word is meant both negatively and positively. Negatively, it should be heard in the absolutely anti-Heideggerian tone in which it was always

sung by Levinas: "Heideggerian ontology subordinates the relation with the other to the relation with the neuter, Being, and it thus continues to exalt the will to power, whose legitimacy the other alone can unsettle, troubling good conscience. . . . This is an existence which takes itself to be natural, for whom its place in the sun, its ground, its site, orient all signification—a pagan existing. Being directs it building and cultivating, in the midst of a familiar landscape, on a maternal earth. Anonymous, neuter, it directs it, ethically indifferent, as a heroic freedom, foreign to all guilt with regard to the other" (Levinas, *Collected Philosophical Papers*, 52–53). Positively, transcendence is a word that Levinas deploys as one of those Jewish words whose very Jewishness will never be overcome, like *hineni*; the "here I am" indicative of the obedient servant. In this way, transcendence indicates the posture of the obedient servant Abraham: "Does not justice consist in putting the obligation with regard to the other before obligations to oneself, in putting the other before the same?" (ibid., 53).

8. Nietzsche, *Thus Spoke Zarathustra*, 89.

9. "The heart has its reasons which reason does not know" (Pascal, *Pensées*, 78). Lest we arouse the suspicions of either romantic and/or irrational appeals here, let it be stated clearly that the ethical relation, as articulated by Levinas, is essentially linguistic. Language connects us to reason, but it does so in a manner that is other than rationalistic by not claiming "the amplitude of an all-encompassing structure or of an ultimate comprehension" (Levinas, *Collected Philosophical Papers*, 153).

10. Nietzsche's idolized eagles swoop down and eat tender lambs, but Tolkien's iconic eagles serve even the lowly likes of Frodo and his half-wit servant. For the significance of "half-wit" see note 23.

11. Levinas, *Collected Philosophical Papers*, 99.

12. Both Nietzsche and Levinas, though they share the suspicion of rationality characteristic of postmodern thinkers, recognize reflection as an integral ingredient to a life worth living. As we shall see shortly, Levinas argues that "will" is basically the "resistance of the unreflected to reflection"; see Nietzsche, *Gay Science*, sec. 2, 3, and 280.

13. "Bilbo rushed along the passage, very angry, and altogether bewildered and bewuthered—this was the most awkward Wednesday he ever remembered" (Tolkien, *The Hobbit*, 18). Levinas described the awkward and estranging impulse behind his masterpiece, *Totality and Infinity*: "The effort of this book is directed toward apperceiving in discourse a non-allergic relation with alterity, toward apperceiving Desire—where power, by essence murderous of the other, becomes, faced with the other and "against all good sense," the impossibility of murder, the consideration of the other, or justice" (47).

14. Levinas, "Diachrony and Representation," 113.

15. Levinas was always clear that the "face" was not meant as a visually perceptible reality situated at the front of my neighbor's head: "Vision is not a

transcendence. . . . It opens nothing that, beyond the same, would be absolutely other. . . . In fleeing itself in vision, consciousness returns to itself" (*Totality and Infinity*, 191). The solipsism of sight and its hegemony will only be broken by the face of another that arrives "as speech" (ibid., 201).

16. Levinas, "Diachrony and Representation," 153.

17. The phrase is borrowed from theologian Frederick G. Lawrence and is meant as a shorthand description of modern/calculating reason's brash claim to truth. By having conformed itself to the scientific ideal, as promulgated by figures such as Bacon and Descartes, inquirers hubristically imagine that as long as they maintain methodological purity in "the abstract and static context dictated by logical clarity, coherence, and rigor," they can and will operate beyond the biases, contingency, and fallibility of the neutral observer. Lawrence comments that "unlike Heidegger, Lonergan brought to light how the liberation of the existential subject occurs in religious conversion; and that falling in love with God is not a human achievement but a divine gift." "Nevertheless," Lawrence adds, Lonergan "stresses that any attainment of human authenticity is always dialectical, because 'it never is some pure, serene, secure possession' but is 'always precarious'" (Lawrence, "Hermeneutic Revolution and the Future of Theology," 351–52).

18. Levinas, *Collected Philosophical Papers*, 99.

19. Ibid., 67.

20. Ibid.

21. This distinction derives from yet another French thinker, Paul Ricoeur.

22. Lawrence reminds us of a similar theme in the work of Lonergan: "I have argued that man exists authentically in the measure that he succeeds in self-transcendence, and I have found that self-transcendence has both its fulfillment and its enduring ground in holiness, in God's gift of his love to us" (Lawrence, "Hermeneutic Revolution and the Future of Theology," 352). Lest we take Lonergan to be overly optimistic with this language of measure and success, Levinas provides a welcome precision regarding the real work associated with such self-transcendence: "Transcendence owes itself to itself to interrupt its own demonstration. Its voice has to be silent as soon as one listens for its message. It is necessary that its pretension be exposed to derision and refutation, to the point of suspecting [in] the *here I am* that attests to it [either] a cry or a slip of a sick subjectivity [or] of a subjectivity responsible for the other!" (Cohen, *Face to Face with Levinas*, 23–24).

23. Sam's real name is Ban. A shortening of Banazîr, meaning "half-wise, simple." Tolkien chose to describe Frodo's closest companion as a "half-wit" servant. I have always thought it was fitting that Sam's name is expunged from the final recounting of the story: "There at last they looked upon death and defeat, and all their valour was in vain; for Sauron was too strong. Yet in that hour was put to the proof that which Mithrandir had spoken, and help came from the

hands of the weak, when the Wise faltered. For, as many songs have since sung, it was the Periannath, the Little People, dwellers in hillsides and meadows, that brought them deliverance. For Frodo the Halfling, it is said, at the bidding of Mithrandir took on himself the burden, and alone with his servant, he passed through peril and darkness and came at last in Sauron's *despite* even to Mount Doom; and there into the Fire where it was wrought he cast the Great Ring of Power" (Tolkien, *Silmarillion*, 303–4). It is worth noting that the last emphasized term "despite" can carry the following connotations: contemptuous treatment, disregard, defiance, and it derives from both the Old French and Latin term: *déspectus*, "view from a height, scorn." For readers of Levinas, this ethical trope will be familiar.

24. Tolkien, *The Hobbit*, 271.

25. Ibid., 9.

26. Ibid., 193.

27. For whatever differences they might have, Nietzsche and Tolkien share a passion for exploring the ethical implications of the word "worm." In English at least, the word suggests both serpents and vermin. Nietzsche's concern for dragons is also worthy of note, especially in *Thus Spoke Zarathustra*.

28. Tolkien, *The Hobbit*, 3.

29. Ibid.

30. Ibid., 194.

31. Ibid., 4.

32. Ibid., 193.

33. Levinas, *Collected Philosophical Papers*, 99.

34. Tolkien, *The Hobbit*, 5.

35. Ibid.

36. Ibid., 18.

37. Ibid., 19.

38. Levinas, *Collected Philosophical Papers*, 112.

39. Tolkien, *The Hobbit*, 11.

40. Ibid.

41. Ibid.

42. *Conatus essendi* is a term that, for Levinas, captures either the natural desire to be or the basic right to existence. Consider his statement in Cohen, *Face to Face with Levinas*:

> The approach to the face is the most basic mode of responsibility. As such, the face of the other is verticality and uprightness; it spells a relation of rectitude. The face is not in front of me (*en face de moi*) but above me; it is the other before death, looking through and exposing death. Secondly, the face is the other who asks me not to let him die alone, as if to do so were to become an accomplice in his death.

Thus the face says to me: you shall not kill. In the relation to the face I am exposed as a usurper of the place of the other. The celebrated "right to existence" that Spinoza called the *conatus essendi* and defined as the basic principle of all intelligibility is challenged by the relation to the face. Accordingly, my duty to respond to the other suspends my natural right to self-survival, *le droit vitale*.

My ethical relation of love for the other stems from the fact that the self cannot survive by itself alone, cannot find meaning within its own being-in-the-world, within the ontology of sameness. That is why I prefaced *Otherwise Than Being or Beyond Essence* with Pascal's phrase, "That is my place in the sun." That is how the usurpation of the whole world began. Pascal makes the same point when he declares that "the self is hateful" (23–24).

43. Levinas, *Collected Philosophical Papers*, 113.

44. Tolkien, *Lord of the Rings*, 40.

45. Tolkien, *The Hobbit*, 6.

46. Ibid. (Emphasis added).

47. Levinas, *Collected Philosophical Papers*, 55.

48. Tolkien, *The Hobbit*, 6.

49. Ibid.

50. Ibid., 12.

51. Levinas, *Collected Philosophical Papers*, 113.

52. Tolkien, *Lord of the Rings*, 2.

53. Ibid., 9.

54. We should never turn away, of course, from ancient convivial truths, even those as popular as this one: "If more of us valued food and cheer and song above hoarded gold, it would be a merrier world."

55. Ibid., 7.

56. In a letter to Amy Ronald, Tolkien points out that Gandalf "did not mean to say that one must be merciful, for it may prove useful later—it would not then be mercy or pity, which are only truly present when contrary to prudence. Not ours to plan! But we are assured that we must be ourselves extravagantly generous, if we are to hope for the extravagant generosity which the slightest easing of, or escape from, the consequences of our own follies and errors represents. And that mercy does sometimes occur in this life" (*Letters*, 253).

57. Tolkien, *The Hobbit*, 6.

58. Ibid., 4: "But the fact remained that the Tooks were not as respectable as the Bagginses, though they were undoubtedly richer."

59. Ibid., 6.

60. Ibid.

61. Ibid.

62. Ibid.

63. "A first step toward transcendence, then, is to reject the mistaken supposition that knowing consists in taking a look" (Lonergan, *Insight*, 658).

64. Tolkien, *The Hobbit*, 200. The narrator suggests that it is "wise" to withhold one's name from a dragon. I suspect that Gandalf certainly knew the risk associated with revealing his proper name to Bilbo, but because he is not completely under the sway of the *libido dominandi*, because he is heedful of the call of infinity, he knowingly opens himself by vulnerably singing his own proper name in front of one (Bilbo) who could be "as fierce as a dragon in a pinch" (Tolkien, *The Hobbit*, 17).

65. Ibid., 6.

66. Ibid.

67. Levinas, *Collected Philosophical Papers*, 53.

68. Ibid., 112.

69. Ibid., 53.

70. Tolkien, *Lord of the Rings*, 242–43.

71. Ibid., 243.

72. Tolkien, *Silmarillion*, 303.

73. The last page of *Silmarillion* attests to Gandalf's power and wisdom: "Thus peace came again, and a new Spring opened on earth; and the Heir of Isildur was crowned King of Gondor and Arnor, and the might of the Dúnedain was lifted up and their glory renewed. . . . Now all these things were achieved for the most part by the counsel and vigilance of Mithrandir, and in the last few days he was revealed as a lord of great reverence" (304).

74. Tolkien, *Lord of the Rings*, 262.

75. Erestor's humility shines in his ability to incorporate Elrond's wisdom in his own reckoning.

76. Tolkien treated this matter decisively in another place. In a chapter called "Of Beren and Lúthien," Tolkien outlined what he called the "Lay of Leithian, Release from Bondage," the second longest song of those that are sung "concerning the world of old" (Tolkien, *Silmarillion*, 162). Lúthien's posture before Morgoth is an exemplary enunciation of the kind of scandalous service we have been hinting at in this whole effort so far: "Lúthien was stripped of her disguise by the will of Morgoth, and he bent his gaze upon her. She was not daunted by his eyes; and she named her own name, and offered her service to sing before him, in the manner of a minstrel" (ibid., 180). Again, the sonority between Levinas and Tolkien on the character of the Release from Bondage could not be more audible, even if we have told the tale here more laboriously, when we might have done it "in fewer words and without song" (ibid., 162).

77. "Heart" as used here refers not to the sentimentality of a Hallmark moment but more closely to the Hebrew *lev*, the center of "thinking and wisdom."

78. Tolkien, *The Hobbit*, 199.

79. Vanier, *Broken Body*, 77.
80. Tolkien, *Silmarillion*, 304.
81. Tolkien, *Annotated Hobbit*, 369.
82. Ibid.
83. Ibid.

BIBLIOGRAPHY

Cohen, Richard A. *Face to Face with Levinas*. New York: SUNY Press, 2007.

Lawrence, Frederick G. "Fragility of Consciousness: Lonergan and the Postmodern Concern for the Other." *Theological Studies* 54 (March 1993): 55–94.

———. "The Hermeneutic Revolution and the Future of Theology." In *Between the Human and the Divine Philosophical and Theological Hermeneutics*, edited by Andrzej Wierciński, 326–54. Toronto: Hermeneutic, 2002.

Levinas, Emmanuel. *Collected Philosophical Papers*. Pittsburgh: Duquesne University Press, 1998.

———. "Diachrony and Representation." In *Time and the Other*, translated by Richard A. Cohen. Pittsburgh: Duquesne University Press, 1987.

———. *Otherwise Than Being or Beyond Essence*. Translated by Alphonso Lingis. Pittsburgh: Duquesne University Press, 1981.

———. *Totality and Infinity*. Translated by Alphonso Lingis. Pittsburgh: Duquesne University Press, 1969.

Lonergan, Bernard. *Insight*. Toronto: University of Toronto Press, 1992.

Nietzsche, Friedrich. *The Gay Science*. Edited by Bernard Williams; translated by Adrian Del Caro and Josefine Nauckhoff. Cambridge: Cambridge University Press, 2001.

———. *Thus Spoke Zarathustra*. Edited by Adrian Del Caro and Robert Pippin; translated by Adrian Del Caro. Cambridge: Cambridge University Press, 2006.

Pascal, Blaise. *Pensées*. Translated by W. F. Trotter; introduction by T. S. Eliot. New York: E. P. Dutton, 1958.

Tolkien, J. R. R. *The Annotated Hobbit*. Adapted by Douglas A. Anderson. Boston: Houghton Mifflin, 2002.

———. *The Hobbit*. London: HarperCollins, 1995.

———. *The Letters of J. R. R. Tolkien*. Edited by Humphrey Carpenter with the assistance of Christopher Tolkien. Boston: Houghton Mifflin, 2000.

———. *The Lord of the Rings*. Boston: Houghton Mifflin, 2005.

———. *The Silmarillion*. 2nd ed. Edited by Christopher Tolkien. Boston: Houghton Mifflin, 1981.

Vanier, Jean. *The Broken Body*. New York: Paulist, 1988.

CHAPTER 9

TOLKIEN AND POSTMODERNISM

Ralph C. Wood

It may seem manifest madness to suggest that J. R. R. Tolkien has any real engagement with postmodern concerns, especially when we recall the many reasons for describing him as a *pre*modern and antiquarian writer. Tolkien regarded nearly everything worthy of praise in English culture to have ended in 1066. He scorned the imposition of a Norman ethos on a vibrant English tradition that had flourished for more than 500 years; he looked upon the Arthurian legends as an alien French import and thus as no fit basis for a national mythology; he lamented Chaucer's penchant for the gently rocking Italian iambic over against the hard spondaic stresses of Anglo-Saxon meter; he also regarded Shakespeare as hopelessly modern, since so many of his characters remain so obsessively subjective in their quandaries. Tolkien also judged the Reformation to be a terrible error, insisting that the cathedrals of England were stolen Catholic property, the booty of what G. K. Chesterton called the sixteenth-century "revolution of the rich." Neither was he happy that his dear friend and companion C. S. Lewis, remained, for the entirety of his life, what Tolkien derisively called "an Ulster Protestant."

The litany of Tolkien's antimodernity could be extended almost endlessly. He was a confessed Luddite, for example, who lamented the Triumph of the Machine, as he described the Industrial Revolution and all its pomps. He refused, moreover, to drive a motorcar once he saw the damage that paved roads and automobiles had done to the English countryside. Tolkien also remained a lifelong Tory and an unapologetic monarchist in his politics, believing that hierarchical distinctions are necessary for the flourishing of any polity, whether academic or ecclesial or governmental. He longed, in fact, for the return of Roman Catholicism as the established state religion of England. In both his poetry and his prose, moreover, Tolkien had repeated recourse to decidedly premodern literary forms, especially epic and romance. As Kenneth Craven has also noted: "J. R. R. Tolkien was an 'Ancient' in the sense that he never wanted to live in the present time, but in saner ages and in eternity. . . . Tolkien [was] as ancient as Treebeard, a mossy poet who lived in the languages and poems of the Dark Ages."[1]

Yet I contend that, for all of his admitted troglodyte sentiments, Tolkien can be shown to have anticipated many of the concerns of the postmodernists—even if he answered them not at all in postmodernist terms. Let it be made ever so clear that I do not regard Tolkien himself as a postmodernist in any intentional or accidental sense, but rather as an author whose concerns often coincide and overlap with those of the postmodernists. Just as Jan Kott revealed more than forty years ago that Shakespeare shares our contemporary *problématique*, so does Tolkien anticipate, in a similarly proleptic way, the vexations and opportunities of the postmodern world. To make this counterintuitive case, I will first seek to define the modernism whose errors Tolkien had so tellingly avoided while doing his work in the midst of the modernist collapse.

THE MODERN "GOD" WHO IS NOT GOD

So convoluted is the program of postmodernism that John Barth has described it as "tying your necktie while simultaneously explaining the step-by-step procedure of necktie-tying and chatting about the history of male neckwear—and managing a perfect full Windsor anyhow." Richard Rorty once suggested that we drop the term "post-modern," so elusive has become its meaning, so crude has been its overuse. Yet there is no avoiding Jean-François Lyotard's celebrated claim that to be postmodern is to be incredulous toward metanarratives. What Lyotard means is not that there can be no overarching Story—even its denial would constitute a new metanarrative—but that the chief modern narratives have been reductive and totalizing. Whether in Hegel or Marx or Freud, human existence is explained so finally and definitively that there is nothing left unaccountable, nothing without remainder, no mystery inviting wonder and endless exploration. Both the pretense and the inhumanity of the modern project were first named by Søren Kierkegaard in the nineteenth century. The great Danish poet-philosopher famously said of Hegel that he built a palace of thought so magnificent that it was uninhabitable—and so he had to construct a shanty outside it to actually inhabit. Kierkegaard was thus one of the first to discern that, without recourse to the divine revelation that makes such a perspective possible, modernity nonetheless attempts to view the universe *sub specie aeternitatis*. At the heart of the Enlightenment project lies the notion that man-*qua*-man can stand above the flux of history to behold the universe from beyond, examining it "under the aspect of eternity"; that is, from a timeless and placeless stance, a "view from nowhere."

The story of this modern delusion has been told many times and in many ways. Suffice it ever so briefly to say that it has its origin in medieval nominalism, especially in Scotus and Ockham. They sought to rid theological language of ambiguity and equivocation, seeking instead "an absolute transparency of the language of every science." They did so by way of semantic reduction and simplification that exalted the denotative over the connotative: "Only the former can be said to refer to existing entities that do not need the mediation of universals either for their existence or for our immediate cognition of them." God, in turn, could no longer be symbolized through nature because nature itself is utterly contingent on a "God" whose will is at once so powerful and arbitrary that He could just as readily have assumed the form of a stone or donkey as the person named Jesus of Nazareth.[2] The upshot of this reversal is that the rich medieval tradition of the *analogia entis*—the "method of predication whereby concepts derived from a familiar object are made applicable to a relatively unknown object in virtue of some similarity between two otherwise dissimilar objects"[3]—was steadily abandoned.

This was no small loss, for the analogical concept seeks to avoid both equivocity and univocity by embracing "the common and the proper, like and unlike, in a community which is logically indivisible. . . . [It] is founded on that community and diversity which is present in every existing thing precisely in its being."[4] Thus, for example, could Aquinas speak confidently of human justice being analogous to divine justice because, though the two terms are far from identical, neither are they utterly unlike. With the loss of such analogical predications of God and his attributes, the imagination itself was impoverished, for nature and history themselves were also desymbolized.[5] Thus did a new conception of space and location arise with Scotus and Ockham. With such a vacating of real significance from both bodies and places, of metaphors and analogies, the universe had been made at once homogeneous and univocal and ultimately godless.

The Nominalists opened the way for Descartes to make God not only beyond analogy but also unnecessary. For him, bodies are nothing but extended things, so that space and matter have the same meaning: "the material world is one infinite continuum, and in fact, all matter is one substance." Whence, then, motion? To say, as Descartes did, that God implanted certain rules of quantity and motion within matter is an empty hypothesis, as Newton complained. In fact, God is not needed at all in a Cartesian universe:

> Matter-in-motion is conceived of by Descartes as devoid of any final cause or aim. But it is even difficult to see how a spirit could intervene in this closed system of causality by motion. If animals are pure *automata*, why not also all the actions of the human body? Finally, Descartes insists . . . on a voluntarism more radical than the most radical Nominalists. God is first and foremost omnipotent and self-caused; all his other attributes depend on his will. If he so willed, he could invalidate our "clear and distinct" ideas; even eternal truths are contingent upon his will.[6]

Despite his well-meant attempt to defend such an arbitrary god as the author of such a mathematical universe, Descartes left the world godless. "Mind, not the universe," writes Michael Buckley, "bears the evidence for the divine existence. Just as the divine truth guarantees the external physical world, so the divine infinity removes from this universe any discernible final order and purpose." What is left, asks Buckley, when final causes are removed from the universe? "A mechanical universe whose entire composition can be explained simply by matter and the laws of nature."[7]

Buckley has traced the ruinous history of those thinkers—especially Isaac Newton, Nicolas Malebranche, and Samuel Clarke—who both embraced and attempted to defend Descartes's "God." The result was unmitigated failure. Whereas the God of Abraham, Isaac, and Jacob was once regarded as the condition for the possibility of the world's existence—so that everything in the world bore witness to God—this newly minted deistic "God" now bore witness to the world. In the lesser tradition that runs from John Toland's *Christianity Not Mysterious* to Matthew Tindal's *Christianity as Old as the Creation* and finally to William Paley's *Evidences for Christianity*, the contradiction was even more drastic, as an impersonal natural order became the alleged basis for belief in the irreducibly personal God. "Let nature," writes Buckley about this tradition, "whether in the inner orientation of things or in the ontological structure of ideas, constitute the evidence for the existence of god; let philosophy be the discipline by which this evidence is analyzed."[8]

What Buckley finds astonishing about the seventeenth and eighteenth century Christian apologists and defenders of the Faith is that, with the exception of Blaise Pascal, none of them appealed either to Christ or Christian experience. They had no recourse whatsoever to the lives of the saints, to mystical prayer and miracles, or to the ordinary Christian devotion and service that were still ingredient to the entire cultural existence of Europe. "Christianity as such," Buckley writes, "more specifically the person and teaching of Jesus or the experience and history of the Christian Church, did not enter the discussion. The absence of any consideration of Christology is so pervasive . . . that it becomes taken for granted."[9] There is little

wonder that Diderot and d'Holbach made short shrift of the so-
called God of deistic Christian philosophy. Even more devastating,
of course, were the critiques that would follow a century later in
Fichte and the Russian nihilists, in Nietzsche and Marx and Freud.
They rightly railed against this Supreme Being who was but one
among other beings, this Old Nobodaddy, as Blake called him, this
omniscient, omnipresent, and omnipotent It, this Nada which art in
Nada and which thus could not possibly have become "flesh and
dwelt among men, full of grace and truth." Far from being the enemies of orthodox Christianity, these great "masters of suspicion," as
Paul Ricoeur called them, killed off a god to which premodern
Christians had never given their devotion in the first place. Hence
Pascal's sharp rejoinder to atheists who believed that they were denying the True God:

> They suppose that [the Christian religion] consists simply in wor-
> shiping a God considered to be great, powerful, and eternal: this is
> properly speaking deism, almost as far removed from the Christian
> religion as atheism, which is its complete opposite. From this they
> conclude that all things combine to establish the point that God
> does not manifest himself to us with all the clarity that he might.
>
> But let them conclude what they like against deism, they will
> conclude nothing against the Christian religion, which properly
> consists in the mystery of the Redeemer, who, uniting in himself
> the two natures, human and divine, saved men from corruption and
> sin in order to reconcile them with God in his divine person.[10]

Such a condensed history of modern atheism may seem far removed from the fiction of J.R.R. Tolkien. Yet I contend that this
deistic no-god whose death Nietzsche first prophesied in *The Gay
Science* is also the deity of modernity, and that Tolkien's work has
immense resonance for our time precisely because he writes in response to this modernity whose deity was already dead. Tolkien has
postmodern resonances in this precise sense: his work addresses the
problem of the dead deity of modernism. He does it, I will argue, in
a variety of ways: (1) in his praise for cultural pluralism as a neces-

sary good in order for particular peoples to prosper; (2) in his refusal of modernist and foundationalist accounts of reason, insisting instead that knowledge and truth are historically located and grounded; (3) in his critique of modern culture as wickedly coercive in its false claims to universality, especially in its resulting warfare; and finally (4) in his demonstration that divine action is never obvious but hidden, in fact so providentially obscure that it is to be found in small communities of the weak and the emarginated who overcome modern self-aggrandizing individualism by refusing all coercive power. Finally, in a brief postlude, I will suggest how Tolkien's work remains radically relevant for the culture of life amidst the culture of death and the deceits of modernity—namely, by enabling Christians to enter the postmodern "tournament of narratives."[11]

TOLKIEN'S EMBRACE OF CULTURAL PLURALISM

In calling Tolkien a cultural pluralist, I do not mean to suggest that he is a cultural relativist. Unlike many postmodernists, Tolkien holds neither to the supposed equality of all cultures nor to the impossibility of making judgments among them. Neither seeking some impossibly Archimedean stance outside the universe (as do the allegedly objective modernists), nor claiming that Western culture has authority only for Westerners (as do the radically subjective postmodernists), Tolkien approaches other cultures as an unabashed Christian. He follows the injunction of the early apologists for Christians to "take the spoils of the Egyptians"—to make Christian use of the many accomplishments left from the Greco-Roman world. Thus does Tolkien retrieve from various ancient northern cultures those virtues that serve his Christian project, just as he largely ignores their many vices: witchcraft, slavery, incest, polygamy, and human sacrifice. Nor do his protagonists employ any of the pungent four-letter epithets that salt the Anglo-Saxon tongue. Some of Tolkien's critics have objected, in fact, to such linguistic sanitation. Tom Shippey wittily complains, for instance, that Tolkien's noble characters "are so virtuous that one can hardly call them pagans at all."[12]

One of the most deleterious effects of modernism has been the eclipse of particular languages and cultures in favor of those forms of speech and social order that rely on unhistorical abstractions, on unnarrated concepts, on words unrooted in either time or place. In the name of such untraditioned political systems and ideas has much if not most of our modern mischief been done. From George Orwell to George Steiner, we have been reminded that the unprecedented bloodletting of the modern age is largely the work of omnicompetent governments both acting upon and legitimated by reiterated slogans and deadly neologisms: *Arbeit Macht Frei*, the triumph of the proletariat, and so on. Words uprooted from their concrete origins and made to substitute for real thought can be wickedly used:

> When you think of a concrete object, you think wordlessly, and then, if you want to describe the things you have been visualizing you probably hunt about till you find the exact words that seem to fit. When you think of something abstract you are more inclined to use words from the start, and unless you make constant effort to prevent it, the existing dialect [i.e., the regnant jargon] will come rushing in and do the job for you, at the expense of blurring or even changing your meaning. . . . Political language is designed to make lies sound truthful and murder respectable, and to give an appearance of solidity to pure wind.[13]

We need not look to modern political rhetoric as proof of this danger; Saruman illustrates it all too well. Knowing that he has earned Gandalf's respect as one whose name befits his character—*wizard* is rooted in *wisdom*—Saruman urges Gandalf to join him in an alliance with Sauron. Together they would use the power of the Ring to accomplish great good. That Saruman's premise is true, there is no doubt. Saruman almost persuades Gandalf because his rhetoric so eloquently disguises the sinister quality of his Sauronic methods, and the evil side-effects that would be the terrible cost of such ill-gained good. He thus urges Gandalf to forgo his alliance with such "weak" creatures as men and hobbits, and to keep silent about the malevolent means necessary to accomplish such high-sounding ideals as Knowledge, Rule, and Order (*LOTR*, 253).[14]

Arguments of Saruman's kind, as Czeslaw Milosz observes, have had immense appeal in the modern world because they simply transplant the Cartesian and Newtonian understanding of nature into the human realm. Just as the Enlightenment had reduced nature to a mechanism of colliding and conjoining forces, so have modern materialists regarded "man [as] a social animal whose thought is the reflection of the movement of matter."[15] Since natural creatures can be improved by overcoming things detrimental while enhancing things beneficial to their material well-being, modern ideologues have sought to apply the same principle to history. They thrust the vagaries of human existence through the sieve of economic and racial and class conflict so as to assure an alleged improvement of the species. Through political and social structures designed to enhance such historical progress, they attempted to create an ideal New Man, one who would not submit to the necessities of physiology and to the shackles of ethnicity, but one who would transform such limits into a world without want and without need, a realm of universal peace. "The result?" asks Milosz. Individuals were homogenized into controllable slaves of the omnicompetent state. There could hardly be an apter description of Sauron's aim and of Saruman's collusion with it.

What astonished Milosz about the collusion of thousands of Eastern European intellectuals with the totalitarian programs of the Leninist-Stalinist regimes was their willing consent. While millions of ordinary people were subjected to the terrors of brute political *force*—often committing unspeakable crimes of their own in allying themselves with their overlords—the intellectuals who unleashed this crushing force deliberately embraced demonic *ideas*. For the first time in history, Milosz argues, the human spirit has been enslaved not by outward and mindless oppression but by inward and highly intellectual *consciousness*. "Never before," he writes, "has there been such enslavement through consciousness as in the twentieth century. Even my generation was still taught in school that reason frees men."[16] What "scientific" reason provided these intellectual totalitarians was absolute *certainty*, and thus an escape from ambiguity and mystery, from fate and luck, from the vagaries of human decision and desire. They sought an earthly salvation, and they envisioned human happiness in entirely material terms.

It is exactly these modern Cartesian-cum-Marxist delusions that Tolkien vehemently rejects. He understands that beauty, like certainty, can be put to evil purposes, and that even the noblest can be self-deceived. He expressed alarm, in fact, that our world finds "it difficult to conceive of evil and beauty together. The fear of the beautiful fay [fairy] that ran through the elder ages almost eludes our grasp. Even more alarming: goodness is itself bereft of its proper beauty."[17] Thus does the remarkable beauty of Galadriel expose the elven queen to unique temptation. If she were to accept the Ring of coercion, she confesses, she would accomplish great good, just as Saruman had promised. But her loveliness would become binding rather than inviting. Everyone would bow down and adore her beauty, hopelessly subjecting their wills to hers—thus putting an end to all true loveliness and liberty. Galadriel would come to preside over a despairing crowd of slaves, she declares, not a living community of souls. She would become a new and worse Sauron, a terrible Queen of Absolute Power.

Saruman is the master rhetorician in his ability to put beautiful words to bestial uses. When he later speaks from his tower called Orthanc ("Cunning Mind"), he addresses the Company with a voice that is suave and sweet in contrast to the seeming ineloquence of others. His enchanting words thus elicit easy agreement—until Gimli suddenly detects what is false in Saruman's mellifluous language. Though dwarves often seem obtuse, Gimli responds as if he were an early George Orwell writing *Animal Farm*. For Gimli penetrates Saruman's perverse attempt to give sinister intentions deceptively pleasant expression, upending the obvious meaning of ordinary terms: "In the language of Orthanc help means ruin, and saving means slaying, that is plain" (*LOTR*, 565).

Tolkien set his face like flint against such linguistic abominations. To preserve the humility implicit in things local and particular, he became the advocate of a cultural pluralism that has considerable postmodern resonances. As John Garth has demonstrated in *Tolkien and the Great War*, Tolkien's philological concerns were moral and historical from the start. His two forms of elvish—eventually they became known as Sindarin and Quenya—were based on the phonological principles he had learned from his study of Welsh and Finnish, respectively. These studies were premised, in turn, on Tolkien's conviction that Celtic and northern cultures enshrined virtues that were largely absent not only from the late modern world but also from the antique cultures of Greece and Rome.

Unlike both Victorian and contemporary enthusiasts for ancient Celtic life—naively believing that it was warmly feminine and spiritually comforting—Tolkien learned from the Celts that nature is teeming with *faery*—with elven creatures who, as ambassadors from the natural world, are rather like the angelic emissaries from the heavenly sphere who appear in scripture: fierce, even frightening. In their close alliance with nature, they reveal it not to be a predictable and benign world, as Newtonian modernity once held, but rather a volatile and dangerous realm, a vital plentitude that invites our awe-struck participation, not a dead Cartesian domain that invites our bullying mastery. Thus do the ents bring us in relation to trees as sentient creatures to be reverenced for the slowness of their growth, the hardiness of their fiber, indeed, for their sheer *otherness*.

As Milosz and others have observed, the first aim of modern totalitarian states is to crush such otherness as it is manifest in local cultures and languages. The Communists immediately made Russian the official language of occupied Lithuania, for example, even though Lithuanian is not a Slavic tongue, and thus Russian was a completely alien idiom to the citizens of Vilnius and other Lithuanian cities. Tolkien, by contrast, was concerned to preserve the languages and cultures of conquered peoples. He believed that the ancient northern cultures enshrined a heroism that is largely absent in both the antique Mediterranean and the modern European worlds—namely, a dauntless human courage in the face of unremitting hostility, a heroic willingness to perish without any hope of postmortal reward.

Tolkien was convinced, moreover, that languages and cultures are inextricably rooted in time and place, that geography is hugely determinative for the way people think and act, that human variety is tied to the knotty particulars of culture, that a people's first products are its myths and stories, and that these narratives are the essential carriers of both religion and morality. He lamented, therefore, the ruthless monoculturalism of the Romans in failing to preserve the northern European cultures that they had overwhelmed. Tolkien had no sympathy, it follows, for Enlightenment-inspired attempts to transcend tradition-grounded locality for the sake of allegedly universal values. He lived long enough, alas, to witness the slaughter of roughly 190 million souls in the name of such putatively timeless and placeless truths. Tolkien also abominated the prospect of English emerging as the new *lingua franca* of the modern commercial world. Such a commodifying of his native tongue would destroy the vitality of the many local languages that English would come to displace, Tolkien complained, while also ruining the rich local dialects of English itself.

Such cultural and linguistic pluralism prevents Tolkien's enterprise from becoming anything hegemonic or triumphalist. On the contrary, there is a postmodernist strain in Tolkien's celebration of cultures and narratives other than his own, his abjuring of abstract ideas and political programs as inherently coercive, and thus his ready confession that we inhabit a world of blessed linguistic particularity and thus of saving cultural limitation. In sum: Tolkien gladly sets the various historical and linguistic worlds in conversation and engagement with each other. Rather than being hermetically sealed off unto themselves, such cultural traditions can be mutually fructifying. Precisely as a writer rooted and marked in the Christian culture of the West could Tolkien engage other traditions than his own, retrieving from them those things that were consonant with his faith while rejecting those that were alien and inimical to it.

TOLKIEN'S REJECTION OF MODERN FOUNDATIONALISM

In addition to his embrace of cultural pluralism, Tolkien shared the postmodern rejection of Enlightenment foundationalism—the Cartesian notion, namely, that we can exercise our reason utterly without presuppositions and completely apart from historical conditions. Here we find, surprisingly, a keen disjunction between Tolkien and his friend C. S. Lewis. Unlike Tolkien, Lewis was devoted to the Socratic Club at Oxford—where he eagerly debated nonbelievers, attempting to flatten their arguments—for two related reasons, as Christopher Mitchell observed. Not only did Lewis want to establish Christian truth; he also sought to restore the Enlightenment ideal of "free inquiry" with its assurance that, by fearlessly "following the argument wherever it led," the truth would surely emerge.[18] Thus would "the marketplace of ideas"—a revealing metaphor itself, enshrining a notion of truth as something purchased—produce a conclusion worthy of common affirmation.

Tolkien did not approve of Lewis the Christian apologist, referring to him derisively as "everyman's theologian." Only a Joe Blow sort of theologian, in Tolkien's estimate, would seek to defend Christianity by stepping outside it and proving its validity from some neutral standpoint above both the church and its cultured despisers. This is not to deny that Tolkien was something of a moral foundationalist himself, especially in his conviction that there *are* ethical assumptions common to all cultures—what Lewis calls "the Tao"—without which human life would not be possible at all. However brutal the pagan north may have been, and though the Romans and the Japanese have both exalted suicide as a moral ideal, all peoples everywhere have held to ideals of honor and friendship and humility before the intractable necessities and contingencies of life. Nowhere do people torture their babies or scorn their own kin. The most obvious evidence for Tolkien's belief in an eternal and unchanging order of truth is found in Éomer's query concerning how, in the midst of such strange times as now beset Middle-Earth, one can judge aright: "As he ever has judged," said Aragorn. "Good and evil have not changed since yesteryear; nor are they one thing among Elves and Dwarves and another among Men. It is man's part to discern them, as much in the Golden Wood as in his own house" (*LOTR*, 428).

It is noteworthy that Aragorn does not suggest that such truth can be discerned in advance or in solitude; and much less can it be descried apart from local communities grappling with particular problems in particular situations. Hence Tolkien's rejection of Lewis's assumption that one must first hold to a supernaturalist worldview before one can engage the Christian Gospel. Without such an allegedly timeless and untraditioned foundation, Lewis believed, Christianity has nowhere to stand. In his fiction, therefore, Lewis creates a parallel universe that readers must first credit in order to enter imaginatively into it. Thus do we move from the natural and ordinary to the magical and supernatural realms as if they were essentially disjunct, even though they are finally knitted together. Lucy and Edmund, Susan and Peter, pass wondrously *through* the back of the wardrobe and *into* Narnia. Ransom travels *from* the earth *to* Malacandra and then Perelandra. In Lewis's fiction, the realm of Deep Magic always lies on the *other* side of the quotidian world.[19]

Not so for Tolkien. He assumes no timeless and spaceless "foundation" on which his imaginative world might be erected. For him, transcendent reality is to be found in the depths of this world rather than in some arcane existence beyond it. Tolkien argued, for example, that fairy stories "cannot tolerate any frame or machinery suggesting that the whole story in which they occur is a figment or illusion." Such devices create a skepticism that undermines the truthfulness of the entire fictional enterprise: "The moment disbelief arises, the spell is broken." Tolkien elects, therefore, to set his readers right down in the midst of Middle-earth. There is no time voyage or space travel in his fiction, no slipping through the back of a wardrobe into a magical realm. Tolkien seeks, instead, to convince readers that his imaginative world is already and utterly real, having no other foundation than its own laws and conventions. The Company of Nine receives its mandate from Gandalf, the wizard who has studied the history of the Ring ever so carefully, and they are bound by concrete ties of friendship and remembrance and trust rather than reliance on abstract principles. When they enter warfare, therefore, they shout not such abstract ideals as "Liberty, Equality, and Fraternity," but simply, "The Shire!"

TOLKIEN'S CRITIQUE OF MODERN COERCIONS
AND ADDICTIONS

A third and even more important conjunction of Tolkien's work with postmodernism is to be found in his conviction that modern cultures are coercive beyond all others, and that their worst coercions have issued in the hideous wars of this the bloodiest of all ages. More people were killed by violent means—most of them by their own governments—in the twentieth century than in all preceding centuries combined: roughly 190 million. As Shippey has shown, Tolkien wrote directly in the face of unspeakable horrors—not only the evil regimes of fascism and Nazism and Stalinism, but also "the routine bombardment of civilian populations, the use of famine as a political measure, the revival of judicial torture, the 'liquidation' of whole classes of political opponents, extermination camps, deliberate genocide and the continuing development of 'weapons of mass destruction' from chlorine gas to the hydrogen bomb."[20]

Garth argues, in similar fashion, that Tolkien's grand *legendarium* was decisively shaped by his participation in the Great War. Yet Tolkien began to construct his huge mythological system well before 1914, largely in response to his early immersion in the languages and literatures of the ancient north, but he radically reshaped it because of the horrors he experienced at the Battle of the Somme. Like Karl Barth and many others, Tolkien came to discern that the Victorian age did not end, nor did the twentieth century begin, with the queen's death in 1901. Something dreadfully new entered modern life in 1914, with this war that was supposed to end all wars. A fundamental cleavage in Western culture occurred at Verdun and Passchendaele, at Ypres and the Somme. These battles were conducted not with swords and catapults and rifles, but with tanks and howitzers and airplanes. Here was revealed the essential modernist legacy: the murderous machine. These new instruments of war were designed no longer to kill individual soldiers but to obliterate entire towns, to blast the countryside clean of forests and farms, and thus to lay waste to nearly every living thing. Thus did Tolkien live to witness the fulfillment of the dire prophecy that Nietzsche perversely celebrated in 1887: "We now confront a succession of a few warlike centuries that have no parallel in history; in short, . . . we have entered *the classical age of war*, of scientific and at the same time popular war on the largest scale (in weapons, talents, and discipline). All coming centuries will look back on it with envy and awe for its perfection."[21]

Unlike Nietzsche, Tolkien did not respond to the nihilistic terrors of his time by recurring to the romanticized idea that warfare can be morally cleansing. Rather did he set out to create a new and redemptive mythology for his own native England, one that would not exalt war. Convinced as he was that the Arthurian legends were not only an inimical French import but also that their exclusively Christian character made them oblivious to the greatness of England's pagan past, how could Tolkien be faithfully English while not also becoming hopelessly chauvinistic, even imperialistic? How, in short, could he retrieve the noblest virtues of his own land and people while avoiding any notion of "England, England, *über alles*"? The answer lay, in part, with his long immersion in *Beowulf* and the *Eddas* and the *Kalevala*. They had taught Tolkien to honor the courage of heroes who face insuperable obstacles without divine assistance. Unlike their Greek and Romans counterparts—heroes whom the gods either aid or impede, often for their own selfish ends—the deities of the aboriginal north are themselves destroyed at Ragnarök. In that final battle, after all social and familial order collapses, everything returns to monstrous chaos and permanent night.

There is a godlessness implicit in the indigenous Nordic cultures, a cosmic vacancy that eerily resembles our late-modern sense of divine absence and abandonment. As the Venerable Bede notes in his *Ecclesiastical History of the English People*, life in the pre-Christian world of the antique north was like that of a sparrow flying into one end of a lighted mead hall and out the other: from the Void into a brief moment of light and warmth back into the Void. The Nazis thus seized upon the dark traditions of the ancient north in order to create their own racist and imperialist myth of national greatness. In defense of a demonic *Blutbrüderschaft*, Hitler slaughtered 7 million

Jews—not to mention the millions of gentiles who died either defending or defeating Hitlerism. As a lover of primeval northern sagas, how could Tolkien avoid the mythic nihilism that the Nazis had exploited? In a remarkable act of cultural and spiritual retrieval, Tolkien found his answer lying in a previously neglected quality of the heroism of the primeval north. The spirit that animates it, he remembered, is not preening victory so much as somber defeat.

If Tolkien were merely antimodern, he would have opposed coercive modern power with its medieval counterpart, perhaps by creating a warrior Christ such as we find in the Germanic recension of the four Gospels called the *Heliand*. Instead, Tolkien made the radically antithetical decision to enshrine *loss* rather than victory at the heart of his massive mythology. Not only would he thus eschew any sort of English triumphalism; he would also make his work thoroughly Christian. Yet its God would not be the arbitrary monarch who acts upon the world from without, as for Newton and Descartes. Nor would divine action be obvious and clear so much as dark and hidden. The Gospel, after all, is not a narrative of conquest but of defeat. The Resurrection does not cancel so much as it vindicates the cross as the essential instrument of Christian vocation. It summons disciples to live in the light of a strange sort of victory—namely, within a community built on apparent weakness rather than obvious strength, embodying a triumph that comes not by seizing but by surrendering coercive power, even unto death.

By granting the Ring a remarkable power to coerce the will, Tolkien reveals what he regarded as the chief evil of the modern world—the various tyrannies that have trampled the human spirit. The most obvious examples are to be found in the assorted totalitarianisms of Germany and China and Russia. Quite apart from the multiplied millions who were slaughtered by their own governments, many more were made to live in constant fear of violating the oppressive system and thus of bringing its terror upon them. Theirs was the daily dread that the Nine Walkers and their allies also confront. Never have fear and coercion been so pandemic, as millions have been murdered for no reason at all, and as countless millions more have been made to practice secret surveillance on their neighbors, lest they themselves be devoured by the gigantic bureaucracy of control and oppression.

We who live in the so-called Free World—the nations of the democratic West—are hardly immune from this worst of modern legacies: mass death. This is not to deny the brutality of many premodern ages and cultures. In addition to practicing human sacrifice and cannibalism, our forebears often chopped heads and lopped hands for trivial offenses, and many of our ancestors lived in constant terror of various royal autocracies. Even so, our age is incomparably Sauronic. Our culture of comfort and convenience can be as subtly coercive as dictatorial regimes are obviously enslaving. In the United States, for instance, we have created a demonic drug culture and an enslaving eroticism that are hardly less addictive than the Ring itself. Could this be the work of the Sauron who was defeated at the Cracks of Mount Doom, but only—as we are told—to assume new and even more sinister guise, still subjecting the human spirit to hideously coercive pressures?

Almost everyone exposed to the Ring experiences its mesmerizing power, even the splendidly innocent Samwise Gamgee. Only Faramir, among our own human kind, remains so pure of spirit as to be totally immune to its magnetic attraction. Yet it is the will of Frodo—the most valiant of the hobbits—that is most severely tested by the Ring. The closer he comes to the place where it was forged, in the very heart of Sauron's evil empire, the greater its power over him. It has not only left Frodo physically emaciated, it has also drained his spirit, overwhelming him with hopelessness. The dread fear that he will not succeed in his mission, especially as the obstacles to his errand increase in fury and horror, afflicts Frodo with a paralyzing pessimism. The Ring takes control of him, both awake and asleep. "I begin to see it in my mind all the time," Frodo confesses, "like a great wheel of fire . . . I am naked in the dark, Sam, and there is no veil between me and the wheel of fire. I begin to see it even with my waking eyes, and all else fails" (*LOTR*, 898, 916).

Having arrived at the Cracks of Doom so weary that he cannot walk, Frodo seems incapable of self-defense, much less of asserting his own self-will. Yet when Gollum leaps on Frodo's back in an attempt to seize the Ring at the last, Frodo flicks him away as if he were an insect. Sam is rightly startled to find Frodo suddenly so strong and so merciless. In an act of seeming bravery, Frodo is seeking to draw strength of will from the Ring in order to keep Sauron from seizing it. So fully is he imbued with a kind of holy severity that Frodo undergoes a virtual transfiguration of his own. Sam is given a sudden mystical vision of his friend. He sees Frodo as a stern and terrible figure, "untouchable now by pity, a figure robed in white" (*LOTR*, 922)— as if he were a new Saruman who has returned to replace Gandalf.

Yet at the very apogee of his mistaken attempt to combat evil with evil, Frodo is overwhelmed by the Ring's bullying power, a force so strong that even Sauron can no longer command it. Frodo becomes, in fact, a virtual puppet for the ventriloquizing Ring. On all other occasions when he has been able to resist the Ring, Frodo speaks in the passive voice, as Tolkien makes clear that he is being graciously acted upon no less than himself acting. But here he speaks in the active voice, loud and stentorian. He does not declare, "I will not" but rather, "I choose not"; for his will still desires to destroy the Ring, but he has no power to enact what he wills. Like the Apostle Paul lamenting that "I can will what is right but I cannot do it. For I do not do the good I want, but the evil I do not want is what I do" (Rom. 7:18b–19), Frodo also lacks the strength to enact his will. Yet it is not his rebellious nature that binds Frodo; it is the coercive power of an evil Other, the Ring itself: "I have come," Frodo declares. "But I do not choose now to do what I came to do. I will not do this deed. The Ring is mine!" (*LOTR*, 924).

This is surely the great and terrible anticlimax of Tolkien's epic fantasy. After his year-long twilight struggle to take the Ring back to the Cracks of Doom, Frodo fails at the very last—not because his will is corrupt but because the Ring finally overwhelms him. Thus does the Quest culminate not in jubilant victory but in dispiriting defeat, as Tolkien deflates the reader's hope for a conventionally "heroic" ending—whether ancient or modern. It's a quintessential postmodern moment, this failure of Frodo at the end of his Quest. For it reveals the hobbit not to be, in typically modernist fashion, an antihero who embodies a sort of upside-down goodness in his very insufficiency. Neither is it a classical moment, for Frodo is no tragic hero like Oedipus, one who is ennobled even in his defeat. Rather is Frodo a thoroughly Christian victor with peculiarly postmodern appeal. For in his very failure, as one finally unable to resist the coercive force of the Ring, Frodo remains a humbled and flawed protagonist who is vindicated only by the silent and invisible Ilúvatar. There is not the least sign of Old Nobodaddy at work here, no Supreme Being bringing sure and final victory to his faithful ones. Not only do we later discover how fully the Shire had gone over to Sauron's side during the Company's year-long absence, but also how Frodo himself is far too wearied and worn by the Quest to enjoy the delights of victory. Instead, he departs for the Grey Havens amidst a tearful and enormously sad farewell.

TOLKIEN'S ANSWER TO MODERNIST INDIVIDUALISM

Why, then, the enormous currency of Tolkien's work in a world hungry for certainty and victory? It is clear that Tolkien rejects much of what the postmodernists reject—especially the Enlightenment conviction that all evils, being humanly generated, can be humanly overcome. On this modernist view, what is broken can be fixed, so that evil itself remains a problem to be solved rather than (as Flannery O'Connor said) a mystery to be endured. Tolkien agrees with the postmodernists that, despite the enormous human benefits accomplished during the modern period, the attendant evils almost outweigh them: cultural and moral disintegration, the collapse of ethical and social standards, genocidal wars of unprecedented scale and ferocity, and new technologies that seem beyond human control. Yet it must be emphasized that, over against such modern evils and ailments, Tolkien does not propose postmodern solutions. Not for him the postmodern fascination with what Stanley Fish has called the "boutique multiculturalism" that scorns historically developed communities while admiring nearly every other culture than one's own: "the multiculturalism of ethnic restaurants, weekend festivals, and high-profile flirtations with the other in the manner satirized by Tom Wolfe under the rubric of 'radical chic.'"[22] Postmodernism of this kind is but hypermodernism, as autonomous individuals create their own identities by fulfilling whatever needs and choosing whatever pleasures they prefer.

Tolkien is certainly a cultural pluralist, as we have seen, but he is most certainly not a religious pluralist. Without apology, he held to the absolute finality of God's act of self-disclosure and definition in the Jews and Jesus and the Church. Yet the self-revealing God is not an obvious God. Thus is Tolkien ever so subtle in his depiction of divine authority and power, lest it appear hegemonic even in its silent and anonymous victory. Tolkien confessed, in fact, his desire to evoke a presence that would be felt by its absence, and this surely accounts for the continuing appeal of Tolkien's work to a world overwhelmed by swaggering power. Tolkien demonstrates, over and again, that there are evils too great for human resistance, forces too powerful for human control, coercions that can be conquered only by the transcendent power of noncoercion.

The destruction of the Ring is accomplished, it is noteworthy, by the operation of secondary causes, not by supernatural intervention. The greed-maddened Gollum, having bitten the Ring off Frodo's finger, dances his jig of joy too near the brink of the volcanic fissure, thus tumbling into the infernal lava that alone can liquefy it. For the undiscerning reader, the Ring is destroyed by Gollum's hobbit presumption and carelessness. For the discerning reader, however, the standard workings of natural causation and human willing are providentially guided. Just as Bilbo was *meant* to find the Ring, so was the Ring *meant* to be destroyed by the very evils that it has spawned. That so many millions of readers, whether Christian or not, have found the scene completely convincing demonstrates the wisdom of Tolkien's strategy. In a world driven by coercive power, only a modest, even a failed kind of valor—"failed" only because it is an uncoercive valor—can have lasting purchase. And the theological metanarrative that undergirds such bravery must have an uncoercive God as its Author and Director and chief Actor.

It is not difficult to discern what is not postmodern in Tolkien's account of Frodo's victory-in-defeat: his insistence that the coercions plaguing late-modern life can best be combated by communities rather than individuals, yet not by strong and dominant communities, but rather noncoercive and perhaps peripheral fellowships, by the little people of the world, the *populi minuti*. The Company of the Nine Walkers is a frail and often broken community. They are sustained throughout their seemingly hopeless struggle not by ties of self-interest, much less by contractual agreement. Their unbreakable bond—the covenant that undergirds their Quest—lies in their forgiving faith and their enduring trust in each other: in their *friendship*. Sauron, by contrast, can form no community. His orc-slaves serve him out of fear, not from devotion. Tolkien is convinced, in fact, that there can be no true company of vice, no fellowship of the wicked, however rigidly loyal its members may remain. Whether in the Taliban or the Mafia, whether in Al-Qaeda or street gangs, their sort of clan-and-tribe dedication to evil makes their singleness of spirit both internecine from within and contemptible from without.

Over against all such aggregations of force, Tolkien poses the Company (literally: the "Bread-Sharers") of the Nine Walkers. They are chosen by Elrond as Middle-earth's answer to the Nine Riders of Sauron—the nine mortal men who, wearing the rings that the sorcerer made for them, have come totally under his power and thus have been turned into the fearsome ringwraiths. But while the Nine Riders have been made into vaporous shadows of an evil sameness, the Nine Walkers are a remarkably diverse assemblage of the unlike. And this surely is one of their most remarkably postmodern qualities. Yet Tolkien makes clear that diversity for its own sake is no virtue. The members of a polyglot group chosen only for their race and class and gender differences would, if lacking any commonality of transcendent and self-surrendering purpose, merely take sides and fight, in a Hobbesian war of all against all—or else they would come to a legal agreement about how best to preserve the self-interest of each individual. And thus would they have undertaken the new undeclared war of constant competition.

Elrond chooses nine radically disparate travelers for this seemingly impossible journey, electing them according to the unique strengths they bring to their singular task. Gandalf is chosen for his wisdom, Aragorn for his royal link to the Ring, Boromir for his manly valor in battle, Legolas for his elvish mastery of the woods, Gimli for his dwarvish knowledge of mountains and mines, and Sam because he is Frodo's closest and most trustworthy companion. When Merry and Pippin also insist on accompanying Frodo, Elrond objects that such youngsters cannot imagine the terrors that lie ahead. Gandalf admits that, if these two youngest hobbits could foresee the dangers that await them, they would surely hold back. Yet they would also be ashamed of their cowardice, Gandalf adds, and thus be made even unhappier at staying than going. Merry promises that they will hold hard to Frodo until the very end comes, no matter how bitter—maintaining their solidarity with him regardless of circumstances and keeping confidences without fear of disclosure. They will not allow Frodo to go off and face danger and difficulty alone. Their deceptively simple reason for wanting to accompany Frodo is voiced by young Meriadoc Brandybuck himself: "We are your friends, Frodo" (*LOTR*, 103). With those four plain monosyllables, had Sauron heard and fathomed them, his mighty fortress at Barad-dûr would have been shaken to its foundations. For this little community of noncoercive weaklings will help throw down, as we discover at the end, the seemingly impregnable strongholds of the master Force-Wielder.[23]

Not only does the Fellowship consist of friendly representatives of all the world's free peoples, it also includes two examples of historic enemies: the elf Legolas and the dwarf Gimli. Yet through their radically communal life of mutual devotion and sacrifice, they become the fastest of friends, even being allowed at the end to spend their lives together in Valinor. The Company also contains its own subverter and betrayer in the overly brave warrior Boromir. As is nearly always the case in Tolkien, community is broken by force. In a foolhardy desire to attack Sauron himself with the aid of the Ring, Boromir tries to seize it from Frodo. For such a heinous act of betrayal, he surely deserves to be ousted from the Fellowship. If his community were merely contractual, he would no doubt have been driven out. But as we have noticed briefly before, covenantal communities cannot be broken, even when egregious evils are committed by one of their own, since they are grounded in a noncoercive source beyond themselves.

Here, then, is Tolkien's most radically Christian move against both the modern and postmodern grain: not only to create a noncoercive community willing to suffer terrible loss, but also to found it on a radical sense of forgiveness. The leitmotiv of the entire epic lies in Gandalf's crucial speech (though virtually ignored in Peter Jackson's films) explaining why Bilbo refused to kill the murderous Gollum, choosing to spare him in pity: "The pity of Bilbo may rule the fate of many." It is important to note that Tolkien is at once unclassical and unmodern in this privileging of pity. In both ancient heroic societies and in so-called modern meritocracies, pity is not a virtue but a vice. The Greeks, for example, extend pity only to the pathetic, the helpless, those who are able to do little or nothing for themselves. When Aristotle declares that the function of tragic drama is to arouse fear and pity, he refers to the fate of a character such as Oedipus. We are made to fear that Oedipus's plight might tragically be ours, and thus do we pity him for his unjust fate. But whether in the ancient or the modern world, pity must not be granted to the egregiously unjust or undeserving, lest they be denied the justice that they surely merit. Yet *Lord of the Rings* is a book imbued with such unmerited mercy and forgiveness. It is extended not only to the unworthy Gollum over and again but also to the far unworthier Saruman, not once but thrice.

Perhaps knowing that his readers would not draw this historical distinction, and perhaps fearing that any overtly Christian allusions would meet with modernist incredulity, Tolkien offered his subtlest and least direct version of transcendent forgiveness in the death of Boromir. This exceedingly courageous warrior would seem to be the Judas of the story, for it is he who breaks the Fellowship by trying to seize the Ring from Frodo. Frodo in turn is forced to wear it in order to escape—not, alas, from orcs or ringwraiths or even Saruman, but rather from his friend and fellow member of the Company.

As soon as Boromir has seen the horror that he has committed, he calls out to Frodo in shame at what he has done, pleading with him to return rather than to flee, explaining that a momentary madness had overtaken him. It is too late in the literal sense, because Frodo has already fled. But it is not too late in the spiritual sense, for in Boromir's death we are shown one truly binding tie that can knit a community of the weak and uncoercive into an unbreakable unity.

When Aragorn and Legolas and Gimli at last hear the sounding horn of the desperate Boromir, they fly to him, only to find him dying from his orc-inflicted wounds, after he has slain many of the enemy in order that Sam and Frodo might go free. Yet Boromir does not boast of his valor, nor does Aragorn accuse him of betrayal. They perform, instead, the ultimately communal act, one that Tolkien conveys with supreme craft and tact—again proceeding with subtle indirection rather than overt theological reference. For Aragorn, the future king with priestly powers, leads Boromir through the three steps of what was once called the sacrament of penance. First, the *confessio oris*, as Boromir admits that he tried to seize the Ring from Frodo. Boromir's oral confession alone would not suffice unless he genuinely lamented his evil deed, which he does, declaring, "I am sorry." Yet this *contritio cordis*, this sorrow of the heart, has validity only if it also issues in *satisfactio operis*, works of satisfaction, as it did in his losing battle against the orcs. Boromir poignantly concludes, therefore, "I have paid."

Aragorn knows that these last words are not Boromir's vain boast that he has bravely recompensed for his community-rending sin; they are his humble admission, on the contrary, that he has paid the terrible price of breaking trust with Frodo and the Fellowship. Hence his final words of defeat: "I have failed." Aragorn reads this admission aright: it is Boromir's final penitential act, and thus a declaration that refutes itself, since it enables his pardon and thus his reconciliation with the Company that he once betrayed. Aragorn thus absolves the dying hero by holding Boromir's hand and kissing his brow, assuring him that his life is not ending in the pain of absolute loss but in the confidence of permanent gain. "You have conquered," says the priest-king. "Few have gained such a victory. Be at peace! Minas Tirith shall not fall" (*LOTR*, 404).

Again, Tolkien offers an indirect affirmation, allowing the discerning reader to see what is sacramental in this reconciling act. Boromir's last gesture, a silent smile, could be construed as his ironic doubtfulness, as if to say: "My people at Minas Tirith will hardly be saved by this ragtag Company, on whom Sauron and his minions will feast like jackals." But Boromir's smile may also be read as an expression of gratitude, a sign that he has received mercy and been restored to the community that he once had broken. On either reading, it is fair to say that Tolkien has placed a multicultural community at the center of his epic. It is not a company united either by high-minded abstractions or by merely private excellences. Rather is it a fellowship bound in unbreakable solidarity by the ultimate remedy to coercion: the act of pity and mercy and reconciliation performed within a reconciled and reconciling company. In a power-driven world characterized by community-denying coercions of all kinds, this noncoercive community built on a willingness to lose and a willingness to forgive is surely the key to Tolkien's postmodern appeal, even as it sets him at a far distance from postmodernism itself.

TOLKIEN AND THE POSTMODERN TOURNAMENT OF NARRATIVES

Our remaining task is to determine how such a community can make its witness to the postmodern world. Tolkien has made the answer plain, though far from easy. It is not by adopting the tactics of modernism, especially not the modern enlargement of the technical and conceptual realm over the narrative and storied world. On the contrary, it will happen as we live and move and have our being in hobbit-like fellowships. Among Christians, such companies will welcome others into the ever-widening circle called the Church Universal. Or else they will be contracted into an ever-shrinking circle by the persecution that truly noncoercive communities nearly always face. Even then, the tiny circles constituted by the blood of the martyrs will always remain the secret seed of the Church.

Literarily, the postmodern task for Christians will consist in the indirect display of the Christian story by means of such carefully crafted works as *Lord of the Rings*. The massively popular reception of Tolkien's epic demonstrates that Christians are able to enter what the late Baptist theologian James Wm. McClendon called "the tournament of narratives." Despite its potential relativism and even nihilism, McClendon discerned that the postmodern revolution enables Christians to set our tradition alongside its various competitors and companions. It also frees us to confess that ours is a fundamentally narrative tradition, that we are sustained by the constant retelling and thus the repeated reenactment of the Christian story via prophetic action and sacramental grace. Even our creeds are but compressed plots, with their beginning and middle and end.

So strong does story figure in Tolkien's work that he makes very few appeals to historical fact. Myth and history come to resemble each other, Tolkien notes, because, like story and truth, they are radically interdependent. Mythical pattern gives form to history, just as historical occurrence gives substance to myth. Story is not merely the "vehicle" of truth. Nor does Tolkien merely clothe Christian "themes" in the pleasant guise of fiction, as if the religious element were the kernel covered by the husk of the mythology. Such a tactic would be a reversion to the "old" modernism. What we see displayed so winsomely in *Lord of the Rings* is a subtle kind of Christian confidence—namely, Tolkien's antinominalist conviction that the world is not only narratable but that it has its true life only by way of analogies. Hence his willingness to retell the Gospel story in an indirect and mythological and anticipatory way, setting his metanarrative right alongside the many others—whether Joycean or Lawrentian, Nietzschean or Marxist, capitalist or socialist, liberal or conservative. Who wins and who loses in this tournament is not Tolkien's primary concern; he desires only that his vision be seen and his voice be heard. His is thus an irreducibly Christian desire, since the metanarrative of the Gospel is built around the one Loss that constitutes the ultimate Victory.

Tolkien remained convinced that the first task of the Church is not to answer critics and to defeat enemies so much as to body forth its story in both word and deed. Nor can these two be separated, for the right deed is nourished and enabled by the right word, the right story. This is the point that Samwise Gamgee, the least reflective of the hobbits, comes to discern. In the Tower of Cirith Ungol, as he and Frodo have begun to doubt whether their Quest will ever succeed—and thus to fear that they will die and be utterly forgotten—Sam seeks to distinguish between tales that really matter and those that do not. There are many competing stories that vie for our loyalty, and Sam is trying to distinguish among them, to locate the one hope-giving Story. It is noteworthy that Sam judges from a stance within his own story, not by seeking to transcend all narratives and to assess them from a delusory eagle-aerie perch above space and time. He declares that, if they themselves had known how hard was the road that lay ahead of them, they would never have come at all. Yet such is the way of stories, he adds, that rivet the mind and of songs that are sung for the ages. They are not about fellows who set out on adventures of their own choosing, Sam confesses, but about folks who found themselves traveling a path that they would never have elected to follow on their own. They were chosen for the quest, but they could have turned back. If they had quailed, no one would have ever sung their story, since those who defect from their calling are not celebrated. What counts, Sam wisely warns, is not that these heroes defeated their enemies and returned home safely to relish their triumph, but that they trustworthily did their bit in the "long defeat," moving relentlessly forward to whatever end awaited them, whether good or ill. And in the Great History later recorded, Sam is not even mentioned by name but referred to only as "a faithful servant."

If it is not a happy ending that matters, then what does? After all, each particular human story—and, by extension, all the stories of all fellowships and companies—will finally end and permanently disappear. Does this mean that all stories are equal—even perhaps equally futile and vain? Not at all, says Sam. What matters is whether our own little story forms part of an infinitely larger story, and thus whether we rightly enact our own little roles within this Great Saga. If we do, Sam adds, then when our own story is done, someone else will take the tale forward to either a better or worse moment in the ongoing drama. Until the end, we cannot stand *sub specie aeternitatis* to see the final outcome. Yet we can know indeed what kind of story we are enacting: whether we are actors in one of the various modern stories of individualist preference or statist coercion; whether in one of the many postmodern dramas of boutique multiculturalism; or whether in the only narrative centering on a community that is publicly called into being rather than privately chosen; and whether, within this latter story we belong to those who, rather than enslaving their enemies, are willing to forgive them because they know themselves to have been forgiven. What we learn from Tolkien is that this infinitely larger story encompasses all the smaller stories, that it retrieves all things worthy from them—even from the story of modernity and its hypermodernist legacy. All of the perversions and distortions of the one true Story can thus be redeemed: "Why," says Sam, "even Gollum might be good in a tale" (*LOTR*, 697). No wonder, then, that so many readers of Tolkien have been converted, albeit often unawares, from their hegemonic and triumphalist modernism—not to an anarchic postmodernism, but to the classically Christian virtues of the hobbits and their friends.

NOTES

1. Craven, "Catholic Poem in Time of War," 145.
2. Funkenstein, *Theology and the Scientific Imagination*, 57–58.
3. "Analogy," 19.
4. Rahner and Vorgrimler, "Analogy," 18.
5. Funkenstein, *Theology and the Scientific Imagination*, 58.
6. Ibid., 76.
7. Buckley, *At the Origins of Modern Atheism*, 97.
8. Ibid., 345. In both Newton and Descartes, Buckley adds, "god functioned as an explanatory factor in a larger, more complete system" (349).
9. Ibid., 33.
10. Pascal, *Pensées*, 170.
11. I should add that, though Tolkien has little affinity with those who would make postmodernism an *answer* to the mistakes of modernism, he shares the postmodernist critique of modernism's chief errors: its endless self-reflexivity and cognitive instability, its domestication of ordinary life into separate domains (e.g., sacred and secular, public and private, work and play, the political and the

individual), its creation of massive bureaucracies through centralized state power, its elevation of impersonal scientific experimentation and proof over religious ritual and sacrament, its enlargement of the conceptual realm over the narrative and storied world, and finally its inadvertent creation—via reaction and rebellion—of an inwardly subjective art and likewise an inwardly experiential religion. It should also be said that Tolkien shares some of the positive goals of the postmodernists: their desire to recover the organic from the mechanical, their elevation of the communal over the individual, their admission that hierarchy is inevitable in every culture, and their reenvisioning of a universe in which everything is mutually referential rather than being divided into precise and isolated spheres. See Benavides, "Modernity," 190.

12. Shippey, *Road to Middle-earth*, 202.

13. Orwell, "Politics and the English Language," 176–77.

14. *LOTR* shall here and henceforth designate Tolkien, *Lord of the Rings*.

15. Milosz, *Captive Mind*, 147.

16. Ibid., 191.

17. Tolkien, *Monsters and the Critics*, 151.

18. Mitchell, "Following the Argument Wherever It Leads," 183, 193. Yet, at least in *The Discarded Image*, Lewis rejected such a flight from history. There, rather than subjecting the medieval worldview to modernist critique, he demonstrates its own internal consistency and integrity, showing that it is as persuasive in its own way as the Darwinian naturalism that has replaced it. The English poet John Heath-Stubbs confessed to me, in a 1988 interview, that he became a Christian largely from hearing Lewis deliver the *Discarded Image* lectures at Oxford in the 1950s. They convinced him that the ancient Christian outlook was more cogent and persuasive than the physicalist worldview of modernity.

19. In *Till We Have Faces*, Lewis locates his narrative in the ancient pagan kingdom of Glome, making its life-world marvelously and chillingly credible. Yet even there, Orual remains torn by the natural-supernatural distinction, as she is forced to decide whether Psyche's heavenly palace is objectively real or just her own subjective delusion.

20. Shippey, *Road to Middle-earth*, 324–25.

21. Nietzsche, *Gay Science*, book 5, sec. 362, 318.

22. Fish, *Trouble with Principle*, 60–61.

23. It is important to recall that, for Aristotle, friendship is not a plebeian but an aristocratic virtue. It can be realized only among those who, by dint of the labor done by others, have been freed to pursue such higher activity. Friendship, by definition, is restricted to the few. Tolkien's friendships, as we have seen, cut all across all "sorts and conditions," so that true mutual fidelity is open to all who will enter it.

BIBLIOGRAPHY

"Analogy." In *The Concise Oxford Dictionary of the Christian Church*, edited by E. A. Livingstone. Oxford: Oxford University Press, 1977.

Benavides, Gustavo. "Modernity." In *Critical Terms for Religious Studies*, edited by Mark C. Taylor. Chicago: University of Chicago Press, 1998.

Buckley, Michael J. *At the Origins of Modern Atheism*. New Haven, CT: Yale University Press, 1987.

Craven, Kenneth: "A Catholic Poem in Time of War." In *A Hidden Presence: The Catholic Imagination of J. R. R. Tolkien*, edited by Ian Boyd and Stratford Caldecott, 145–72. South Orange, NJ: Chesterton, 2003.

Fish, Stanley. *The Trouble with Principle*. Cambridge, MA: Harvard University Press, 1999.

Funkenstein, Amos. *Theology and the Scientific Imagination from the Middle Ages to the Seventeenth Century*. Princeton, NJ: Princeton University Press, 1986.

Milosz, Czeslaw. *The Captive Mind*. Translated by Jane Zielonko. New York: Vintage, 1981.

Mitchell, Christopher. "Following the Argument Wherever It Leads: C. S. Lewis and the Oxford University Socratic Club, 1942 to 1954." *Inklings Jahrbuch fur Literatur und Asthetik* 17 (1999), 172–96.

Nietzsche, Friedrich. *The Gay Science*. Translated by Walter Kaufmann. New York: Vintage, 1974.

Orwell, George. "Politics and the English Language." In *A Collection of Essays by George Orwell*. New York: Doubleday Anchor, 1954.

Pascal, Blaise. *Pensées and Other Writings*. Translated by Honor Levi. New York: Oxford University Press, 1995.

Rahner, Karl, and Herbert Vorgrimler. "Analogy." In *Theological Dictionary*, edited by Cornelius Ernst; translated by Richard Strachan. New York: Seabury, 1973.

Shippey, Tom. *The Road to Middle-earth*. Rev. and expanded ed. Boston: Houghton Mifflin, 2003.

Tolkien, J. R. R. *The Lord of the Rings*. Boston: Houghton Mifflin, 1994.

———. *The Monsters and the Critics and Other Essays*. London: Allen & Unwin, 1983.

Peter M. Candler, Jr., lives and writes in Asheville, North Carolina. He earned his B.A. from Wake Forest University and his M. Phil. and Ph.D. from Cambridge. His first book is *Theology, Rhetoric, Manuduction, or Reading Scripture Together on the Path to God* (Eerdmans, 2006).

Phillip J. Donnelly is Associate Professor of Literature in the Honors College at Baylor University, where he also directs the Great Texts Program. He holds degrees from the University of British Columbia (B.A.) and the University of Ottawa (M.A., Ph.D.). He is author of *Milton's Scriptural Reasoning* (Cambridge University Press, 2009) and *Rhetorical Faith* (English Literary Studies, 2000). His major area of research is Renaissance literature, but his published work ranges from St. Augustine and postmodern critical theory to the fiction of Wendell Berry.

Helen Lasseter Freeh lives with her husband, daughter, and son in Lander, Wyoming, where she is an independent writer and editor. She received degrees in political philosophy (B.A.) and American Studies (M.A.) from the University of Dallas, and she holds a doctorate in English from Baylor University. Her dissertation was a study of Tolkien's recasting of ancient Icelandic and Scandinavian epics into fresh mythic forms, showing how they engage modern questions of determinism and fatalism.

Dominic Manganiello earned a B.A. at McGill University and a D.Phil. at Oxford. He is Professor of English Literature at the University of Ottawa, having taught previously at Laval University and Augustine College. He is the author of *Joyce's Politics* (1980),

T.S. Eliot and Dante (1989), and co-author of *Rethinking the Future of the University* (1998). He has also written extensively on the culture of modernism and modern writers. He serves on the editorial boards of the *James Joyce Quarterly* and the *Joyce Studies Annual*.

Scott H. Moore is Associate Professor of Philosophy and Great Texts at Baylor University. He is the author of *The Limits of Liberal Democracy: Religion and Politics at the End of Modernity* and the co-editor of *Finding a Common Thread: Reading Great Texts from Homer to O'Connor.*

Joseph Tadie is Associate Professor of Philosophy at Saint Mary's University of Minnesota in Winona. He holds a B.A. in philosophy from Saint Mary's College and M.A. and Ph.D. degrees, also in philosophy, from Boston College. Tadie has regularly taught courses and presented papers on Tolkien, most notably at "The Festival in the Shire" in Pontrhydfendigaid, Wales.

Michael D. Thomas, Professor of Spanish, and formerly Director of the Division of Spanish and Portuguese at Baylor University, holds B.A. and M.A. degrees from the University of Northern Iowa and received his Ph.D. from the University of Kansas. He has done post-doctoral study at the Université Paris-Sorbonne, Dartmouth College, and Yale University. He has also published on methods of teaching foreign languages, New Testament studies, modern Spanish literature, and Spain's chief medieval epic, the *Cantar de mio Cid*. His book on the Spanish post–civil war novel was published by Peter Lang in 2014.

Germaine Paulo Walsh is Professor of Political Science at Texas Lutheran University in Seguin. She holds a B.A. in government from the University of San Francisco, an M.A. in political science from the University of California, Santa Barbara, and a Ph.D. in political science from Fordham University. She has published on Aristotle's *Nicomachean Ethics* and Jane Austen's *Mansfield Park* and *Persuasion*. She regularly teaches a course titled Fantasy and Political Philosophy: The Works of J.R.R. Tolkien.

Ralph C. Wood is University Professor of Theology and Literature at Baylor University. He has earned degrees at Texas A&M University-Commerce (B.A., M.A.) and the University of Chicago (M.A., Ph.D.). He taught at Wake Forest University from 1971 to 1997. In addition to *The Gospel According to Tolkien: Visions of the Kingdom in Middle-earth*, his other main books are *The Comedy of Redemption: Christian Faith and Comic Vision in Four American Novelists*, *Flannery O'Connor and the Christ-Haunted South*, and *Chesterton: The Nightmare Goodness of God*.

INDEX

The index includes the names of many fictional characters from Tolkien and other writers.